Corporate Resou

Corporate Resource Allocation

Financial, Strategic and Organizational Perspectives

Cyril Tomkins

Basil Blackwell

Copyright © Cyril Tomkins 1991

First published 1991

Basil Blackwell Ltd
108 Cowley Road, Oxford, OX4 1JF, UK

Basil Blackwell Inc.
3 Cambridge Center
Cambridge, Massachusetts 02142, USA

British Library Cataloguing in Publication Data
A CIP catalogue record for this book is available from
the British Library

Library of Congress Cataloging in Publication Data
Tomkins, Cyril,
Corporate resource allocation: integrating finance and strategy /
Cyril Tomkins.
p. cm.
IBSN 0–631–14528–1 (hardback) — ISBN 0–631–17822–8 (pbk.)
1. Corporations—Finance. 2. Cost effectiveness. 3. Investment
analysis. 4. Strategic planning. I. Title.
HG4026. T64 1991
658.15—dc20
90—765 CIP

Typeset in 10 on 12pt Times by TecSet Ltd
Printed in Great Britain by T. J. Press Ltd, Padstow, Cornwall

To Dorothy, Neil and Stephen

Contents

Figures

Preface

This book would not have been written at all had David Cooper not asked me to write 'something on divisional performance' for the Blackwell series. The request was couched in general terms; enough material for about five classes at final undergraduate level was to be the objective. The resulting book is nothing like that requested!

Personal background and motivation

On various occasions over the last sixteen years I have thought of updating my 1973 book *Financial Planning in Divisionalized Companies* and correcting a few errors in it, but other activities seemed of more interest. Other books and articles got written, other controversies were enjoyed and my own background broadened. Consequently, when I came to consider David's offer, it was clear that I could 'knock off', quite quickly, a limited student text on the accounting dimensions of divisional control along traditional lines, to include the use of return on investment as a control device, inconsistencies between *ex ante* and *ex post* financial appraisals of investment, transfer-pricing, and so on. These are still important topics, are included in my current teaching and are to some extent referred to in this book. I considered, however, whether I could not offer something rather different. Could I not make better use of the fact that I have spent the last fifteen years working in a School of Management rather than a Department of Accounting and Economics?

During these fifteen years I have come to see, far more clearly than I did before 1973, how different academic disciplines involved in the broad field of management address the same or similar issues in quite different ways. Could I not attempt to show accounting students with narrower backgrounds (like mine in 1973) how their studies, particularly on the question of resource allocation and control in large organizations, relate to thinking in other disciplines? The accounting notions already taught on divisional performance and control are merely a subset of these broader issues. Seeing them in the broader context might suggest developments of accounting and finance in ways not widely perceived. Moreover, what is needed now of accounting and finance has to be seen in the context of the developments in other literature and in business practice over the last decade.

On the other hand, I was very aware that attempting to look at these issues from the viewpoint of a range of disciplines was ambitious, perhaps too ambitious. Until very recently, little effort had been made to intregrate finance and accounting, business strategy and organizational analysis, and there still has not been much progress in that direction. This book does *not* claim to make great advances at integrating these differing perspectives; in fact, one of my students who read an early draft suggested that I shouldn't have tried to integrate them! Each specialist, she thought, should present that specialism and leave managers to decide which blend of advice to use in reaching decisions. She added that managers have the responsibility for blending the different business functions, not accountants. She may have a point, and certainly I am aware that anyone trying to write a book from the viewpoint of various different functions or disciplines is likely to meet with criticism from all of them and little praise from any. Nevertheless, I am sufficiently 'long in the tooth' now not to worry unduly about criticism, *provided that* a worthwhile debate ensues which provides better insights into the relationships of the different perspectives to each other. My student's observation, it seemed to me, assumed a static field of knowledge or at least one in which future boundaries were clearly delineated. It did not take account of the indeterminate way in which knowledge develops. What are now separate fields of study or business functions may well evolve into some hybrid form. By searching across disciplines we may find common foundations. For example, developments in science in the understanding of chaos (see Gleick, 1987) show that different disciplines do have points in common. Also, according to a recent report on management education (EFMD Working Group, 1989), more countries than not expect that in five years' time the trend in business faculties will be towards generalists with cross-functional knowledge and problem-solving skills, with fewer specialists in narowly defined academic subjects. Consequently, my objective became one of searching my own (limited) knowledge of different disciplines on the question of resource allocation and then reflecting upon any implications which might arise for developing accounting and financial management. I hope the result indicates to others that this is a path worth pursuing. If it does not, the exercise has simply been a personal indulgence which I have, nevertheless, enjoyed.

While obviously a considerable amount of reading is needed in preparing a book such as this, it must be stressed that my view of the different disciplines concerned is based on my own knowledge, which inevitably is limited – especially outside the area of accounting and finance. Significant progress towards the objective set out above can really only be achieved by collective action. No one person can have adequate knowledge of all the disciplines involved. In that sense this small book hopes merely to encourage group exploration and criticism.

While the book is written principally for accounting and finance students, it may be of some value to those operating in other fields, by helping them to appreciate how important accounting and financial management are in running organizations and how their own studies might be enriched by a knowledge of other disciplines. This, however, is a secondary objective. I have set out to write a small, but speculative, book for senior undergraduates and postgraduates studying accounting and finance and for financial managers and executives. The aim is to provide *them* with selected insights into the fields of corporate strategy and organization behaviour, as a stimulus to reflection on where accounting and financial management may be improved or changed in relation to major resource-allocation decisions. Given the apparent trend in the accounting profession towards qualifications more akin to financially oriented MBAs, this approach may be appropriate for the 1990s. It is stressed, however, that this book does not attempt to review the *whole* of financial controllership in the light of other disciplines. It addresses operating-control questions only as far as it seems necessary to see how they affect major resource-allocation decisions. A *complete* mapping of financial control from a multi-disciplinary stance would be a huge task.

The structure of the book

In setting about my task, I first thought that I needed to describe key elements of each separate discipline and then draw them all together in one grand combination. In an earlier draft I followed that format, but decided, on reflection, that the result was rather a muddle. I needed to act more incrementally, taking first the disciplines I know best (accounting and finance) and then trying to integrate them with corporate strategy before adding in, finally, organization-theory perspectives. I hope that this gives the text better continuity and a sense of mission and direction. I puzzled over how to fit in the production perspective, which has become so important with the development of new technologies. I decided that the best way with that was to integrate it as and where needed – principally in discussing product-costing and project appraisal in chapters 5 and 6.

The first three chapters stay within what may be loosely termed the finance function. Chapter 1 summarizes the current state of the theory of finance with regard to investment appraisal. Starting with a review of the principles of the capital asset pricing model (CAPM), it discusses the difficulties met in determining required yields for corporate divisions and projects, and extends the analysis to consider the theoretical complications of foreign investment, multi-period projects and dealing with inflation. The chapter tries to be critical and to emphasize where the literature needs clarification: notably in relation to errors in adjusting investment appraisal routines for inflation, suspect advice regarding the derivation of divisional cut-off rates, and the dangers of incorrect specification of required yields for foreign investment and projects with a significant element of research and development.

The text then reviews some aspects of financial modelling, bearing in mind the theory of finance set out in chapter 1. Well-established techniques such as simulation, decision trees and Monte Carlo analysis are discussed, but it is also shown how care is needed to prevent use of those techniques in ways which are inconsistent with finance theory. Hence, some limited attempt at an integration of different perspectives is introduced as early as chapter 2. This chapter also shows students how to construct Monte Carlo analyses on a simple spreadsheet without even using a macro. In practice, one would normally use a package like @Risk, but students can benefit in their initial exposure to the subject from workings which are completely visible on the screen. The disks and Solutions Manual referred to in chapter 2 may be obtained from Blackwell using the order form at the back of the book.

A distinction is then made in chapter 3 between the theory of finance and what corporate accountants and financial managers actually do when they undertake the financial appraisal of projects. This comparison also includes a consideration of where practice in accounting relating to performance measurement – using return on investment (ROI) and residual income – is inconsistent with the theory of finance. Most of the literature considered here is relatively old, but recently proposed solutions are also examined and criticized from a practical viewpoint. Finally, the chapter considers how cost-accounting practices are changing and stresses that it is only by understanding them that one can obtain the correct data for investment decisions. Chapter 3 therefore tries to draw together concepts from the different areas of financial management (the theory of finance, divisional performance measurement, and product-costing).

Up to this point the informed student of accounting and finance will notice no major departure from other books in the field. The material will be familiar, though possibly with some added insights about where care is needed. The departure from accounting and finance occurs in chapter 4 with an analysis of developments over the last twenty years in the areas often broadly described as 'corporate strategy'. Again the discussion attempts to be critical of the subject matter from *within* its own perspective. Then, in chapters 5 and 6, there is a lengthy consideration of this form of strategic analysis and how it compares first with accounting methods (chapter 5) and then with the theory of finance (chapter 6). These chapters provide a number of indications of where more integrated thinking across 'finance' and 'strategy' may be beneficial, and propose some specific forms of analysis to which accountants and finance theorists might pay more attention. These chapters also address the influence of new manufacturing technologies upon corporate resource-allocation decision processes and calculations.

In the next chapter the book takes a step in quite a different direction. So far the discussion has all been about analysis for decision-making. Chapter 7, in contrast, describes the development of the literature over the last two decades in the organizational *behaviour* field. This literature provides a stark contrast with the logical-deductive emphasis of chapters 1–6. It highlights the incremental and interpretative aspect of corporate decision-making. It emphasizes the impossibility of *completely* rational analysis in investment decision-making and discusses the processes by which human beings try to operate in complex situations. It also emphasizes the pluralistic pressures and influences on major outcomes in organizations.

Chapters 8 and 9 were the most difficult to construct, for it was here that I had to face the challenge of reflecting on all the different perspectives addressed up to chapter 7 and then trying to set them all, in a more integrated fashion, within the broader organization reality of chapter 7. First, in chapter 8, an attempt is made to integrate thinking from organizational theory with that from the more economics oriented aspects of corporate strategy. The result, in outline, is figure 8.1. Also, perhaps controversially, a defence of the much-maligned strategic portfolio grid is launched from the perspective of its value as a focus for debate and interactive decision-making. From figure 8.1 a further review of accounting and finance is then launched in chapter 9. The first result is a series of thoughts about how, in a pluralistic organization, the risk/return attitudes of different stakeholders should be approached. This also leads to the proposal that, despite the CAPM, a financial manager wishing even to maximize *shareholder* wealth must have due regard for entity risk. The concept of 'relevant-entity risk' is developed for each stakeholder group to substantiate this. The discussion then goes on to consider the varying role of ROI depending on the location of responsibility for strategy formulation, and the role of accounting as a setter of organization schemas – models of how we should act which, while becoming internalized so that following them sometimes seems merely a matter of ritual, nevertheless do have an underlying logical derivation. The chapter and the main text of the book end with a consideration of the problems likely to be faced where changing accounting systems and analysis presents a challenge to embedded schemas.

I do not pretend that I am completely satisfied with the eventual outcome of the book, but the time comes when one must take action and publish and not procrastinate and analyse any longer. That is, one must be action-rational – see chapter 7. But more thought and analysis is needed – especially at the level of chapters 8 and 9. I should like this book to stimulate a 'Chapter 9 Club' committed to seeing accounting and finance in its full organizational context, but with the *manager's* problems in mind. Such a managerial perspective need not imply the pursuit of just one stakeholder view: rather, it means developing financial management and accounting practices to enable the resource-allocation process to operate more smoothly *within* corporations. It is managerial too in the sense that it is not content just to describe how accounting practice is influenced by its environment, but tries to help managers *make resource-allocation decisions* in full awareness of the organizational context of their actions. Clearly, however, the more we know about the former, the more we should be able to do the latter.

Finally, I am acutely aware that this book presents no new empirical evidence of its own (apart from a few anecdotes here and there). At other times, I have urged accounting and finance academics to spend more time in business organizations and in talking to executives to learn what happens 'out there'. I still stand by that advice and try to follow it myself. It is not, however, an argument against reflecting on the academic analyses available, attempting to synthesize them and puzzle over linkages and possible further developments. Progress in developing academic knowledge in accounting and finance needs a balanced interaction between analysis and a sense of what is achievable and relevant in real organizational decision-taking situations. This book offers a contribution to the analytical side of things. This problem of balancing analysis against practical considerations is also the theme upon which this book on corporate resource allocation ends, in a few concluding thoughts in chapter 10.

Cyril Tomkins

References

EFMD Working Group, Report 1989: *Management Teacher Supply and Demand in Europe*. Brussels: EFMD.
Gleick, J. 1987: *Chaos: making a new science*. London: Cardinal.

Acknowledgements

Thanks are due to Trevor Hopper, who read and commented very usefully on the whole of an earlier draft; to Mario Levis, who looked at chapters 1 and 2 for me; and to Mike Saren, who offered comments on chapters 4 and 6. None of them, of course, is any way responsible for such errors as may remain, especially since the text was radically revised after they saw it.

I should also like to thank Angela Price for coping with all the drafts, corrections and final typing. After fifteen years of working with me, she is as committed to her task as ever and provides considerable secretarial support. Thanks are also due to my son, Neil, who compiled the index.

1

Investment Appraisal: A Theory of Finance Perspective

In this opening chapter the current state of the art of resource allocation will be summarized and reviewed from the perspective of the corporate-finance literature. Resource allocation is interpreted as relating to the distribution of the main funds for investment over competing claims.

Measuring returns from an investment

The basic concept underlying the whole theory of finance is that required returns on investment are a positive function of the degree of risk to be faced in undertaking that investment. Companies use a variety of different ways to assess returns on the investment as well as the risks associated with them. Common methods of measuring returns which readers will have met previously include accounting rates of return, the payback period, the internal rate of return, and the net present value. Most finance theorists prefer the **net present value** (NPV) measure, which may be defined as

$$NPV = \sum_{j=1}^{n} \frac{c_j}{(1 + k)^j} - c_0 \qquad (1.1)$$

where c_j represents the net cash flow (negative or positive) in each period j, c_0 represents the cash flow (usually negative) at the current time and k is assumed to be the rate of return that the investor requires to just compensate for the risk involved. NPV is then interpreted as the addition to the value of the company which can be obtained by making the investment. Hence, projects with positive NPVs should be accepted.

NPV is, of course, one type of discounted cash-flow calculation which recognizes that the more distant in time that a sum of cash due to us is, the less it adds to our current wealth. Put another way, the availability of cash now, rather than the same sum tomorrow, means that we shall have more tomorrow because interest can be earned on the sum received today by investing it until tomorrow. The payback method and accounting rates of return do not adequately take into account this concept of the time value of money.

The **internal rate of return** (IRR) is an improvement on these other non-discounting methods, but is still often less satisfactory to use than the NPV concept. The internal rate of return, defined as the solution r to the following expression

$$\sum_{j=1}^{n} \frac{c_j}{(1 + r)^j} = c_0 \qquad (1.2)$$

may be awkward to use in practice for two main reasons. First, there may be multiple solutions to r if there are alternating signs in the series of c_j. Second, the above formulae ignore the possibility that investors may require different spot rates of return for investments of different periods, due to the existence of the term structure of interest rates. Also, it may be necessary to use different discount rates in respect of cash flows arising in different years of the project's life because of the changing nature of risk as the project develops. Projects with research or development phases are often in this category. With this type of project the uncertainty associated with the cash flows often decreases markedly after the research or development stage. In such a situation it is difficult to compare an internal rate of return, r, with a series of different ks in order to try to assess whether the IRR on the project exceeds the required rate of return. There are no such difficulties with the NPV formula, because the relevant value of k can be inserted into equation 1.1 for each period and the NPV will still indicate that one should invest if it is positive.

The NPV concept is also attractive in the sense that a company manager may act to maximize it without worrying whether the time-stream of benefits from investment satisfies any particular investor's desired time pattern of use (or consumption) of his funds. This holds provided that there is a perfect capital market in which everyone can borrow and lend in order to convert actual timestreams of cash returns from the investment to the desired consumption pattern. Whatever time pattern of consumption is required, the larger the present value of one's wealth, the more one will be able to consume within that pattern. Capital markets are not perfect, but they are quite efficient in developed countries, and so, for practical purposes, one may recommend this view to company managers making investment decisions in the interests of maximizing their shareholders' wealth. (This is not the place to set out these arguments in full. Readers who need to be reminded about them can refer to almost any good corporate-finance textbook.)

Of course, in real live companies investment decisions are not made with only the increase of shareholders' wealth in mind, but for the moment let us concentrate on this viewpoint. Indeed, the current theory of corporate finance goes no further. Other possible interested parties rarely receive more than a brief mention.

Given this very brief review of the measures of return derived from the theory of finance, consideration now needs to be given to the way in which this theory suggests that risk should be taken into account.

Assessing the relationship between risk and return for one-period investment

When, in the early and mid 1960s, I first learned concepts from the theory of finance, I was taught that there were basically two ways of taking risk into account in project appraisal. The first was to incorporate a premium for risk into the discount rate to be used in the NPV calculation. Crude as the explanation may seem now, it was stated that a project with an NPV which was just positive would then still have a 'buffer of present value' in hand to allow for errors and uncertainties. The second approach was to use a discount rate which contained no element of risk premium and then to assess risk separately by looking at the distribution of possible NPVs. Let us focus discussion on the problem of determining the appropriate risk premium to incorporate into the discount rate with which the expected series of cash flows should be discounted.

The theory of finance has moved forward very rapidly since my student days. Now there is a very well developed modern portfolio theory relating to the determination of risk premia. This is based on the recognition that shareholders do not hold just single assets but hold portfolios of them. Consequently, the total risk that they face is the total risk possessed by the whole portfolio of their assets. It follows that the risk attached to an individual security or share which is of concern to a security-holder is the extra risk which that security adds to his (or her) portfolio and not the total risk faced by that share in isolation.

The current dominant theory which formulates this notion is the **capital asset pricing model** (CAPM). This defines portfolio risk as the variance or standard deviation of expected returns associated with a given portfolio. Using this definition, one could in theory, plot all possible portfolios of shares as a shaded area on a graph with axes labelled 'Expected return' (strictly the arithmetic mean of the distribution of expected returns on a one-period investment) and 'Standard deviation of returns', as shown on figure 1.1.

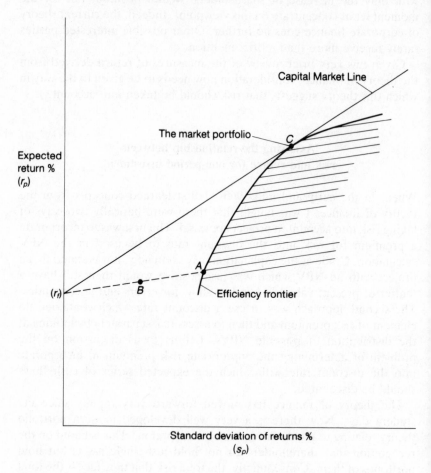

Figure 1.1   Portfolio risk: the efficiency frontier and the Capital Market Line

Any portfolio is said to be efficient if it offers the largest expected return for a given degree of risk measured by the standard deviation of the distribution of expected returns. If there were no efficient capital market, investors would simply choose a particular portfolio on the efficiency frontier which happened to match their attitude towards balancing risk with return. However, with an efficient capital market in which one can freely borrow or lend at a risk-free interest rate r_f, an investor can always achieve a higher expected return for a given degree of risk from a portfolio which consists of a proportion of risky assets and a proportion of risk-free lending or borrowing. This theory also implies that all investors will hold the same portfolio of risky assets irrespective of their attitudes towards taking risks.

To justify these statements, consider an investor who has invested in portfolio A and who then realizes that he may be able to improve his position by lending some of his wealth at a risk-free rate while retaining that part of his wealth invested in equity in portfolio A. That investor has then available to him a range of different combinations of risk-free and risky investment as indicated by points along the line $r_f A$. Clearly, the investor may consider himself to be better off at B than he was at A. Observe, however, that, if the investor held a mixture of portfolio C and risk-free investment, he could be even better off, because $r_f C$ always offers higher returns than $r_f A$ for any degree of risk except at the intercept r_f itself.

A similar form of logic can be used to demonstrate that an investor wishing to accept more risk than investment in portfolio C alone provides can improve his position by borrowing at a risk-free rate to increase his total investment in portfolio C rather than moving to a different, more risky portfolio on the efficiency frontier of risky assets.

It follows that all investors will invest in the same portfolio of risky assets but combine this with different proportions of risk-free investment (borrowing being considered as negative investment). This common risky portfolio is called the **market portfolio** and the line indicating the possible combinations of risk-free investment and the market portfolio is called the **Capital Market Line** (CML). The CML is, in fact, the basis for establishing a formula for the risk premium. In fact the mean return required on a portfolio (r_p) can be expressed as

$$r_p = r_f + \frac{m - r_f}{s_m} \cdot s_p \tag{1.3}$$

where m is the expected rate of return of the market portfolio, s_m is the standard deviation of returns of the market portfolio and s_p is the standard deviation of the appropriate risky portfolio.

From the CML expressed in 1.3 a **Security Market Line** can be derived which indicates the equilibrium condition between the risk and return of an individual security. This in fact is the formula for calculating the required rate of return (k_e) on an individual company's shares which does take into account the fact that this share will be held in a widely diversified portfolio. The formula is

$$k_e = r_f + (m - r_f) \cdot \frac{\text{Cov}(k_e, m)}{s_m^{\,2}}$$

$$= r_f + (m - r_f) \cdot B_e \tag{1.4}$$

where k_e is the expected return for the particular security in mind and $\text{Cov}(k_e, m)$ is the covariance of that security's returns with those of the market portfolio. (See any basic finance text, e.g. Brealey and Myers, 1984, ch. 8, for the derivation of this formula from the equation for the CML.) k_e is used here rather than just k because, as will be seen below, it is very important to distinguish between the required return for equity-holders and that for the firm as a whole. k_e therefore denotes the cost of equity capital and only equals the returns required on the firm's total assets if the firm is wholly equity-financed. B_e, called the share's (equity) **beta value**, measures the contribution which that share makes to the risk of the market portfolio.

The holder of a widely diversified portfolio can use a security's beta as a measure of the extra risk he faces as a result of acquiring that security. Beta represents the amount of uncertainty in the distribution of expected returns from a security which cannot be diversified away, and this is called the **systematic risk** of the security. Hence, given estimates for r_f, m and a security's beta, a corporate finance officer can estimate the yield that shareholders require on the company's shares over the next period. Furthermore, to re-emphasize the point, this value of k_e, often called the company's cost of equity capital, can be determined without any need to consider the degree of aversion which the share-holders have towards risk. It also follows that the company gains nothing on behalf of the shareholders by diversifying its activities. The theory and its associated assumptions of perfect markets imply that a company should focus on maximizing its present value. If it uses the correct risk-adjusted discount rate, it need not worry about diversifica-tion. If the shareholders do not like the resulting risk profile, they can easily arrange a diversification package of their own.

More importantly for the purposes of this book, the theory provides a clear formulation of the trade-off between return and risk in the market. Hence, it is a big step forward in comparison to the considerable vagueness generated by adding risk premia to discount rates as practised before the development of the CAPM.

Estimating a company's beta in practice

The beta for a company's shares depends on the extent to which it varies along with returns on the market portfolio, which in practice are usually taken to be the returns earned on an equity stock-market index. Consequently, the regression coefficient obtained when the share's returns are regressed on the index returns is that share's beta coefficient. For example, suppose that over the last twelve years the returns of the share and the index have been as shown in table 1.1 and figure 1.2. Note that the returns have been expressed as excesses over the risk-free rate to allow for variations in the risk-free rate itself over that period.

Table 1.1 Estimation of a share's beta

Year (1)	Excess return on share (k_{et}) (2)	Excess return on index (m_t) (3)	$(3)^2$ (4)	$(2) \times (3)$ (5)
1	6.0	11.0	121.0	66.0
2	6.1	9.0	81.0	54.9
3	7.0	11.0	121.0	77.0
4	7.3	12.0	144.0	87.6
5	8.0	14.0	196.0	112.0
6	8.7	16.0	256.0	139.2
7	6.0	13.0	169.0	78.0
8	6.3	10.0	100.0	63.0
9	8.6	14.0	196.0	120.4
10	9.0	14.0	196.0	126.0
11	10.4	13.8	190.4	143.5
12	8.5	10.0	100.0	85.0
Sum	91.9	147.8	1870.4	1152.6
Mean	7.66	12.32		

Note: For purposes of this table and equation 1.5 only, k_{et} and m_t represent *excess* returns over the risk-free rate.

The results of the regression are as follows:

$$(\text{Col.2}) = 2.56 + 0.414\ (\text{Col.3}) \qquad R^2 = 0.382$$
$$(0.166)$$

The share's beta is 0.414. (In fact this value of beta would be rather low in practice. Between October and December 1989, the London Business School Risk Measurement Service found beta to vary between 1.74 and -0.04, but only in a very few cases did it go above 1.5 or below 0.25. Also, R^2 rarely went above 0.5 for the individual companies and was usually somewhat lower.) The regression line, with the share's beta as its slope, is called the share's **characteristic line**.

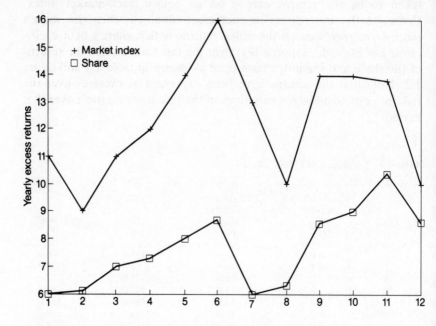

Figure 1.2 Hypothetical movement of returns on a share and market index over twelve years

In this example only 38.2 per cent of the variation in this company's excess returns was explained by the variation of excess returns on the market index. Consequently 61.8 per cent of the variation in this share's excess returns is accounted for by specific factors affecting this share alone and not general market movements. The risk attached to a share can therefore be divided into two parts: **systematic risk** (the risk faced in terms of general market fluctuations) and **non-systematic risk** (the specific risk faced by individual shares).

Instead of running the regression, it is possible to calculate the estimated beta directly, using formula 1.4.

$$
\begin{aligned}
B &= \frac{\mathrm{Cov}(k_e, m)}{s_m^2} = \frac{\Sigma_t \, (k_{et} - \overline{k})(m_t - \overline{m}) \, / \, n}{\Sigma_t \, (m_t - \overline{m})^2 \, / \, n} \\
&= \frac{\Sigma_t \, k_{et} m_t - 12.\overline{k}.\overline{m}}{\Sigma_t \, m_t^2 - 12.\overline{m^2}}
\end{aligned}
\tag{1.5}
$$

where the bar over a variable indicates a mean value and n is the number of observations.

In terms of the example above this provides

$$B = \frac{1152.6 - (12 \times 7.66 \times 12.32)}{1870.4 - (12 \times 12.32 \times 12.32)}$$

$$= 0.410$$

which, apart from rounding errors, is the same as the regression coefficient calculated above.

It will be noted that the share's beta is below 1.0. This means that, in comparison to the returns on the market index, the share has a smaller rise in a bull market, when share prices generally are rising, and a smaller fall in a bear market, when share prices generally are falling. Such shares are sometimes called 'defensive' stocks. In contrast, 'aggressive' stocks have betas of more than 1.0 and fluctuate more than the market index as the whole market moves up and down.

It should be noted, however, that many of the largest companies quoted on the London Stock Exchange have betas close to 1.0. Moreover, in calculating the cost of equity for those companies, variations in betas between companies only affect the $m-r_f$ component of equation 1.4. If one takes the long-run value of m even as high as 15 per cent and the risk-free rate (as in December 1989) at about 7 per cent, a company with a beta of 0.7 (e.g. British Telecom) will have a cost of equity of 12.6 per cent, which is only about 4 per cent different from British Aerospace with a beta of 1.22 and a cost of equity of 16.76 per cent.

How good is the CAPM at explaining investment-market behaviour?

Before proceeding further with this model, it is worth briefly considering the extent to which it has been shown to explain real world behaviour in asset-pricing. There have been extensive tests of the CAPM (mainly in the USA), and, in general, empirical studies have established a positive and linear relationship between risk and return. On the other hand, tests to date have not shown an exact relationship with systematic risk as the theory would predict, and some recent evidence suggests that the risk premium may not always be positive when year-end effects are excluded.

In the USA, 'year-end effects' occur in January (in the UK in April), when investors adjust their portfolios to optimize their tax positions (see

Corhay et al., 1987). If this January effect is excluded from CAPM tests in the USA, there is doubt whether a positive relationship between return and risk can be established empirically. In the UK this year-end effect has similarly been shown to be enhanced (see Levis, 1985) with respect to small companies. There is also UK evidence to suggest inconsistencies in market behaviour between small and large firms. Smaller companies have been shown to have larger returns than larger companies, while the large companies have higher betas (even though accounting earnings per share are more volatile for smaller companies). This suggests that investors have perceptions of risk related to smaller companies which are not adequately captured by correlation with the market index returns. Perhaps other factors need to be introduced to explain investment risk. Alternatively, or perhaps even consequently, this small-company effect may be due to the thinness of trading in such shares.

This does not necessarily mean that the *theory* is wrong. First, the CAPM defines the market portfolio as comprising all types of risky assets which individuals may hold, including land, property and securities. The empirical tests have used market indices of common shares as proxies for the market portfolio, and the degree of error associated with this cannot easily be rectified. For example, one of the largest investments many people hold, even quite wealthy people, is their residence, or residences. The desire to acquire a residence certainly cannot be attributed solely to the search to be mean-variance efficient. The existence of non-wealth-maximizing objectives as motivation for holding at least part of one's total asset portfolio makes it impossible to test the applicability of the CAPM on that portion of assets which are held with wealth maximization in mind.

Secondly, the CAPM defines returns and risks in terms of expectations. The empirical tests have assumed that historic data give an adequate indication of expectations. If one then adds other difficulties, such as the assumed equivalence of borrowing and lending rates and the fact the Treasury bill rate, often used as the risk-free rate, is not riskless in real terms, the difficulty of specifying tests which leave the validity of the theory in no doubt is obvious. Also, some tests have been criticized for paying inadequate attention to the problem of statistical bias, but this need not be dwelt upon here because none of this means that the CAPM is necessarily wrong. If the CAPM could be tested properly, it might represent a reasonable representation of market behaviour. But, then, it might not!

It is important, therefore, to consider whether there is an alternative theory upon which to base risk–return relationships. A recent rival to the CAPM, called the **Arbitrage Pricing Theory** (APT), has been claimed to explain a greater part of market behaviour: 'In all of the performance comparisons with CAPM of which we are aware (whether done by researchers who have hopes for the model . . . or by those who question its empirical foundation . . .) APT outperformed CAPM' (Bower, Bower and Logue, 1986). Some consideration of APT is therefore necessary.

Ross (1976) introduced the APT on the premise that returns on securities vary from those expected according to their sensitivity to *unanticipated* changes in various basic economic factors or forces. These basic forces are thought to have a systematic effect on all securities. The returns of individual securities (or portfolios or individual assets) may therefore be expressed as a funcion of three elements:

$$k_e = E + \sum_{i=1}^{n} b_i f_i + e \qquad (1.6)$$

where E is the expected return of the security;

b_i is the sensitivities of the security returns to the economic forces f_i; and

e is the residual, non-systematic risk associated with idio-syncratic factors which affect the individual companies' returns.

As with the CAPM theory, it may be assumed that an investor may diversify away the non-systematic risk due to idiosyncratic factors. Hence, a company manager should look to earn a rate of return on investment equal to the expected return for these assets plus adjustments for the sensitivity to these prime economic forces.

Tests of the APT have used factor analysis to determine 'economic factors' which explain security returns (see Bower, Bower and Logue, 1986). Unfortunately this is a statistical artefact which does not provide an *economic* explanation of what these factors are. Moreover, different researchers have established different numbers of factors – from two to nine. This makes it difficult to accept the APT as an established theory, even if it were known what the economic meaning of the factors is. It is also tempting to argue that through statistical manipulation some statistical factors will *always* be identified, and that identification of factors devoid of empirical meaning justifies no theory at all.

Roll and Ross (1984) report, however, that, through attempts to estimate the economic factors directly, the following four seem to be dominant:

- unanticipated change in inflation;
- unanticipated industrial production;
- unanticipated change in risk premia (the difference between yields of low- and high-grade bonds);
- unanticipated changes in the term structure of interest rates.

The first two factors are deemed to affect the cash-flow numerators in NPV calculations, while the last two affect the discount rates in those same calculations. If this can be substantiated through wider testing, it at least provides some tentative alternative logic. However, when it comes to testing the APT in order to try to explain share-price movements, there remain data problems and it is difficult to separate out anticipated from unanticipated factor movements (see Roll and Ross, 1984).

So what may one conclude regarding the APT? That some argue that it is better at explaining security returns than the CAPM, but that the results of empirical tests of the APT may be largely a statistical artefact devoid of much economic logic. If, however, the argument of Roll and Ross (1984) with regard to the four factors identified can be substantiated, corporate managers may have an alternative basis upon which to estimate required returns for their corporate groups. They need, in principle, to modify the expected return according to the perceived sensitivity towards these basic economic factors. Bower, Bower and Logue (1986) think that corporate planners will not be able to do this until the basic factors have been identified more precisely and books similar to 'beta books' have been made readily available for the APT's b_i.

The fact that the APT has not yet been developed into a form in which it can readily be used by company finance managers, plus some severe doubts about whether it is likely, in the near future, to provide economically recognizable, consistent and proven basic factors with stable coefficients (b_i), persuaded me to retain the older CAPM theory as the basis for the finance theory in this work. However, it must also be recognized that the CAPM is still a *theory*. Increasing evidence has shown that it cannot be proved by reference to historic data on securities. Despite widespread adoption in elementary financial management texts, the CAPM has not been justified beyond doubt and so further reference to it in this book must take this into account. All that one can say is that this book is trying to look at corporate resource allocation from the viewpoint of different disciplines. The fact is that, while financial academics have not yet been able to prove definitely and empirically *any* theory (i.e. CAPM or APT) showing the positive relationship between risk and return, despite many years and hundreds of computer hours of trying, this is the current state of the finance literature. Moreover, the CAPM is the best *theory* available and, in attempting to compare and contrast the approaches of different disciplines, one has little option in using the CAPM to represent finance theory. Hence the emphasis will still be on the CAPM, although some brief reference will be made to the APT in chapter 6, where possible links between a corporate-strategy perspective and the theory of finance will be considered.

In fact, for the purposes of this book, the problems of adhering to the CAPM may be less serious than they seem. When considering investment in industrial projects within companies, it will become clear that the *concepts* derived from this theory and its rational analysis of risk are rather more important than the precise determination of beta values based on historic data. Nevertheless, enough has probably been said to warn readers to keep conclusions in this book derived from the CAPM in perspective. The strength of the theory is that it takes our understanding of the risks faced by shareholders considerably beyond what it was before the development of the CAPM, and managers do need a *conceptual apparatus* in order to handle the problem of balancing risk against return. Also, much of our human behaviour is governed by much poorer theories about cause and effect. But the CAPM still remains at the level of deductive theory and is not a complete empirical explanation of shareholder and investor behaviour.

Moreover, while it has already been noted that the cost of equity capital is not highly sensitive to variations in beta, the CAPM is very useful for indicating the general level of equity costs. It shows quite clearly that the rates of return on investment sought by many large companies (25–30 per cent), or the hurdle rates implied by very short payback periods, are far too high. This further suggests under-investment in UK industry. While this view is often stated in the financial press, it is not often justified by reference to the CAPM theory.

Separating business risk from financial risk

It has been stated above that k_e is not the required rate of return on the total assets of the company unless the company is financed totally by equity. If there is debt in the capital structure, equity-holders face two types of risk: **operating business risk** and **financial risk**. The former refers to the uncertainty associated with cash flows to be received from investment in physical assets. Equity-shareholders face more risk to the extent that debt-holders have a prior claim to returns. The higher the financial gearing, the higher is the financial risk. The company has to take into account the returns required by both equity-holders and debt-holders in deciding what return must be earned on total assets, and the classical formula used to establish this rate of return (ignoring taxes for the moment) is

$$k_o = D.k_d + E.k_e \tag{1.7}$$

where it is assumed that there are only two types of finance, debt and equity. k_d is the required return on debt, k_e is the required return on equity, and D and E are respectively the proportions of debt and equity in the capital structure. If it is then recognized that the cost of debt can be estimated using the CAPM just as the cost of equity can, this formula can be rewritten

$$k_o = D \left\{ r_f + B_d \left(m - r_f \right) \right\} + E \left\{ r_f + B_e \left(m - r_f \right) \right\} \tag{1.8}$$

where B_d and B_e are the betas for debt and equity. This then simplifies to

$$k_o = r_f + B_o \left(m - r_f \right) \tag{1.9}$$

where $B_o = B_d.D + B_e.E$

It follows that the classical weighted average cost of capital is exactly the same as the risk-free rate plus a risk premium based on the beta value derived from the covariance of the firm's total returns (before deducting interest) with the market portfolio. The CAPM does not invalidate the traditional formula: it enhances it by giving it a more precise basis of measurement.

Often analysts assume that B_d is near enough to zero to ignore it. Then

$$k_o = r_f + E(k_e - r_f)$$

$$= D.r_f + E.k_e \tag{1.10}$$

With debt risk-free, its cost, k_d, obviously becomes equal to r_f.

Hence, still ignoring tax effects for the moment, with a risk-free rate of 8 per cent, a 30 per cent debt-financed company with a cost of equity of 16 per cent needs to earn

$$k_o = 0.3(0.08) + 0.7(0.16) = 13.6 \text{ per cent}$$

on its total assets. If the excess market return is 7 per cent, this implies a B_o of 0.8 and an alternative calculation for k_o:

$$k_o = 0.08 + 0.8(0.07) = 13.6 \text{ per cent}$$

Required rates of return from divisions and projects for one-period investments

While it may seem unrealistic to consider investment in a division or capital project over only one period, it is necessary to work through the implications under such assumptions in order to provide a proper theoretical basis for moving on to consider multi-period investment.

First, formulae 1.9 and 1.10 are not appropriate discount rates for assessing whether the returns earned on corporate divisions or individual projects are adequate, unless the division or project has exactly the same risk profile (i.e. beta value) as the company as a whole. This will hardly ever be the case. In practice, therefore, one can either estimate k_o and then adjust it to take into account the higher or lower risk faced by the division or project, or, alternatively, estimate the divisional or project required rate of return directly using the following formula

$$k_o' = r_f + (m - r_f) . \frac{\text{Cov}(k_o'm)}{s_m^2}$$

$$= r_f + B_o'(m - r_f) \tag{1.11}$$

where k_o' is used instead of k_o. k_o' stands for the expected return of the division or individual project, as appropriate, and B_o' represents the divisional or project beta.

In fact, formulae 1.10 and 1.11 are not really two different methods, because, if the corporate cost of capital, k_o, is adjusted for the different risk faced by the division or project, the correct adjustment is

$$k_o' = k_o - (B_o - B_o') (m - r_f) \tag{1.12}$$

In other words, there is no alternative to making an estimate of the divisional or project beta. At least, there isn't if one wants to justify the adjustment on the basis of some established theory, rather than admit that it is a complete guess.

On the other hand, it must be stressed that the required divisional or project rate of return cannot be determined precisely. Some judgement is required, but it is suggested that judgement will be assisted by using the CAPM to focus attention on the relevant matters to be considered.

If one requires a divisional discount rate, it is sometimes argued that it is easier to get a more reliable estimate of it than of the yield required on the company's total returns. This is because the company as a whole will represent a unique mix of different risky assets located in different industries. Consequently, the total corporate required yield can only be derived from past data relating to this particular company, and the beta will then be estimated on a small sample of observations with possible high estimate errors. If, in contrast, a division can be identified as a member of a fairly homogeneous industry, unlevered betas can be calculated for all members of that industry and the average unlevered industry beta can be taken for use as the divisional cost of capital (i.e. applied to discount the total operating cash flow of the division before deducting interest). The advantage in this procedure is that estimating-errors will tend to cancel out when betas for a number of companies are estimated and then averaged to determine the industry beta.

There is reason, however, not to rely upon this argument too readily. Firms are allocated to industries using a standard classification, and the procedure usually adopted is to assign firms to the industry according to their main line of business. This can mean that an industry beta has actually been derived from returns of members of an industry which incorporate effects of operating in industries other than the one to which they are assigned in the classification. This problem will not be lessened by taking finer industry classifications, because the problem lies with the definition of an 'industry' at whatever level of detail one is operating. The corporate financial analyst can check whether this problem is likely to be serious by examining the dispersion of unlevered beta values in the industry, rather than just accepting the average industry beta without question. A low dispersion will probably indicate that this problem may be ignored and that the companies concerned are sufficiently homogeneous for that industry's beta to be used as the divisional beta.

Even so, the analyst should also explicitly consider whether his (or her) own division has an anticipated stream of returns which is likely to vary with the returns of the market portfolio to the same extent as the average industry returns. There will be no share-price data on which to make estimates of the beta for the division, but accounting returns or cash flows could be used as surrogates for stock-market returns and there is some evidence that a reasonably good correspondence exists between such accounting or cash-flow betas and betas based on market returns for companies. If the analyst can obtain segmented earnings statements of the other companies in the industry, he might even be able to get a better idea of the 'pure' industry beta by basing the estimate of the industry average upon accounting returns.

To summarize, the best procedure would probably be to make divisional estimates on the basis of formula 1.11 using past accounting returns or cash flows (both calculated before interest) and then comparing the results with the average industry unlevered beta if it is clear that the division largely operates within that same industry and that that industry has a low dispersion of unlevered betas.

It might also be noted that, if market returns are used to calculate betas for the industry, some regard is being paid to companies' earnings from industries other than the one under which they are classified. Hence, it may mean that the average industry beta is a better estimate of the total firm beta than of the divisional beta. This would be so if the firm in question had a spread of activities with similar systematic-risk characteristics to other firms classified under that industry. This may seem unlikely, but, if so, it seems just as unlikely that the industry beta will reflect the same commercial activities as a 'pure industry' division. There is no substitute for careful thought around these issues, and casual use of the CAPM formula is not recommended.

The estimation of an individual project beta is obviously far more problematic. Projects are rarely duplicates of those undertaken before, especially the major elements of multi-business investment programmes, which are the subject of this book. It is therefore virtually certain that it will not be possible to base project betas on historic figures. The analyst has no alternative but to consider the possible covariance of returns from the project in each period with economic activity generally as reflected in movements of the stock-market index. This will involve considering cost and revenue factors within the project. It is now beginning to become clear why modern portfolio theory and its derivative the CAPM offer a conceptual basis for considering the nature of risk attached to individual corporate projects but do not offer very precise figures to use for the yields required from those projects.

In thinking about the yield required from a project, it would also be sensible to see to what extent costs are 'fixed'. If it is known that some costs will not change in each period, they will obviously have a beta of zero. Hence, one would use higher betas with projects with higher operating leverage (i.e. a higher percentage of fixed costs), because the project rate of return after deduction of fixed costs will be more responsive to general market movements. Care is still needed, however, because fixed costs as defined by accountants are those costs which do not change with changes in the level of output. There may be some 'fixed' costs which do change with economic activity in general.

Multi-period discounting in the appraisal of projects

It was stated earlier in the chapter that the NPV could more easily accommodate the use of different discount rates for different periods of the investment's life. It was also stated that this might be necessary because of the term structure of interest rates or the changing nature of a project's risk at different stages of its life. The same might apply to a division taking into account the different stages of product and industry life-cycles. It is therefore important for the analyst to remember that the discount rate arrived at using the CAPM is only the required rate of return for one period, despite the fact that the covariance of market and asset returns is estimated on the basis of a time series.

Strictly the analyst needs an estimate of the appropriate risk-free rate, the expected market-portfolio rate of return and project beta value for each separate period of the investment being considered. As regards the risk-free rates, the analyst could take the range of different spot rates on Treasury bills. The term structure implied by those rates could also be used in estimating the market-portfolio return for different periods, by modifying the expected return in the current period in proportion to the difference between the relevant spot rate and the current risk-free rate.

The estimation of a beta for each separate period is even more problematic. The analyst needs to consider whether the covariance between the project's cash flows and the market portfolio's returns is likely to change over time. A precise judgement here will be impossible, but that does not mean that the exercise is pointless. There may be marked changes in the nature of activities, expenditures and revenues during the life of a project, and these may reflect changes in the level of general economic activity in the economy as a whole. In most types of industrial investment this will probably not be a significant factor, at least once the project is on stream and producing positive cash flows, but a little thought around this issue may identify situations which do require some adjustment to the implied use of a standard beta throughout all periods of the calculation.

It is also clear now that, if a project has a large initial research or development stage, the outcome of which is much more uncertain than the subsequent earnings will be if the R&D is successful, discounting cash flows back over this initial period does not necessarily have to be done at a higher rate. It will only be necessary to use a higher discount rate to the extent that the outcome of the initial experiments is correlated with the returns of the market portfolio in that period. They may not be highly correlated with the market returns if the success of the R&D depends upon specific technological factors. In other words, if both the actual expenditure and the success of the R&D phase of the project depend very little upon the way the general securities market behaves, the correct way to value the whole project is as follows. First, the cash flows which will occur if the R&D phase is successful must be discounted back to the end of the R&D phase of the project using a discount rate which reflects the beta appropriate to those operating flows (i.e. using the beta value which does not take account of the R&D phase itself). Second, both that value of the future cash flows calculated as at the end of the R&D phase and the R&D expenditure itself must be discounted back to the beginning of the project life at a rate which is based on the beta appropriate to just the R&D phase. The beta for the R&D phase may be quite low due to its low systematic risk. (The precise form of calculation required will be shown in chapter 2 when discussing decision trees.)

This conclusion has very wide implications. R&D investments are often looked upon as very risky and it is suspected that practising managers will therefore use higher discount rates, not only for the initial R&D stages of investment, but also for the subsequent earnings stages. This will probably be done even though the outcome of the R&D is determined by scientific or technical factors which are likely to have a beta near to zero. Such technical risks would be totally diversifiable according to the CAPM theory and hence by definition not part of systematic risk. It is therefore interesting to speculate whether industrialists are not making errors and undertaking less apparently risky projects than the market would permit.

Of course, another interpretation is that they do not see the CAPM and systematic risk as the only dimension of risk that they face, especially when considering both their own managerial position and the welfare of company employees. Such issues will be addressed in chapter 9. The point to note now is that, once again, a clear recognition of the concepts involved could lead to a constructive debate amongst corporate decision-makers about the extent to which they wish to satisfy different parties' interests and leave shareholders to fend for themselves in arranging their own risk diversification. The end result will not be a precisely determined discount rate, but the debate is likely to lead to one which is more defensible and to make it clearer why the firm is going into the project, in terms of its impact on the fundamental interests of the corporate shareholders.

**Other complications: cash flows after corporate taxes,
adjusting the required return for the tax benefits from debt finance,
capital allowances, subsidized loans and inflation**

A few other complications need to be considered before conclusions can
be drawn about the current state of finance theory with regard to
determining the required rate of return on investment.

Cash flows after corporate taxes

We have seen that it is appropriate to discount the cash flows of a
project by an unlevered rate determined by reference to the project's
beta. It has not been made clear, however, that the cash flows must be
defined as those arising after corporate taxes. Also, due allowance must
be made for time lags between the point at which cash flows into the
company and the point at which it flows back out again in the form of
taxes. Moreover, the usual practice is to assume that the tax paid is
calculated by applying the tax rate to the total operating cash flows (i.e.
before deducting interest), even though the tax authorities do allow
interest as an expense for tax-calculation purposes. The tax benefit
arising from the deductibility of interest is then dealt with separately,
either by adjusting the cost of debt or by the method explained in the
next subsection. The latter method is a more precise practical tool,
because it is difficult to allow for time lags in the receipt of the tax
benefit using an adjustment to the cost of debt.

The tax deductibility of debt-interest payments

Suppose now that the company has a target financial-gearing ratio of 40
per cent such that its investment each year is financed with 40 per cent of
debt and 60 per cent of equity. Then it seems appropriate to assume that
40 per cent of the expenditure on the project will be financed by debt. In
contrast to dividends, interest payments are fully deductible in calculating taxable income. This means that, at a corporation-tax rate of 40 per
cent, for every pound paid in interest the company recovers 40p from
the Inland Revenue provided that it expects regularly to pay mainstream corporation tax. Consequently, the project gives rise to a tax
shield which has some real economic benefit. If it may be assumed that
the situation is as simple as just described, an easy way to incorporate
this tax benefit into the appraisal of the project is to adjust the NPV of
the project (calculated using the project unlevered rate) by adding to it
the present value of the tax-shield benefit. The present value of the tax

shield for an x per cent debt-financed project which will last four years and which repays the initial loan principal at the end of four years will be

$$\sum_{n=1}^{4} \frac{x.I.k_d.T}{(1 + k_d)n} \tag{1.13}$$

where I is the capital outlay and T is the marginal corporate tax rate. It may not be correct to use k_d as the discount rate, because that is supposed to reflect the risk attached to the tax stream, which includes uncertainty about future tax rates and liability, and is not supposed to relate only to future payments of interest. Whether the discount rate is much above k_d will, strictly, depend upon the covariance of the tax-shield benefits and the market-portfolio returns. Also, strictly speaking, allowance must again be made for time lags between paying the interest and receipt of the tax benefit. These time lags can arise through the company having a temporary non-liability to mainstream corporation tax or simply through delay in making assessments and collecting the tax due. The latter can usually be ignored, but many companies have experienced several years without paying mainstream corporation tax through possessing an excess of tax allowances over current needs to cover assessed income, and so that form of time adjustment can be of critical importance.

To summarize, the project's **adjusted present value** (APV) is the correct value to adopt in appraising the investment, where the APV is equal to (1) the base NPV calculated by discounting the after-tax operating cash flows (i.e. before deducting interest) by the project's unlevered rate, plus (2) the present value of the tax-shield benefit which arises through using debt finance.

Unfortunately, doubts about the precise value of the discount rate to use for the tax-shield stream are far from the most problematic aspect of such an adjustment to the base NPV. While this is not the place to discuss whether a company has or does not have an optimal capital structure, and the relevance of taxation to that question (matters discussed in any basic finance text), it is clear that academics hold a considerable range of views on the value of T. This is due to the existence of significant differences in personal tax rates, and questions related to the relationship between those tax rates and the demand and supply of finance for the economy as a whole. Given the current state of knowledge, I would suggest that, provided the marginal project is not going to change significantly its corporate financial leverage position, an individual company can assume that the market rates of return required on both debt and equity will remain unchanged and that these reflect both financial-risk and personal-tax positions. In such a situation, the individual company can probably assume that, unless the project is huge, it will have minimal effect on its market position as a whole, and so from its individual viewpoint it can use the full marginal corporation-tax rate for T or something fairly close to it. It is appropriate, however, to point out to students that some academics have a different view and that a rigorous consideration requires reading beyond this text, which places far more emphasis on investment decisions than on financing decisions. The vagueness results from our inadequate state of knowledge on the issue. In one sense this makes the APV approach to valuation more attractive, because the estimated effect of the tax shield can be seen quite separately, instead of being wrapped up in an after-tax discount rate for debt. If the acceptability of the project clearly and crucially depends upon the tax-shield gain, it is a signal to look very carefully at whether the project really is so attractive and, at the very least, to test the sensitivity of both the APV and the NPV of the tax shield for reasonable variations in T.

Other adjustments using the APV method

The APV approach is also a useful vehicle for allowing for the effect of tax allowances. In addition to the tax shield one may simply add in another term equal to the NPV of the benefit of the tax allowances. It is usually a simple matter to estimate the expected cash savings through having such allowances; the difficult part, once again, may be to know exactly what discount rate to use to reflect the uncertainty attached to future tax policy. Much depends upon the nature of the tax allowances involved and how long it will be before their benefits materialize.

This approach may also be used to calculate the benefit from special subsidized loans which are specific to the project, i.e. loans at subsidized interest rates that are only available if the project is undertaken. Suppose that such a loan carried an interest rate of 6 per cent when the company's usual debt cost 10 per cent. Then the NPV of the benefit from the subsidized loan would be the difference in gross interest payments discounted at the cost of debt, 10 per cent, less the present value of the lost tax shield through having lower interest payments also discounted at 10 per cent. This would be correct if the previous tax-shield adjustment in the APV had been calculated assuming an unsubsidized rate of interest on all borrowing.

Inflation and the discounting of cash flows

All the discussion so far has assumed that there is no such thing as inflation. Fortunately, while the business problems associated with inflation may be severe, the extra technical problems introduced into the appraisal calculations of investment analysis are not too complex. By far the most straightforward way to allow for inflation is to use market (nominal) discount rates expressed in money rather than real terms and use those rates to discount the actual money flows expected from the project in each year. Of course, in order to estimate the actual money flows to be derived from the project, estimates will have to be made of the rates of price changes which are likely to occur in respect of items of expenditure used in the project, and the changes that will be possible in the prices of the company's products. Similarly, care must be taken not to inflate cash flows which are fixed over time irrespective of the rate of inflation. Nevertheless, the key point is that there is no need to convert those estimated future money flows to a real value if the discount rates are also expressed in money terms. This assumes that investors take inflation into account in demanding money rates of return.

In fact the treatment of inflation is often discussed very loosely. One hears or reads (for example, in Brealey and Myers, 1984) that expected future *money* flows may be discounted at market nominal rates, or that the future money flows may be converted to real terms and discounted by a discount rate expressed similarly in real terms. Taken literally this is correct, but care is needed in interpreting the statement. If adopting the second approach, it is vital to recognize that the real rate must be expressed in terms of the real value of money *to the providers of finance*. It must take into account *their* opportunity cost in real terms. Hence it is *not* correct simply to assess future cash flows in terms of current *company* price levels and discount those by a real rate. A simple example will demonstrate this point.

Suppose that investors require a real rate of return of 5 per cent and that general inflation is expected at 10 per cent. Assume also that the net cash inflow one year hence from a one-year project *at current prices of the company's sales and costs* will be £100 and that the current outlay of that project is also £100. Finally, assume that the company will be able to achieve a money net cash inflow of £120 in one year's time due to specific price movements in its industry. That project will have a positive NPV as follows:

$$\frac{£120}{1.05 \times 1.1} - 100 = +3.9$$

The project should be accepted (i.e. the market nominal rate inferred is 15.5 per cent). The ability of the firm to increase prices in excess of the general rate of inflation for goods and services purchased by investors is greater in scale than the 5 per cent real rate required. In contrast, simply discounting the cash flows expected at current company prices by the real rate will give the wrong answer:

$$\frac{£100}{1.05} - 100 = -4.7$$

It is wrong because it makes no attempt to assess the cash flow in terms that are real to the investors who provide the finance.

If the analyst wishes to work in real terms, the future cash flow in real terms must be calculated by adjusting the future *money* flow expected by the general rate of inflation (i.e. the rate relevant for the investors' opportunity costs). Hence the year-one cash flow in real terms *to investors providing finance* is

$$\frac{£120}{1.1} = 109.1$$

and the NPV is then, obviously, +£3.9:

$$\frac{£109.1}{1.05} - 100 = +£3.9$$

Discussions with practising financial controllers have indicated that this is often not understood, and most basic financial-management text-books do not make the distinction clear.

We have now concluded discussion of the basic elements from the theory of finance which relate to the discounting of expected returns by a risk-adjusted discount rate in order to maximize shareholders' wealth. Despite the elegance of the basic CAPM theory, a range of uncertainties have been raised, mainly in terms of identifying the appropriate discount rates and the benefit of financial gearing. These are not trivial problems, for a small variation in the discount rates used for a long-lived investment project can have a substantial impact upon the APV. Moreover, so far no mention has been made of investment overseas. The discussion has effectively assumed investment solely within a domestic economy. Given that this book is aimed at the analysis of resource allocation in large multi-business companies, this omission must be rectified.

Extra complications with foreign investment

As soon as one considers the possibility of investment in foreign countries, it appears that the difficulties involved in arriving at a reliable estimate of NPV (or APV) escalate rapidly. Depending upon which foreign country one is thinking of investing in, there may be a considerable risk of political upheaval or even an expropriation of the company's assets. Also, the value of any remittances back to the parent will depend upon the prevailing exchange rates and any action taken by the company to protect itself against exchange-rate losses. Moreover, some foreign countries block, either completely or partially, the remittance of funds back to the parent company. Foreign taxation may also depend upon the form in which funds are transmitted. Finally, various financing deals may be arranged, not as the pure provision of finance, but as a means of partial protection against political risks. For example, I have observed how leasing arrangements may be routed through a major bank so that ownership of the asset rests with the bank, rather than with the company operating abroad; the foreign government may thus be deterred from expropriating the asset through fear of foregoing future financial assistance.

Despite all these significant practical implications, the basic theoretical issues are relatively clear. It must be borne in mind that in the current theory of corporate finance, and in this chapter so far, the analysis relates wholly to the maximization of shareholder wealth. It, therefore, does not matter what the investment is in, or where assets and operations are located; the expected returns to the parent company should be discounted at a rate which reflects the beta associated with the expected covariance of those returns with the market returns. It will be more difficult, in practice, to provide reliable estimates of cash flows back to the parent company and a reliable project beta when the increased uncertainties of foreign investment are involved, but the basic theory is clear.

Various authors state that projects should also be appraised at the level of the subsidiary, in the currency of that country. This may well be required, but, if so, it is owing to practical organizational requirements or objectives other than the maximization of the wealth of the main shareholders. (The latter objectives are discussed in chapter 9.)

Once one considers operating in an international environment, there arises the additional question of what the market portfolio is, even if, incorrectly, it is interpreted as being only a portfolio of risky traded securities. Is it the UK market portfolio or, supposing that the company is investing in Japan, the Japanese? Or is it some average of the two? The answer is that the market concerned should be the one in which the company shareholders deal. This does not yield an easy practical solution, because clearly some investors diversify their asset-holdings abroad and some do not. As stock markets internationalize, one might argue that the expected returns and variation of those returns on the leading stock exchanges of the world will come closer together, but it will be some time before the corporate analyst can assume that beta based on a market portfolio will be the same regardless of the market in question.

It should be noted, however, that, although this problem always seems to be raised in textbooks in relation to the complexities of foreign investment, it really has nothing to do with the company's decision to invest in a project located abroad. Exactly the same problem arises with corporate domestic investment if the shareholders are assumed to hold securities which are diversified across international capital markets. The physical location of the company investment is totally irrelevant in selecting the market portfolio to use. The target country for corporate investment is only relevant as a factor in selecting a discount rate in so far as the beta should be calculated on the expected covariance of returns on that foreign corporate investment and on the market portfolio selected.

It is very clear from focusing on the implications of the CAPM that the practice by some multinationals of increasing the required rate of return for foreign projects may well be wrong – at least in terms of maximizing shareholder wealth. The relevant concept of risk for determining required yields is systematic risk, not total risk. Hence, a project in a developing country which may carry significant risk when viewed in isolation may have significant risk-diversification properties and be properly discounted at a lower rate than that used for domestic investment. Whether this is so will depend on what that project contributes to the variance of a well-diversified portfolio. In fact, if the extra risk associated with a foreign, as opposed to a domestic, project is mainly attributed to the risk of expropriation or other extreme aspects of political risk, the company should look long and hard at whether there is any reason at all for such events to be associated with the movement of share prices on the relevant capital market. If there is no such association, shareholders should be able to protect themselves perfectly against such risks by diversification and there will be no need to adjust the discount rate at all in respect of political risk. On the other hand, some projects in developing countries may well have expected returns which are highly correlated with world markets (see Shapiro, 1988).

In respect of political and other general uncertainties associated with foreign projects, there is, therefore, no reason to depart from the fundamental valuation principles already described. It will be more difficult to provide reliable estimates of expected cash flows back to the parent company and their underlying probability distributions, but that is what has to be provided by corporate analysts. Given the greater uncertainty, companies may well want to indulge in more sensitivity analysis to determine how the attractiveness of the project will change if forecasted events are wrong, but that is a different matter. The resulting series of expected cash flows should then be discounted at the appropriate rate of return required for the project as determined by formula 1.11 using a specific project beta. Often this beta need not be substantially different from those for similar projects in other parts of the world. The difference in political risk, for example, will be treated as a risk attached to the expected cash flow *per se*, and probabilities of different political events would be used in estimating the expected cash flows. This also has the benefit of facilitating a separate consideration of the effect of political risk on the project, which would be difficult if it were wrapped up in an arbitrarily determined higher discount rate.

The question of which exchange rate to use does not give rise to major conceptual problems, although it may give rise to considerable anxiety in practice in forecasting what the exchange rate will be. The treatment required is no different from that needed when considering any uncertain variable which can affect the outcome of an investment. One has simply to estimate the expected cash flow in the currency being used as the basis of the evaluation and determine the project NPV. If the corporate treasurer decides to take steps to hedge against exchange-rate movements, the expected cash flows must be estimated after allowing the expected benefits and costs of such protective action.

The handling of foreign-government regulations blocking remittances also needs consideration. First, it needs to be recognized that, while dividends to a parent company may be blocked, it may still be possible to transmit funds back by other means, such as royalty payments or inflated prices for goods and services, though it must be borne in mind that there are also limits on such pricing behaviour. Even so, suppose that funds are unlikely to be remittable for fifteen years. Then, according to strict theory, an investment abroad with a life of only five years cannot be looked upon in isolation. The correct procedure is to consider how the proceeds from the five-year investment will be reinvested, in order to see what sum will be remittable after fifteen years. If the NPV of this 'combined investment' is positive, the company should go ahead. It is obvious that the first five-year project cannot be seen in isolation. Suppose that on its own it has a huge positive NPV, but that funds cannot be transmitted within fifteen years and it is certain that within that period a new government will come to power and sequestrate all foreign-held assets. Obviously the huge positive NPV will be of no value.

It might be argued that the statements in the last few paragraphs are satisfactory provided that the shareholder's objective is to maximize his (or her) wealth in terms of a specified currency – for instance, the US shareholder is interested in maximizing wealth in US dollars. This may still be true for many shareholders, but it is increasingly not the case for large shareholders. They think in terms of a diversified wealth holding in securities denominated in various currencies (Flight and Lee-Swan, 1988).

It may be argued that shareholders who follow such an internationally diversified strategy have no *strict* conception of wealth maximization in a single currency at all. Nevertheless, as with diversification aross different corporate stocks, the shareholder can be assumed to take care of his own diversification requirements over different currencies. Also, one may still assume that he will require more rather than less wealth generation from any single source. Moreover, in order to construct an appropriately diversified international position, the shareholder must have estimates of what income and capital gains may be expected from each asset held *and in what currency those proceeds will be received*. It follows that the corporation should decide in which currency gains will be transmitted to the shareholder (usually one may assume the currency of the parent company) and attempt to select projects which maximize wealth in that currency. The shareholders will then be best able to make their own diversification decisions. I believe that it also follows that there is no need to revise any of the arguments of earlier paragraphs in this section: foreign investments need to be evaluated in terms of the NPV of projected cash flows achievable in the parent company's currency if that is the currency in which shareholders will receive benefits from the investment. This applies whether the shareholders are perpetually diversified over assets denominated in different currencies or not. That much seems relatively clear. The difficult issue is deciding, in practice, what the relevant market portfolio is and in what currency its returns should be stated in order to calculate the appropriate beta for the cash flows as just defined.

A final problem to consider in this section is the question of subsidized loans and other interactions between investment in the project and financing arrangements which arise when a company develops activities abroad. It is probably best to deal with these complications by adding terms to the APV formulation. Again, there is no theoretical difference when foreign activities are involved, although the relevant figures to use may well be more difficult to estimate.

A brief summary of resource allocation from the shareholder's view based on the CAPM

It is clear that there now exists a considerable body of theory relating to the valuation of securities, risk diversification, required rates of return and project analysis. It is also clear that this theory has been extremely valuable in identifying key concepts and issues to be addressed in corporate-project appraisal. The state of our knowledge is still such, however, that risk-adjusted discount rates for individual projects, divisions or total groups cannot be specified precisely with any high degree of assurance. Certainly with 'beta theory' we are in a better position to understand the basic concepts that we should be considering than we were before it was available, but many instances have been given above of difficulties which arise in applying the theory in practice. Perhaps we can be more certain about the returns required from divisions of companies that are squarely in a specified industry in comparison with returns required from whole groups or individual projects, but even there misconceptions are possible, through ignoring the process by which statisticians classify companies as belonging to a particular industry. It is plain that corporate analysts will not wish to rely on single estimates of the discount rate, but will prefer to assess the NPV of projects using a range of likely rates. The result will usually be presented in the form of an investment profile like that shown in Figure 1.3.

The uncertainty does not necessarily arise only with the total-asset beta. The discount rate for various separate elements of an APV calculation may also be subject to doubt, in which case analysts may

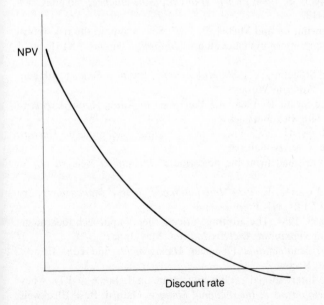

Figure 1.3 Sensitivity of NPV (or APV) to discount-rate variations shown by an investment profile

want to produce a separate investment profile for each element of the APV. It would then be possible to run a simulation allowing for the uncertainties attached to each discount rate to produce a probability distrubution of APVs. A case seems to be building up for the use of some sort of financial modelling to help evaluate doubts about a project's discount rate.

Financial modelling with regard to corporate resource allocation will be the subject of chapter 2, but there are already some signals that modellers may not be acting in ways consistent with the theory of finance, principally when dealing with risk assessment. The discussion on modelling must, therefore, avoid falling into that trap and give due regard to the theory outlined in this chapter.

References

Bower, D., Bower, R. and Logue, D. 1986: A primer on arbitrage pricing theory. In J. Stern and D. Chew (eds), *The Revolution in Corporate Finance*. Oxford: Basil Blackwell.

Brealey, R. and Myers, S. 1984: *Principles of Corporate Finance*, 2nd edn. New York: McCraw-Hill.

Corhay, A., Hawawini, G. and Michel, P. 1987: Seasonality in the risk–return relationships: some international evidence. *Journal of Finance*, XLII, no. 1 (March).

Eitman, D. K. and Stonehill, A. 1986: *Multinational Business Finance*, 4th edn. Reading, Mass.: Addison-Wesley.

Flight, H. and Lee-Swan, B. 1988: *All You Need to Know About Exchange Rates*. London: Sidgwick and Jackson.

Hodder, J. and Riggs, H. 1985: Pitfalls in evaluating risky projects. *Harvard Business Review*, January–February.

Levis, M. 1985: Are small firms big performers? *Investment Analyst*, no. 76 (April).

Rodriques, R. and Carter, E. 1984: *International Financial Management*, 3rd edn. Englewood Cliffs, NJ: Prentice-Hall.

Roll, R. and Ross, S. 1984: The arbitrage pricing theory approach to strategic portfolio planning. *Financial Analysts Journal*, May–June.

Shapiro, A. 1986: *Multinational Financial Management*, 2nd edn. Boston, Mass.: Allyn and Bacon.

Shapiro, A. 1988: International capital budgeting. In J. Stern and D. Chew (eds), *New Developments in International Finance*. Oxford: Basil Blackwell.

Problems and discussion questions

1.1   The financial controller of the Husky PLC has asked you for advice on the discount rate he should use for investment-project appraisal. You decide, first, to estimate the cost of equity for the company from the following historic data

Period	Excess returns on market index (%)	Excess returns on Husky shares (%)
1	7.2	5.2
2	7.9	11.0
3	8.3	(2.3)
4	10.6	4.8
5	13.4	17.5
6	3.2	2.0
7	5.6	6.5
8	(2.4)	1.2
9	7.8	2.4
10	3.4	(8.9)
11	17.8	14.7
12	12.0	11.9
13	6.9	3.2
14	11.7	18.7

(a) Estimate the cost of equity for Husky PLC assuming an expected risk-free rate of 7 per cent and an expected rate of return on the market index of 15 per cent. What is Husky PLC's systematic risk?
(b) Assuming the company is all equity-financed, is your result in (a) appropriate for estimating individual project cash flows? Explain fully.
(c) If Husky PLC was thinking of moving to a target debt ratio of 30 per cent, how would that be likely to affect the beta for Husky's equity. What would be the effect on individual project discount rates? Discuss fully.

1.2   The Husky PLC is considering whether to invest in a project with the following anticipated cash flows

Year		£
0	Capital outlay	10,000
1	Net cash inflows	1,000
2		4,000
3		6,000
4		4,000
5		3,000

(a) You have decided that the discount rate should be somewhere between 16 and 21 per cent. To what extent does your inability to know exactly what discount rate to use affect the desirability of the project? How does a knowledge of the IRR help you avoid worrying about the precise specification of the discount rate?

(b) Now suppose that you realize that the cash-flow estimates above are merely means of probability distributions of each year's cash flows. State how you would need to revise the project investment profile.

1.3 The ABC company is thinking of investing in a completely new venture which is expected to generate operating cash flows of £40,000 per annum over six years in return for an initial capital outlay of £60,000. ABC headquarters has indicated that the new venture must be completely 'stand alone'; it cannot expect debt finance from the parent, although the parent will provide initial funds for investing in the project, provided that a return of 21 per cent can be earned on the project's unlevered cash flows after tax. The company's effective tax rate is 30 per cent.

The proposed manager of the new venture also discovers that the local authority is very keen for this project to go ahead and will provide a subsidized loan with interest at 10 per cent, as against the 12 per cent that the company would otherwise expect to pay. The local-authority loan will, however, contain a clause specifying that operating earnings (before interest and tax) must be 7.5 times the interest payments and that no other debt is to be used to finance the venture. If the local-authority loan is taken out, it will be outstanding for six years, at the end of which period the principal must be repaid. Interest is payable annually in arrears.

For purposes of calculating tax, the company is allowed to write off depreciation on the straight-line basis over six years. Tax payments are made one year after the year for which they are assessed.

The new manager seeks your advice. He must satisfy the parent-company requirement of 21 per cent on the unlevered after-tax cash flows. He himself feels that the requirement is wise, because he does not want to enter into a venture which is fundamentally unsound as a business risk. On the other hand, if he can increase profits by using subsidized lending and taking advantage of the tax benefits derived from the debt capacity of the project, he will do so. He wants, however, to see the financial benefits of this calculated quite separately.

The manager also asks you to specify the maximum amount of subsidized loan he can get from the local authority. When you tell him, he says that the amount suggests a very high leverage in balance-sheet terms for a £60,000 project.

Make some calculations and advise the manager. He says that he would want interest to be covered 7.5 times by earnings even if he borrowed at 12 per cent in the market.

1.4 Husky PLC, whose shareholders hold portfolios mainly in UK securities, is going to invest in an underdeveloped country where there is believed to be considerable risk of political upheaval which could result in the complete expropriation of the project's assets and net revenues. Discuss carefully the conceptual issues to be considered in setting a required rate of return for this project.

1.5 How, in theory, should your answer to 1.4 differ if Husky's shares are held by shareholders who themselves hold portfolios of securities balanced across different currencies and who do not attempt to maximize their own wealth in any single currency?

1.6 As far as the largest UK companies are concerned, the CAPM is more useful for checking the *general level* at which they should try to earn returns for shareholders than for calculating precise differences between them in the returns required. Discuss this statement fully.

1.7 In calculations to discount cash flows, it does not matter whether one allows for inflation by discounting cash flows in real terms by a real discount rate or does so by discounting projected money flows by a nominal discount rate. Discuss fully.

2

Financial Modelling in Project Appraisal and its Relationship to the Theory of Corporate Finance

In chapter 1 resource allocation was reviewed from the viewpoint of the theory of corporate finance. It became clear that, even with developments such as the capital asset pricing model (CAPM), the making of major investment decisions can be a very complex matter. It is in such a situation, where a considerable number of calculations need to be made in order to view a project from a number of different perspectives, that computers have proved valuable decision aids, and, following the explosion of distributed computer power in recent years, their importance in this regard seems bound to increase.

By far the best way to appreciate what computer models can offer is to gain some experience in running some models and interacting with them in the decision process. This chapter will outline several different types of model, but the reader who has not gained any direct experience of running a computer model is urged to work the end-of-chapter exercises. These offer fairly simple models, but they do illustrate the basic principles of some of the types of model used in practice.

All the models illustrated by the end-of-chapter problems were developed using Lotus 1-2-3 (Release 2) on a portable IBM computer with 512 RAM. Such facilities are very modest now and will be available to most students. It is not suggested that large companies will be able to meet all their capital-investment modelling needs using Lotus and a microcomputer – even with Release 3 and a more powerful computer. Rather the purpose is to try to give students a closer insight into what they can do with financial models and the most modest of equipment. If Lotus and the micro do not give adequate capacity for real-world applications, the student will find the transition to increased computer power relatively painless once he or she has acquired an understanding of the basic principles involved. In any case, a surprising range of financial modelling does seem to be carried out in companies using Lotus on either a micro or main-frame computer, and so the exercises do offer a path into practical modelling and are rather more than just classroom demonstrations. Also, as computer power expands, it is likely that more and more modelling will be feasible at the micro level.

The models described in this chapter and illustrated by the problems at the end of the chapter attempt to incorporate correct theoretical considerations derived from the theory of finance. In this sense they tend to diverge somewhat from the way such models are often currently used in practice. The models described include simple '**what if**' models, **goal-seeking** models, **decision trees** and **Monte Carlo analysis** in relation to the appraisal of single projects. The text describes these models in outline, but, to repeat, deeper understanding really comes from working the exercises.

Simple 'what if' and goal-seeking models to appraise individual projects

The simplest type of financial model for project analysis merely uses a computer to calculate the net present value (NPV), internal rate of return (IRR) or other criterion deemed relevant by the company. With large projects, a range of assumptions is often needed to estimate the various components of the project's future cash flows and perhaps the project discount rate itself. By setting up the calculation on the computer, the analyst simply provides a way of quickly repeating the calculation under a range of different assumptions. In this way he (or she) can see how sensitive the projected NPV, IRR, and so on, are to changes in assumptions and gain some insight into the critical factors associated with the project's projected profitability. One can then focus on those key factors to consider how much uncertainty surrounds them. Note, however, that the 'what if' questioning itself does not really address uncertainty – project profitability may be very sensitive to one factor and yet that factor's value may be virtually certain. Hence, all 'what if' questioning does is to direct the decision-maker to factors likely to have a significant influence on the outcome of the project; he then needs to give some careful thought to the uncertainty surrounding them. The model itself does not usually incorporate an assessment of uncertainty.

I have just said 'usually' because it is possible that the modeller does know the range of the probability distribution and, indeed, may consider that distribution to be fairly flat with relatively equal probabilities of different factor values occurring. In that case, one could infer that a 'what if' exploration process, which varies the input value for a given factor by taking alternative values at constant intervals within a set range into the model, does incorporate an implicit recognition of the probability distribution attached to that factor. To make sure that the decision-maker can properly evaluate the modelling output, the modeller must clearly indicate what assumptions he is making in the sensitivity tests.

Lotus 1-2-3 also possesses a command called **Data Table** which enables the analyst to undertake a wide range of sensitivity tests without having to keep resetting the input value for the variable(s) on which the sensitivity analysis is being conducted. Using that command, the analyst can set a range of values over which certain key parameters are to be varied and the computer then supplies results (in terms of NPV or whatever is of interest) for each and every variation in those parameters. Moreover, Lotus 4-5-6 now provides various forms of 'add-on' packages to enable the analyst using Lotus 1-2-3 to manipulate data in various ways. For example, packages called **Goal Solutions** and **Impact Solutions** make it possible to set threshold levels which the company feels must be achieved for specified outcomes from the model, and the computer will then indicate the level that specified inputs to the model must reach to achieve those outcomes. In this way the analyst may be saved much time searching for critical levels of any of the parameters in the model. The computer provides the critical information, without any need to rely on trial and error.

For example, the analyst could set a target or goal that indicated that the project IRR must not fall below x per cent and ask the computer the largest annual percentage increase in wage rates that can be allowed without violating that goal. The package would indicate the answer. Moreover, one can set more than one goal, although this increases the chances of one or other of the goals being infeasible within the logic of the model. The Goal Solutions package, upon finding that the analyst has set an infeasible target, will indicate what the right value must be to get as near as possible to the target. It may be a little less straightforward if numerous goals are set and several of them are mutually incompatible, but the package will at least indicate the 'absurdity' of the request.

There is a theoretical difficulty to watch out for in this type of modelling (see Brealey and Myers, 1984). It is often argued that a sensible approach to risk analysis is to form a probability distribution of NPVs based upon applying the same discount rate to annual probability distributions of project cash flows. For example, suppose that an analyst is faced with the prospective project cash flows shown in table 2.1, and that, after deciding upon the appropriate project beta and using it, he

Table 2.1 A hypothetical one-year investment project

| Capital outlay in year 0 | | Cash inflows in year 1 | |
Probability	£	Probability	£
1.0	100	0.2	110
		0.5	220
		0.3	330
		mean	231

comes to the conclusion that the project discount rate should be 10 per cent. It would then be quite incorrect to discount all the possible outcomes to arrive at the following distribution of the project NPVs

Probability	NPV	
0.2	0	$(110/1.1 - 100)$
0.5	100	$(220/1.1 - 100)$
0.3	200	$(330/1.1 - 100)$

and then try to look at this complete distribution to assess risk and take the decision. From the diversified shareholder's viewpoint, systematic risk has been taken into account in setting the discount rate and that rate should be applied to the *expected* cash flows from the project. Hence, the expected cash inflow of £231 should be discounted at a rate of 10 per cent and the capital outlay of £100 deducted to arrive at an NPV of £110. The project should be accepted.

So, if, by playing with 'what if' assumptions or a Data Table, the analyst is exploring the nature of the probability distribution of cash flows in terms of its dependence on underlying factor distributions which are likely to apply in each period, he should not use the project's risk-adjusted discount rate to convert all the possible outcomes of cash flows into a probability distribution of NPVs, even though this is often advocated. To repeat, the discount rate should be applied to the *expected* values of the cash flows in each period.

This does not, however, mean that the practical analyst can ignore the possible variation in cash flows. Indeed, he may well need to undertake some form of sensitivity analysis in order

1 to understand and assess the likely cash-flow distribution for each period in the first place, and
2 to consider how those distributions will co-vary with the market-portfolio returns, which in turn will be a basic determinant of the risk-adjusted discount rate.

Consequently, to be theoretically correct, the 'what if' analysis or Data Table should be confined to establishing the likely variability of cash flows to be derived from the project *in each period*. With that information, a view should then be taken upon the appropriate discount rate to be applied to the mean net cash flows for each period. In other words, the sensitivity analysis on the cash flows should *precede* the selection of the discount rate and the discounting process.

Of course, having conducted the sensitivity analysis on the cash flows, it is still far from easy to specify exactly what the correct discount rate for each project should be, as discussed in chapter 1. Hence the analyst might want to conduct a second sensitivity analysis allowing for variations in the discount rate to be applied to the *expected values* of the cash flows for each period. This would then give a possible range of NPVs, but that range would only reflect the uncertainty attached to the estimation of the discount rate itself. The uncertainty attached to the project cash flows is already incorporated into the discount rate. It is important to distinguish very clearly between these two types of sensitivity analysis and to understand exactly what each of the analyses is designed to achieve.

If the company prefers to work with the IRR criterion, it will also be theoretically valid to use sensitivity analysis to develop an understanding of the variability of cash flows, in order to calculate an expected value for the IRR. This expected IRR can then be properly compared to the correct risk-adjusted discount rate based on the project's beta. Also, the insights gained from conducting the sensitivity analysis will probably be useful in gaining a view on the project beta. This is subject, of course, to the reservations expressed in chapter 1 about use of the IRR criterion.

If one uses Goal Solutions, rather than a sensitivity test, to find the critical level of discount rate to yield a positive NPV, this will obviously be the IRR and exactly the same logic applies. However, in using such a package as Goal Solutions, there is still a need to show care for conceptual clarity.

Suppose, instead, that the point of the Goal Solutions analysis is to establish a critical level of some parameter determining the mean cash flow, which can then be assured by some form of subcontracting or insurance. In this case, as often happens in practice, the company is not just analysing risk but attempting to manage it. The adoption of that critical value into the analysis is likely to change the project beta, which means that the discount rate will have to be re-estimated. If the cash flow which is to be 'fixed' is a cost, operating leverage will increase and the project beta may well increase along with the correct discount rate, as explained in chapter 1. Hence, the critical NPV may not be achieved after all (the impact on the NPV depends, of course, on how the mean of the cash-flow distribution is shifted, as well as on the change in the discount rate).

It is doubtful that many companies are alive to these theoretical points. Where sensitivity analysis takes place, and it is in widespread use, it is common for analysts to vary any of the cost or revenue parameters in the model using the same discount rate without giving careful thought to how the discount rate should be modified in the light of changes to the implied distribution of cash flows and its associated beta.

Decision trees applied to individual projects

Some types of project are particularly amenable to analysis by decision trees. This is particularly the case where projects can be divided up into stages, and where critical decisions to be made at the end of each stage have a major influence on the direction of the project beyond that point. A typical project of this kind has a fundamental research phase followed by product development, initial production, product launch and regular production stages. A failure to recognize the critical turning-points in the project and the possibility of bailing out or modifying the direction of the project at a subsequent date can obviously lead to incorrect investment decisions. So can a failure to appreciate that different stages of the project may have quite different risk characteristics, implying different discount rates for different stages. An example of this has already been touched on in chapter 1, where reference was made to the errors probably being made in practice through not distinguishing between betas appropriate to research phases and those appropriate to subsequent operating phases.

The following simplified description of a consultancy project that the author and a colleague were involved in illustrates these points. The company in question wished to develop a method to evaluate its investments in major R&D projects which were nevertheless directed towards products with fairly clear technical specifications. After discussion with company executives and scientists, it became clear that the projects could normally be divided up into several stages as follows:

1 'applied' research
2 product development
3 product tests
4 regular production and sales

The probability of success was different for each stage, and stages 1, 2 and 3 all had clear success or failure outcomes. In the event of failure, the whole project would be terminated at the end of that stage. In such a situation it was obviously incorrect to estimate the probability distribution of cash flows for each stage independently of the previous stages and to discount the means of those distributions by a single discount rate. (In fact the firm, a major UK company, had previously used a single-point estimate of costs and revenues in each phase, using a broad estimate of the likely volume of sales; did not use discounting at all; and, at least in terms of its formal analysis of single projects, did not explicitly recognize the possibility of bailing out at the end of the earlier stages.)

In such a situation it is important to distinguish between two types of uncertainty. Uncertainty type 1 relates to the chances of a successful outcome to each phase of the project, while uncertainty type 2 relates to the potential variability of the cash flow within each year.

The correct treatment may be illustrated by the project described in table 2.2. For the sake of simplicity, assume that each phase takes one complete year. It is also assumed, for simplicity, that sales only occur in one phase (year 4), and that cash flows arise at the end of each phase, but the expenditures for phases 1–3 have to be spent before it is known whether each phase has been successful and the project may continue to the next phase. The correct NPV may be built up by multiplying the expected cash flows by the appropriate discount factor for the corresponding year.

Consider first the activities and cash flows of year 1. The phase is certain to occur and so the expected cash flow of −£1,200 should be discounted back to time 0 at a discount rate which reflects the covariance between the cash flows in that period and the market

Table 2.2   Characteristics of a hypothetical multi-phase project

Uncertainty type 1

Phase (i.e. year)	1	2	3	4
Probability of successful phase	0.4	0.6	0.9	
Probability of phase commencing	1.0	0.4	0.24	0.216

Uncertainty type 2

Phase (i.e. year)	1		2		3		4	
	Prob.	£	Prob.	£	Prob.	£	Prob.	£
Cash flows	0.1	−1,000	0.2	−2,000	0.3	−2,500	0.5	20,000
	0.8	−1,200	0.6	−2,400	0.7	−3,000	0.5	30,000
	0.1	−1,400	0.2	−2,500				
Expected within phase if occurs		−1,200		−2,340		−2,850		25,000

portfolio – i.e. that covariance is based on events which give rise to the uncertainty type 2 distribution.

Prob.	*£*
0.1	−1,000
0.8	−1,200
0.1	−1,400

Let us call this discount rate $_cd_1$; the subscript c indicates that the beta will be based on the covariance of the within-period cash-flow distribution shown. This discount rate might reflect uncertainties over material costs, labour costs, and so on, in that period.

Now consider year 2. Using the same logic as for year 1, the within-period expected cash flow of −£2,340 must be discounted back to the beginning of year 2 using a discount rate which reflects the covariance between the distribution

Prob.	*£*
0.2	−2,000
0.6	−2,400
0.2	−2,500

and the market porfolio – i.e. $_cd_2$. Now, however, we have to consider how to discount the expected value of the year 2 cash flow as at the *beginning* of year 2 back to the beginning of year 1.

The expected value of the year 2 cash flow at the beginning of year 2 will be

$$0.4 \left(\frac{-2,340}{1 + _cd_2} \right) + 0.6(0)$$

The appropriate discount rate to convert this to a present value at time 0 is the discount rate reflecting the covariance of *the likely success of phase 1* with variations in the economy in general. It reflects the systematic-risk element attached to the likelihood of success in the applied research of phase 1 – that is, the 0.4 success, 0.6 failure distribution. Hence the present value at time 0 of the year 2 cash flow will be

$$\frac{0.4 \left(\dfrac{-2,340}{1 + _cd_2} \right)}{1 + _sd_1}$$

where $_sd_1$ reflects the beta for the research-outcome distribution – that is, it reflects the degree of association, if any, between the factors affecting the success of the research and the factors causing the market-portfolio returns to vary.

Similarly, the present value at time 0 of the year 3 cash flow is

$$\frac{0.4 \times 0.6 \, (-2,850)}{(1 + {_c}d_3)(1 + {_s}d_2)(1 + {_s}d_1)}$$

Hence the NPV at time 0 for the whole project may be calculated as shown in Table 2.3

Table 2.3   Calculation of the NPV of a multi-phase development project

Year			Expected cash flow (£)	× *Discount factor*
1			−1,200	× $1/(1 + {_c}d_1)$
2	−2,340 × 0.4	=	−936	× $1/(1 + {_c}d_2)(1 + {_s}d_1)$
3	−2,850 × 0.24	=	−684	× $1/(1 + {_c}d_3)(1 + {_s}d_2)(1 + {_s}d_1)$
4	25,000 × 0.216	=	5,400	× $1/(1 + {_c}d_4)(1 + {_s}d_3)(1 + {_s}d_2)(1 + {_s}d_1)$

The aggregate NPV is the sum of the expected cash flows for all periods times their discount factors shown on the right hand side of this table.

While this type of calculation does not need a computer model, the use of one makes it much easier – especially in more complex real-life projects where there are more years involved and almost certainly some sensitivity analysis is required. (Of course, the earlier warning about the selection of discount rates in sensitivity tests must be borne in mind.)

It would probably be mathematically possible to derive a single discount rate to be applied to all cash flows which yielded the same NPV figure for the whole project. In principle this would reflect in some way the covariance of outcomes of projects of this sort as a whole with the market portfolio. However, the probabilities of success or failure in R&D are often highly specific to the project at hand, and breaking down the consideration of uncertainty into its various elements as indicated is a powerful mechanism for gaining understanding of the differing risks faced in the project. By applying this general approach in the consultancy contract mentioned above, the dominant risk was discovered to be the likelihood of getting foreign-government contracts, and, more importantly, this bore little relation to movements of share prices in general on the London Stock Exchange. Thus a large discount rate was not warranted for this risk – at least, not from a shareholder's perspective.

Of course, it may be extremely difficult to put precise numbers on all the different betas, but discussion of the concepts may help to get betas and discount rates which are at the same time good enough and yet avoid crude errors by ignoring the changing risks as each phase elapses. For example, often one might suppose for some types of project that all $_sd_i$ have betas of near zero and so they all may be equated to the risk-free rate (r_f). If, for the numerical example in table 2.2, we take r_f as 5 per cent and the $_cd_i$ as, respectively, 6 ($_cd_1$), 6 ($_cd_2$), 5 ($_cd_3$) and 15 ($_cd_4$) per cent, the project NPV calculation simplifies to

$$
\begin{aligned}
\text{NPV} &= -\frac{1,200}{(1+_cd_1)} - \frac{936}{(1+_cd_2)(1+r_f)} - \frac{684}{(1+_cd_3)(1+r_f)^2} + \frac{540}{(1+_cd_4)(1+r_f)^3} \\
&= -\frac{1,200}{1.06} - \frac{936}{(1.06)(1.05)} - \frac{684}{(1.05)(1.05)^2} + \frac{5,400}{(1.15)(1.05)^3} \\
&= +\pounds1,496.2
\end{aligned}
$$

The project has a positive NPV, which it might well not have done if the management had assessed the uncertainty of normal operating cash flows at 15 per cent and then, recognizing the considerable uncertainty associated with the R&D phases in this project, decided to apply a higher rate of discount to all the expected cash flows. (For interest, a universal rate of 25 per cent applied to all the expected cash flows shown above reduced the NPV to £305. Hence, conceptual errors with discount rates can lead to significant differences in NPV.)

As indicated at the end of the previous section, it is tempting to dismiss these sorts of arguments as mere refinements that have insignificant effects compared to the necessary strategic analysis to identify the nature of desirable projects in the first place. The fact is, however, that these 'refinements' can have significant effects on the NPV calculation and management's perceptions of the profitability of projects from the shareholders' viewpoint. Moreover, if a thorough strategic analysis is undertaken which identifies all the key risks, it will at least be possible to discuss and think about the discount-rate issues raised here, since the basic data for doing so will be available.

Monte Carlo analysis for individual projects

A more systematic and comprehensive form of 'sensitivity testing' is called Monte Carlo analysis (MCA). This technique calls for the prior specification of probability distributions attached to all key variables in calculating an IRR, NPV or other index of desirability for a project. (MCA can be used to explore the uncertainties attached to any form of calculation.) This section will provide a brief description of MCA, illustrate how such an analysis may be run using a Lotus 1-2-3 spreadsheet, and finally evaluate MCA from a practical standpoint.

It is often suggested that MCA should be used to generate a probability distribution of NPVs at a given discount rate taking into account the uncertainty attached to a number of subsidiary cash flows underlying the project. As mentioned earlier, Brealey and Myers (1984) have shown this to be a conceptual error. An allowance for risk is included in the discount rate if it has been detemined by reference to 'beta theory'; the discount rate should be applied to the expected cash flows of each period. Hence, a probability distribution of NPVs at a given discount rate makes no economic sense. This point will be fully recognized in the analysis here, but, before showing how MCA can be validly used in relation to uncertainty attached to NPV calculations, it is necessary to understand the technique itself. It is for this reason that the method of MCA will be explained first by reference to the construction of a simple probability distribution of total operating costs for a single period and then in relation to simple break-even analysis and profit calculations also for a single period. With the technique clearly in mind we can return afterwards to consider investment decisions and more complex matters.

Suppose that a company wishes to estimate the probability distribution of total costs where there are the following probability distributions of the two main elements of costs, with each probability distribution being completely independent of the other.

Cost element 1		Cost element 2	
Prob.	*£*	*Prob.*	*£*
0.2	30	0.3	80
0.6	50	0.4	100
0.2	70	0.3	120

The expected total cost is obviously £50 + £100 = £150, but, if cost element 1 is independent from cost element 2, one can approximate the complete probability distribution of total cost by the following procedure.

Step 1   Attach a number in the range 0–9 to the different possible cost levels as follows

Cost element 1			Cost element 2		
Prob.	*£*		*Prob.*	*£*	
0.2	30	0, 1	0.3	80	0, 1, 2
0.6	50	2, 3, 4, 5, 6, 7	0.4	100	3, 4, 5, 6
0.2	70	8, 9	0.3	120	7, 8, 9

Note that, where the probability is 0.2, two digits are assigned; where it is 0.3, three digits are assigned; and so on.

Step 2   Using a set of random numbers, select a number in the range 0–9. Suppose that it is 4, then you will assume that the cost of element 1 is £50.

Step 3   Repeat the use of the random number table. Suppose you then select 2, then let it be assumed that the selection relates to cost element 2, which will now be assumed to cost £80. Hence, by adding the cost of the two elements, total cost is estimated to be £130.

Step 4   Repeat steps 2 and 3, say, 100 times to give 100 estimates of total cost. Note that, while each selection is made from the probability distributions of the cost elements at random, over 100 selections from each distribution this technique makes individual cost-element selections recognizing the shape of the individual cost-element distributions. For example, for cost element 1, one would expect over many selections that the cost of £50 would be selected three times as often as either the costs of £30 or £70.

Step 5   Form the 100 estimates of total cost into a probability distribution. This distribution will then illustrate the uncertainty attached to the total cost position, given the uncertainties attached to the separate cost elements.

This example is obviously extremely simple and in practice one might have rather more probability distributions and want to use the computer to run the MCA. It will now be explained how a Lotus 1-2-3 spreadsheet can be used to operate MCA.

Many analysts wanting to use MCA may well prefer to use Lotus macro facilities to write their own MCAs. Alternatively, there are Monte Carlo packages available for the microcomputer: for example, 4-5-6's **Simulated Solutions** and **@Risk** packages. The @Risk package, in particular, is sophisticated and easy to use. It also incorporates an abridged form of MCA (called the **Latin hypercube method**) which is faster to operate and provides a good approximation of a full Monte Carlo simulation. It also has a good graphic representation of results. In practice, this package would always be preferred to the approach to be described, which may appear rather cumbersome. Nevertheless, it is possible to use Lotus and run MCA without the use of a macro, and this has the benefit of making every part of the process visible on the screen. This undoubtedly helps students to visualize exactly what the computer is doing. In my view, it is better for the student to construct a relatively simple MCA in this way, to get a thorough grasp of what is going on, than to move directly to a package which tends to work like a 'black box'.

Perhaps, more importantly, for relatively simple analyses, this approach would have the further benefit of making it easier to explain analyses to managers and getting them to interact more closely with the model – simply because everything is visible on the screen. Given that no model can actually take decisions and that models are designed to help managers understand the decision situation a little better, these qualities seem quite important. On the other side of the argument, a practical disadvantage of writing a specific model such as the one described below is that it applies to only one narrowly defined type of application, whereas a package has the flexibility to cover a range of applications. The choice between a specific and fully visual model and a flexible 'black box' model will in practice depend upon the business situation. Here the fully visual model is adopted primarily because I have found it valuable as a way of teaching newcomers exactly what is going on inside the model.

Using Lotus 1-2-3 to run Monte Carlo analyses

Suppose that a company called Taylors Shirts wishes to explore the degree of uncertainty attached both to its profitability over the next year and to its ability to break even during that period. It has decided to use MCA to explore this question.

Taylors produce leisure shirts with a printed design. The selling price and production costs are as follows

	£
Selling price	5.4
Cost of shirt (purchased)	2.5
Printing (labour only)	1.5
Allocation of factory overheads	1.0
Production cost per unit	5.0

Printing inks and other materials are not charged out directly to each shirt, but are included in the overhead allocation.

Before deciding to conduct the MCA and specify the probability distributions given below, production volume and factory overheads were planned for the next year as

	£
Variable	
Printing inks and materials	50,000
Electricity for equipment	40,000
Fixed	
Depreciation	59,000
Light and heat	26,000
Factory cleaning	25,000
	200,000

Planned production volume 200,000 shirts

Non-manufacturing costs for the next year were planned as

	£
Variable	20,000
Fixed	40,000
Total	60,000

Upon deciding to use MCA, Taylors' management said that it was quite certain about all figures except the achievable sales volume, the variable factory costs and the fixed manufacturing costs. Their view of the impact of the uncertainty attached to these three variables upon variable cost per unit and total fixed costs was then expressed as follows.

Sales quantity		Variable cost per unit		Total fixed costs	
Prob.	*Volume*	*Prob.*	*£*	*Prob.*	*£*
0.1	140,000	0.2	4.45	0.1	130,000
0.2	170,000	0.3	4.50	0.7	150,000
0.4	200,000	0.4	4.55	0.2	170,000
0.3	230,000	0.1	4.60		

Assume that you have been instructed to run a Monte Carlo analysis with 100 iterations. As a first step you need to be clear about the exact form of the calculations needed to determine profit and the break-even point. These are obviously as follows.

Calculation A   Break-even quantity based on original budget

$$\frac{\text{Fixed costs}}{\text{Contribution per unit}} = \frac{£150,000}{£5.4 - 4.55} = 176,471$$

Calculation B   Estimated profit at 200,000 units of production

	£
Contribution (200,000 × 0.85)	170,000
Less fixed costs	150,000
Profit	20,000

Next one needs to decide how to lay out the Lotus spreadsheet. A map of the spreadsheet is shown as Figure 2.1 together with numbers illustrating the first five iterations of the MCA. In the top left-hand corner of the spreadsheet are the basic calculations of the break-even quantity and profit as just described. The information on the probability associated with sales volume, unit variable cost and fixed cost are shown in I1 to Q6. There is one new matter to be explained here with regard to the way these probabilities are used within Lotus 1-2-3. Immediately to the right of each column of probabilities there is a column headed 'Compare'. In this column the probabilities are converted to cumulative integer form to enable the use of the Lotus @**VLOOKUP** command. For example, the probabilities for sales volume and the assignment of integers starting with 0 and within the range 0–9 to each possible outcome are as follows:

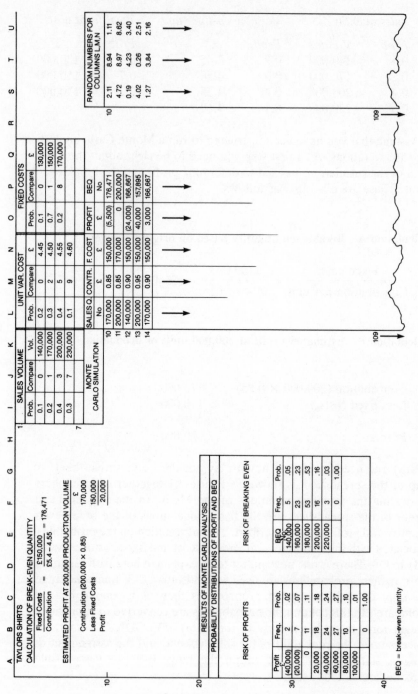

Figure 2.1 Map of Monte Carlo spreadsheet for Taylors example

Prob.	Volume	
0.1	140,000	0
0.2	170,000	1, 2
0.4	200,000	3, 4, 5, 6
0.3	230,000	7, 8, 9

The 'Compare' figures are then simply the first integer in the row of those assigned to each outcome. Hence, the 'Compare' column for sales volume is 0, 1, 3, 7. The @**VLOOKUP** command then takes the number generated by the random-number table and compares it with the 'Compare' column. It will select the sales volume where the randomly generated number equals the 'Compare' number or the next-nearest below it. For example, the random numbers for 100 iterations on sales volume have been placed in column S10 to S109. This was achieved by the use of the Lotus @**RAND** command (multiplied by 10 because the Lotus command selects random numbers in the range 0–1.0). Hence, the computer notes that for the first iteration the random number for sales volume is 2.11; it then examines columns J3–J6 and selects 1 as the next-nearest integer below 2.11. It then further selects the corresponding volume of 170,000 for the first iteration on that variable and places it in L10.

Exactly the same procedure is followed to select the values for the first iteration in respect of unit variable cost and fixed costs. The resulting values are then placed in M10 and N10, respectively. Formulae have been placed in O10 and P10 to calculate profit and the break-even quantity given values placed in L10–N10, with the resulting loss of £5,500 and a break-even quantity of 176,471 for the first iteration.

This method of using the spreadsheet to run an MCA does not require any programmed looping to produce successive iterations. One can fill the whole of the range L10–P109 with appropriate formulae to make the 100 different calculations, and then, as soon as the random numbers are inserted into the complete range S10–U109, all the 100 iterations of profit and the break-even quantity are calculated immediately. (It is very easy to assign random numbers and formulae to the many cells involved by use of the Lotus **Copy** command. Consequently, this can be done in only a few seconds.)

Given the 100 different calculations of profit and break-even quantity, it now simply remains to form frequency distributions of them. This has been done in B30–B38 and F30–F35 using the Lotus **Data Distribution** command. The frequencies are divided through by 100 to convert them to probabilities and the task is complete.

With this model it is also extremely simple and takes very little time to generate several hundred iterations if one feels that, given the problem at hand, 100 are not enough to generate a stable distribution. The Lotus @**RAND** command has the property that it will be reactivated, i.e. new random numbers will be selected, each time the spreadsheet is recalculated. Hence, it only takes a press of the Calc key to generate another 100 iterations. Summation of the successive frequency distributions gives the distribution over as many iterations as one wants.

It has been shown how straightforward the principles of Monte Carlo analysis are and how easy it is to run such models on a microcomputer. Of course, the example just described is an extremely simple one, but, having understood the principles, readers will be able to tackle the more complex investment-appraisal problem involving MCA which is given in the end-of-chapter examples (problem 2.3).

An evaluation of Monte Carlo analysis in investment analysis

When one has learned how to develop a Monte Carlo analysis, it is quite easy to use it in investment appraisal. The underlying factors which determine the probability distribution of cash flows for each period can have probability distributions assigned to them. Then, using MCA, the probability distribution of each period's cash flows can be developed and the mean, or expected, value of each period's distribution estimated, to be discounted by the appropriate discount rate for each period. Summing all the discounted cash flows for all periods obviously yields the project NPV. Remember the earlier warning, emphasized by Brealey and Myers (1984), that one should not use the MCA to produce a probability distribution of NPVs.

Also, as stated earlier, it is theoretically valid to use MCA to produce a probability distribution of IRRs, but, if different periods have different discount rates assigned to them, it will be difficult to incorporate them into the analysis and decision process. It will not be clear what the appropriate cut-off point for the IRR ought to be.

Complex projects may involve various different parts of the organization. The structure of an MCA easily allows the expert in each area of operations to produce his (or her) estimate of the factor probability distribution about which he knows most. Different expert advice relating to different facets of the project can therefore be easily assimilated into the model. Separate identification of the uncertain factors underlying each period's cash flows may also be a critical step in thinking about the likely covariance of cash flows in that period with the market-portfolio returns, and, hence, the appropriate discount rate. MCA may therefore facilitate a more thorough inquiry into the thorny problem of deciding upon the appropriate project discount rate.

It is, however, becoming clear from this discussion that a full MCA for a large and complex project will involve considerable analytical and modelling effort. There may be a large range of factors to be considered for each period, and they may be interconnected instead of separate, as assumed in the simple Taylors example. Consequently, one must beware of being seduced by the elegance of the basic model and not assume that it is suitable for general use on all projects. MCA has been widely known in business circles since at least the mid-1960s (see Hertz, 1964) and yet it has not been that widely used except in very important projects – for instance, oil development projects. Even in such cases, where it is obviously worth expending considerable effort to analyse a project before accepting it, some analysts have become disillusioned about its value and there seems to be less use of MCA than there used to be. Of course, MCA will never be useful unless the underlying factor probability distributions and their interconnections are carefully ana- lysed and specified, but there is a further practical problem in the tendency of top management not to place much reliance on it. This is an attitude that applies to many operations-research models. With MCA, the real benefit comes from 'getting inside' the model and interacting with it to test out one's doubts and anxieties.

Until very recently, MCA was only available on main-frame or mini-computers and so the workings of such a model were often a mystery to many top managers. Even if they understood the simple basis of the model, they were not likely to interact with it to any great extent during the decision process. The coming of the microcomputer and the rapid growth of desk stations may change all that. Many top managers are now becoming familiar with interactive computing and, as younger managers take over top positions, the proportion of top managers who feel comfortable in a modelling environment will rapidly increase. One would not expect them to prepare the models, but the ability to see the workings of the model on the screen (as required) will facilitate interaction between the decision-maker, the modeller and his model. Consequently, it is my view that it is too early to write off MCA as an over-elaborate business tool. If care is taken to confine the uncertainty analysis of underlying factors to those which are really critical (with top decision-makers only becoming involved when the analyst has deve- loped a model which contains the essential matters and is comprehen- sible), an MCA can considerably aid business judgement. Given the power of current generations of computers, it is almost as little effort to run a well-thought-out and structured MCA as it is to embark upon a series of finger-stabbing 'what if' inquiries. Also, if uncertainty relating to some factors is so great that no sensible attempt can be made to assign a probability distribution to it, it is quite possible to combine 'what if' analysis with MCA in an interactive way using a spreadsheet. Problem 2.3 at the end of the chapter illustrates how this can be done.

I feel sure that the explosion in distributed computing power will lead to a reassessment of models such as MCA for use in investment appraisal. That is not to say that one should ignore the experience of the past. It will be as necessary as ever to consider how to get top managers interacting with these models to enhance their own understanding of the risks involved. The difference now is that the technology is rapidly becoming available to enable this to be done more practically. MCA will never be a tool for coping with all types of risk analysis, but its value in analysing projects or parts of projects where the uncertainty is fairly structured (i.e. approximate probabilities can be assigned) has still to be appreciated by many companies.

Individual projects in the context of the corporate portfolio

The theory of finance outlined in chapter 1 emphasizes individual project analysis and holds that, from a shareholder wealth-maximization viewpoint, there is no need for corporate managers to worry about corporate diversification. Shareholders can arrange their own diversification to avoid specific risk. Hence, given a project discount rate based upon the CAPM, all projects with positive NPVs should be accepted. Later in this book, in chapter 9, it will be shown how financial managers may have to interpret this extremely carefully when needing to take into account the interests of multiple parties, but for the moment let the argument continue with this assumption.

Even where projects can be accepted upon analysis in isolation from diversification effects on the total company position, financial managers will still need to assess the total financing needs of the company. Consequently, corporate modelling sometimes follows a two-stage process. First, the project is viewed in isolation. Second, its impact on the total corporate position is assessed – usually in terms of its impact upon projected liquidity and gearing positions, often shown by projected outline balance sheets.

In addition, the practice of corporate financing has also seen the gradual development of a greater range of financial instruments beyond the traditional simple dichotomy between equity and debt. These new instruments often have an explicit purpose of enabling the financing policy-maker to match cash inflows with outflows through time and thereby reduce the likelihood of financial distress. It seems pointless developing this degree of financing sophistication unless the ability to analyse total corporate projected cash flows is also sophisticated. It seems highly likely, then, that models showing the impact of major projects on the total corporate position have a key part to play in enabling financial directors to take full advantage of these newer financing instruments.

Of course, the theory of finance would suggest that this second stage of modelling should never affect whether a project is accepted or not. The decision to accept the project can be entirely separated from the financing decision. In that sense, one could argue that the second-stage modelling is irrelevant to this book, which is concerned with allocating major resources – i.e. investment and divestment decisions. When, however, we move beyond the perspective of the current theory of finance, it will become apparent that the continued viability of the whole corporate entity may be a major concern of financial managers and that this may affect the investment decision. Furthermore, even within the realms of the current theory of finance, the total corporate position must also be considered before taking an investment decision if the company is in a capital-rationing situation. On the other hand, most finance theorists tend to pay little attention to capital-rationing, on the assumption that one can, in efficient markets, always find finance for projects with positive NPVs. Both the issue of perspectives beyond that of the current theory of finance and the question of capital-rationing will be taken up later. For the present, the reader is asked to take it on trust that, especially where major projects are involved, there may well be a need for the financial manager to consider the impact of that project upon the total corporate position. The reasons for this will be explored when other disciplines' approaches to resource allocation have been considered.

References

Brealey, R. and Myers, S. 1984: *Principles of Corporate Finance*, 2nd edn. New York: McGraw-Hill.

Hertz, D. B. 1964: Risk analysis in capital investment. *Harvard Business Review*, April–May.

Schlosser, M. 1989: *Corporate Finance – a Model-Building Approach*. Englewood Cliffs, NJ: Prentice-Hall.

Students are also encouraged to experiment with the various 4-5-6 packages referred to in the chapter.

Problems

2.1　Data Table simulations and Goal Solutions

The Model Company is considering whether to invest in a new project which has a predicted income in each of the next five years as follows.

	£'000
Sales	240
Less cost of goods sold	100
other expenses	40
Net profit before tax	100
Taxation (30 per cent)	30
Net profit after tax	70

The cost of goods sold is made up of approximately 60 per cent variable costs and 40 per cent fixed costs; the latter include £20,000 for depreciation. The other expenses are 50 per cent fixed and 50 per cent variable costs; the fixed element includes £10,000 for depreciation. Assume that tax is payable in the year in which it is assessed.

Now perform the following tasks.

(a) Prepare a simple Lotus 1-2-3 spreadsheet and calculate the expected IRR of the project.
(b) Use the Lotus 1-2-3 Data Table commands to discover

    (i) how the IRR will vary with changes in sales from −20 per cent to +20 per cent (all else unchanged);
    (ii) how the IRR will vary with a change in the tax rate from −20 per cent to +20 per cent of the current rate (all else unchanged);
    (iii) How the IRR will vary with simultaneous changes in both tax rates and sales levels through these ranges.

(c) Suppose now that the manager wishes to find the level of sales per annum which will produce an IRR of 30 per cent and an annual net profit after tax (at 30 per cent) of £100,000. Use the Enfin Software Corporate 'Goal Solutions' package to discover the answer. (Note: it is most unlikely that there will be a feasible solution to provide an IRR exactly equal to 30 per cent when net profits are £100,000 per annum, but ask Goal Solutions to do it and watch what happens.)

2.2 Discounting multi-phase investments

Pimlico are considering whether to invest in the following project, which has three distinct phases.

Phase 1   Initial research   (year 1)
Phase 2   Field trials   (year 2)
Phase 3   Commercial selling   (years 3–5)

The anticipated cash flows in each phase are as follows.

	Prob.	£'000
Phase 1	0.2	−9
	0.6	−10
	0.2	−11
Phase 2	0.3	−5
	0.4	−6
	0.3	−7
Phase 3	0.2	+18
(in each	0.3	+20
of years	0.3	+22
3–5)	0.2	+24

Assume the distributions in each year are independent of each other.

The probability of success of the initial research in phase 1 is only 50 per cent. If the research is unsuccessful, the project will be terminated at the end of phase 1. If phase 2 is undertaken, it has a 90 per cent chance of successful field trials. If phase 2 is unsuccessful, the project will be terminated at the end of that phase.

It is assumed that there is zero correlation between the *likelihood of success* in phases 1 and 2 and returns on the market index. The relevant discount rates reflecting the covariance between the annual cash flows *within* each phase (assuming it occurs) and the market index are 10 per cent in phases 1 and 2, and 20 per cent in phase 3.

Calculate the project NPV if the risk-free discount rate is 7 per cent. What is the maximum loss on the project and its likelihood of occurring?

2.3 The KL Manufacturing Co: combined Monte Carlo and 'what if' analysis

[*Note.* A problem such as this will rarely be run with a spreadsheet in the form illustrated now that packages such as @Risk are available. This example was constructed for *classroom* purposes to illustrate some pitfalls and simple conceptual points associated with this general type of modelling. The model is not very user-friendly.]

The KL Manufacturing Co. produces small electrical appliances. Recently it has become clear that there would be a market for a completely new form of product, and KL is one of several companies that could produce it. It is anticipated that the market will be very competitive, such that any supplier will have very little control over selling price, and there is little scope for genuine product differentiation. Competition will come mainly from making the market aware of the attributes of the product through advertising.

Miss Winnie Lee is personal assistant to the managing director of KL. She suggests to him that the investment opportunity facing KL could be analysed using Monte Carlo analysis. After all, the managing director has already indicated that there are many variables to take into account in launching a completely new product such as this one and that there is considerable uncertainty associated with each one of these variables. 'What I would like,' he said, 'is a method which takes into account all these uncertainties and gives me some idea of the variation in profitability I could expect from a new venture such as this.' He also said, 'Winnie, can't you construct a spreadsheet model on your new personal computer that will do this for me? And, if you do, I want to be able to play with it to see what effect is achieved if I make a range of different assumptions about the level of advertising expenditure and its impact upon our market share.'

Winnie decides first that she needs to draw a diagram of the important variables involved in estimating the profitability of the proposed project. After some discussion with a range of managers, she draws up the diagram shown in figure 2.2. This indicates that, if she had information on seven basic variables,

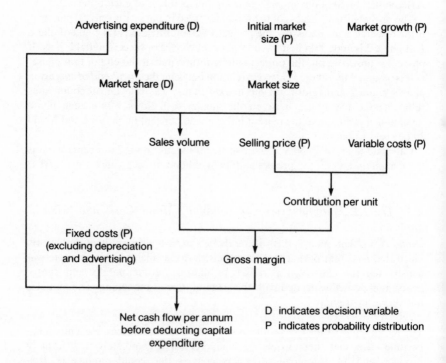

Figure 2.2 Determinants of net cash flows in each period

she could calculate the resulting net cash flow in each year from the project. These basic variables are initial market size, market growth rate, advertising expenditure, market share, selling price, variable costs per unit and fixed costs.

As the managing director had expected, the various functional directors and their staffs state that 'with a new product like this' they cannot be sure about the appropriate values of any of these factors. Consequently, Winnie embarks on a series of interviews to try to capture the degree of uncertainty associated with each of these factors, except that she feels that advertising expenditure is a decision variable controllable by the company and as such should be left as a specific input to be made by the company managers rather than included as an 'uncertainty variable'. Also, the likely market share is so uncertain that Winnie decides that it is best to leave this as a specific value to be put into the model by the company management, so that they can conduct a series of 'what if' sensitivity analyses on market share. She decides, however, that the remaining five key variables are largely 'givens' that (assuming a reasonably efficient production basis) cannot be influenced by the company to any great extent but are still subject to some uncertainty. Further discussions with various functional managers produce assessments of the degree of uncertainty associated with the following factors.

1 Initial market size in year 1

Sales volume (i.e. physical units)	Prob.
20,000	0.1
30,000	0.2
40,000	0.5
50,000	0.1
60,000	0.1
	1.0

2 Market growth in year 2

Growth rate (decimal)	Prob.
0.10	0.2
0.15	0.6
0.20	0.2

But there is much doubt expressed by the sales director about the prospects for the market beyond year 2. He suggests that, if the market growth is strong in year 2, it can be assumed to be somewhat stronger in year 3. He feels, however, that by the end of year 3 the market will have stabilized and that there will be no further market growth in years 4 onwards, or, at least, that this should be the assumption made for purposes of evaluating the investment. Also it is decided that Winnie should assume a ten-year project life.

Eventually, he suggests that Winnie should use the following indicators of uncertainty in market growth in year 3.

(a) If the market growth in year 2 is 10 per cent:

Year 3 market growth rate	Prob.
0.10	0.1
0.15	0.5
0.20	0.4

(b) If the market growth rate in year 2 is 15 per cent:

Year 3 market growth rate	Prob.
0.10	0.2
0.18	0.4
0.20	0.4

(c) If the market growth rate in year 2 is 20 per ent:

Year 3 market growth rate	Prob.
0.12	0.2
0.20	0.5
0.30	0.3

3 Selling prices

The sales staff are also asked to provide estimations of future selling prices. They do not believe that sales volume will be very sensitive to selling price, but there is some doubt as to the level at which selling prices will settle. The best estimates are

Year 1		Year 2		Years 3–10	
Price (£)	Prob.	Price (£)	Prob.	Price (£)	Prob.
14	0.1	15	0.1	16	0.2
15	0.2	16	0.1	17	0.5
16	0.5	17	0.6	18	0.1
17	0.1	18	0.1	19	0.1
18	0.1	19	0.1	20	0.1

Some escalation in prices to allow for inflation was considered in those projections.

4 Direct material costs per unit

Year 1		Year 2		Years 3–10	
Amount £	Prob.	Amount £	Prob.	Amount £	Prob.
2.2	0.1	2.4	0.1	2.6	0.1
2.4	0.2	2.6	0.1	2.8	0.2
2.6	0.3	2.8	0.6	3.0	0.2
2.8	0.3	3.0	0.1	3.2	0.3
3.0	0.1	3.2	0.1	3.4	0.2

5 Direct labour costs per unit

Year 1		Year 2		Years 3–10	
Amount £	Prob.	Amount £	Prob.	Amount £	Prob.
3.0	0.1	3.0	0.12	3.0	0.1
3.5	0.2	3.5	0.08	3.5	0.2
4.0	0.2	4.0	0.2	4.0	0.2
4.5	0.3	4.5	0.1	4.5	0.2
5.0	0.2	5.0	0.5	5.0	0.3

6 Other variable costs per unit (including distribution costs)

Year 1		Year 2		Years 3–10	
Amount £	Prob.	Amount £	Prob.	Amount £	Prob.
2.8	0.1	3.0	0.1	3.2	0.2
3.0	0.2	3.2	0.2	3.4	0.2
3.2	0.2	3.4	0.2	3.6	0.2
3.4	0.1	3.6	0.3	3.8	0.2
3.6	0.4	3.8	0.2	4.0	0.2

7 Fixed costs (manufacturing and non-manufacturing)

Year 1		Year 2		Years 3–10	
Amount £	Prob.	Amount £	Prob.	Amount £	Prob.
21,000	0.2	22,000	0.3	24,000	0.2
22,000	0.2	23,000	0.1	26,000	0.2
23,000	0.2	24,000	0.1	28,000	0.2
24,000	0.3	25,000	0.2	29,000	0.2
25,000	0.1	26,000	0.3	30,000	0.2

Winnie is assured that she should allow separate estimates for these different elements of costs. There is no reason, for example, why labour costs should be subject to the same rate of increase or uncertainty as material costs.

Winnie decides to construct the Monte Carlo model on Lotus 1-2-3 (Release 2) and constructs the model PROJRISK outlined in figure 2.3 (map of the spreadsheet) and table 2.4. A week later she presents the managing director with the results of her analysis, in the form of four graphs of frequency distributions showing

1 the likely variation of NPV of the project using a discount rate of 16 per cent;
2 the likely variation of the project IRR;

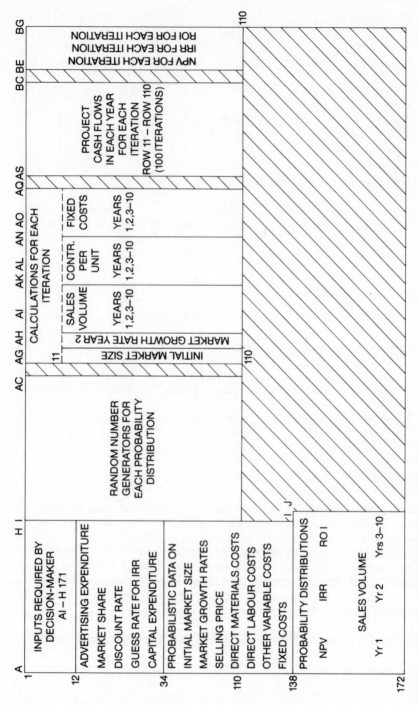

Figure 2.3 Spreadsheet layout for PROJRISK

Table 2.4 PROJRISK: Monte Carlo Simulation. Inputs required

Inputs required	
Advertising expenditure	D15–F15
Market share	D18–F18
Discount rate	D23
Guess rate for IRR	G23
Capital outlay	C29–H29
Probabilistic data	
Initial market size	C42–D46
Market growth rates: year 2	E55–E57, H54, H63
year 3	G58–H60, G65–H67, G71–H73
Selling price	C81–H85
Direct materials costs	C93–H97
Direct labour costs	C105–H109
Other variable costs	C117–H121
Fixed costs	C130–H134
Probability distributions	
NPV	A144–A154
IRR	D144–D154
ROI	I144–I154
Sales volume	A162–A171, D162–D171, G162–G171

3 the likely variation of accounting ROI (calculated as the sum of the cash flows, before deducting capital expenditure, divided by the number of years of the project's life and expressed as a percentage of the capital outlay);
4 the likely variation in sales volume in year 1, year 2 and years 3–10.

The managing director also tells her to assume the following for the first run of the model.

	Market share	Capital expenditure at the beginning of each year (£)	Advertising expenditure amount (£)
Year 1	0.4	400,000	5,000
Year 2	0.4	200,000	4,000
Years 3–10	0.5	–	4,000 p.a.

Winnie also remembers in constructing the model to change the form of these probability distributions so that the @VLOOKUP command can be used (this avoids complex nests of 'if' statements).

The managing director and the functional directors are delighted with the idea of the model. They all agree that now that they can have such a model they can analyse very complex structures of uncertainty very quickly. They are not quite so enthusiastic, however, about some of the inputs to the model. Also, they feel that further work is required to allow for inflation. The finance director points out that inflation has been allowed in selling prices and cost elements up to and including year 3, but that no allowance has been made for it through years 4–10. He sees that this implies a much greater series of inputs (i.e. separate input probability distributions for each of the ten years), but he wonders whether there is anything Winnie can do to allow for that. Winnie is pleased with her success, but a little chastened to realize that she has made some basic errors.

You are now asked to work through the following tasks and problems.

(a) Explain how the probability distributions need to be changed to use the @VLOOKUP command.

(b) Use the PROJRISK file (floppy disk available from Blackwell; ask for Student Disk No. 1) to generate the four frequency distributions which Winnie produced and provide an interpretation of this output. (The model has already been developed for you. You need only understand how the model works and insert the correct data.)

(c) Explore how sensitive the results are to changes in market share. How do you know that it is not the revised set of random numbers causing the changes in the distributions rather than the variation in market share? How would you test for this?

(d) Discuss the problems involved in establishing the probability distributions which underlie the Monte Carlo process.

(e) Where are the indicators that Winnie may have been concentrating too much upon the technique and not enough on the reasonableness of the inputs? What further questions need to be asked to improve the inputs to the model?

(f) Make some reasonable assumptions to remove some of the likely errors in Winnie's probability distributions. Does this affect the attractiveness of the project significantly?

(g) How should Winnie deal with the inflation problem raised by the finance director?

(h) The model has generated a probability distribution of NPVs. Why is this theoretically inconsistent with the theory of finance? What relatively simple adjustment can be made to the model as it stands in order to calculate the project NPV?

(i) What other factors might be relevant which have not been considered in the model, and how would you attempt to take them into account?

Instructions for use of PROJRISK
• File-retrieve PROJRISK. It takes time; be patient!
• Enter inputs as specified above.
• Note that the spreadsheet is set on manual recalculate so that the spreadsheet is not recalculated every time a new input item is entered. It

takes a little time to recalculate the spreadsheet. This means that when all input data has been provided you must press F9 to recalculate the spreadsheet.

- Recalculating the spreadsheet does not automatically revise the frequency distributions. You have to do this by manually operating the /**DD** command. The value range for NPV, for example, is BE11–BE110 and its bin range is A144–A154.
- Note also that, after recalculating and reusing /DD, you have to operate F9 again to calculate the revised probabilities in decimal form (as distinct from frequencies).
- You can convert probability distributions to graphical form using the /**Graph** command.

Spreadsheets can be set to manual calculate by /**WGRM** or reset to automatic calculate by /**WGRA**.

2.4   Taylors Shirts revisited: an illustration of the @Risk package

[*Note*. In contrast to the model used in problem 2.3, this problem illustrates the use of the @Risk package. Students who first become acquainted with Monte Carlo simulation through explicit spreadsheet models such as the one used in problem 2.3 quickly become familiar with the pitfalls of treating Monte Carlo simulations too casually. @Risk is a powerful package, but the newcomer to simulation is in danger of seeing it as a wonderful 'black box' and not thinking carefully enough about the basic underlying concept of this type of simulation. *Before setting this problem, class tutors will probably need to give instruction in using the @Risk package.*]

The Taylors Shirts problem described earlier in this chapter was put, with slightly modified probability distributions, into the Lotus 1-2-3 @Risk spreadsheet shown on Student Disk No. 2 as TAYLORS.WKI. (The disk is available on application to Blackwell.)

  The aim of the model is to generate probabilistic data for both breaking-even and profits based on the probability distributions provided for variable cost per unit, fixed costs and planned production.

  The basic data for this problem are as follows.

Selling price	£5.40
Variable cost per unit	£4.50*
Fixed costs	£150,000*
Planned production	£200,000*

Stochastic variables are marked *; see cell formulae.

Calculation of break-even production level	166,667
Anticipated profit	£30,000

Now perform the following tasks.

(a) Examine the spreadsheet TAYLORS.WK1 so as to understand the form of the model.

For example, place the cursor on E6 and note how to put the following probability distribution into an @Risk spreadsheet.

Probability	Variable cost per unit (£)
0.2	4.45
0.4	4.5
0.3	4.6
0.1	4.7
1.0	

The appropriate entry is

@DISCRETE (4.45, 2,4.5,4,4.6,3,4.7,1,4)

The 4 at the end of the instruction indicates to the computer that there are four discrete values for the distribution.

Examine also the probability distributions entered for fixed costs (E7) and planned production (E8).

(b) Produce simulations to show the uncertainty attached to breaking-even and profitability using the Latin hypercube option. (The Latin hypercube is an abridged form of Monte Carlo analysis which is faster to run and has been shown to give a good approximation to a full Monte Carlo simulation.) Your results should be similar to those shown in figure 2.4 (obviously each simulation is slightly different).

(c) Now file-retrieve TAYLCONT.WK1. This is the same problem except that distributions are now expressed in normal continuous form. For example, place the cursor on E6 and you will see the instruction @NORMAL (4.5,0.3), indicating a normal distribution of 4.5 and a standard deviation of 0.3. Similar instructions are in E7 and E8.

Run the simulation again with TAYLCONT.WK1.

2.5   KL Manufacturing revisited

[*Note.* This problem should be set only after students have thoroughly worked and discussed problems 2.3 and 2.4. Familiarity with the @Risk package is necessary. Before students tackle this problem, tutors will probably need to give some more instruction in the use of @Risk, especially on how to allow correlations between variables.]

After extensive discussion of the Monte Carlo model in problem 2.3, Winnie decided to modify the inputs to her model. She also learned about the availability of the @Risk package and persuaded her company to acquire it. After a few practice runs, Winnie decided that she could generate results far more quickly and gain a considerable range of supporting statistics for her results. Also, after further discussion, she decided to construct a spreadsheet in the form shown on Students Disk No. 2 as KL.WK1. (The disk is available on application to Blackwell.)

She substantially increased the expenditure for advertising and allowed for a product life-cycle by including a 'market decay rate' to indicate an expected percentage decline in sales volume after year 5. An inflation rate was inserted for years 3–10. It was decided that she could not do better than apply this rate to both costs and selling prices. She also simplified and modified the probabilistic data; the exact form of each probability distribution can be seen by examining the formulae behind each cell in the basic spreadsheet. Note, too, how Winnie provided for correlations between some of the variables. She also looked more carefully at the specification of the discount rate incorporating the CAPM approach and decided that it should be about 20 per cent. Moreover, in view of the results from the previous PROJRISK simulations, it was clear that the products had to be modified. As a result of this and the increased advertising, it was felt that selling prices and market growth rates could be significantly increased, although production costs remained more or less at the same general level.

Now perform the following tasks.

(a) Examine the spreadsheet on Students Disk No. 2 and try to understand it. It is in Lotus 1-2-3 @Risk form.
(b) Use the model to simulate the uncertainty attached to the cash flow in each year and the IRR. Interpret your data. Your output should be similar to that shown in figure 2.5

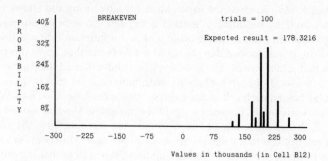

Simulation statistics: BREAKEVEN (in Cell G12)

```
  Probability of result >    0.00 = 100.0%
                        > 142.50 =  97.00%
     Values in thousands > 165.00 =  79.00%
                        > 187.50 =  22.00%
                        > 210.00 =  15.00%
                        > 232.50 =   2.00%
                        > 255.00 =   0.00%
```

Simulation statistics: BREAKEVEN (in Cell G12)

```
  Probability of result < 136.84 =  0%   < 166.79 = 35%   < 187.54 =  70%
                        < 144.48 =  5%   < 166.89 = 40%   < 187.66 =  75%
     Values in thousands < 157.61 = 10%   < 166.98 = 45%   < 188.94 =  80%
                        < 157.85 = 15%   < 178.81 = 50%   < 189.32 =  85%
                        < 162.55 = 20%   < 179.25 = 55%   < 212.64 =  90%
                        < 166.60 = 25%   < 187.31 = 60%   < 214.56 =  95%
                        < 166.70 = 30%   < 187.43 = 65%   < 242.86 = 100%
```

Simulation statistics: BREAKEVEN (in Cell G12)

```
Expected/mean result = 178321.6        Range of possible results = 106015
Maximum result       = 242857.1        Minimum result            = 136842.1

  Probability of positive result = 100.0%
  Probability of negative result =   0.0%

Standard deviation = 21687.16          Skewness             = .5694558
Variance           = 4.703331E+08      Kurtosis             = 3.30777
```

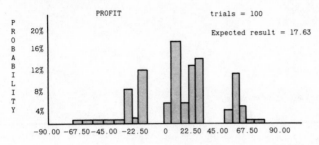

Simulation statistics: PROFIT (in Cell G14)

Probability of result >   0.00 = 74.00% Probability of result <= 0.00 = 26.00%
                      >   9.00 = 69.00%   < −9.00 = 24.00%
Values in thousands   > 18.00 = 52.00%   < −18.0 = 13.00%
                      > 27.00 = 47.00%   < −27.0 = 9.00%
                      > 36.00 = 25.00%   < −36.0 = 5.00%
                      > 45.00 = 19.00%   < −45.0 = 3.00%
                      > 54.00 = 16.00%   < −54.0 = 2.00%

Simulation statistics: PROFIT (in Cell G14)

Probability of result < −72.000 = 0% < 10.123 = 35% < 34.287 = 70%
                       < −31.072 = 5% < 10.457 = 40% < 34.733 = 75%
Values in thousands   < −24.452 = 10% < 11.728 = 45% < 40.083 = 80%
                       < −14.019 = 15% < 20.288 = 50% < 56.500 = 85%
                       < − 9.9400 = 20% < 30.041 = 55% < 57.002 = 90%
                       < − 8.2012 = 25% < 30.350 = 60% < 68.638 = 95%
                       < − 3.4350 = 30% < 30.658 = 65% < 88.500 = 100%

Simulation statistics: PROFIT (in Cell G14)

Expected/mean result = 17630   Range of possible results = 160500
Maximum result   = 88500   Minimum result   = −72000

Probability of positive result = 74.0%
Probability of negative result = 26.0%

Standard deviation = 31585.65   Skewness   = −.3313498
Variance   = 9.976536E+08   Kurtosis   = 2.853034

Figure 2.4   @Risk output: TAYLORS.WK1

REVISED K L MANUFACTURING CO.

DATA

Years		0	1	2	3-10
MARKET SHARE (What if)			0.4	0.4	0.5
		£	£	£	£
ADVERTISING EXPENDITURE (What if)			90,000	75,000	40,000
CAPITAL EXPENDITURE (What if)		400,000	200,000		

MARKET DECAY RATE AFTER YR5 (What if)	0.30
DISCOUNT RATE	0.20
GUESS RATE FOR IRR	0.30
INFLATION RATE YEARS 3-10	0.05

PROBABILISTIC DATA	Years	1	2	3-10
INITIAL MARKET SIZE		40,000		
MARKET GROWTH RATES			0.2	0.2
SELLING PRICE		22	23	24
UNIT VARIABLE COST		10	11	12
FIXED COSTS		23,000	25,000	27,000

CALCULATIONS

YEAR	SALES QU.	PRICE	REVENUE	VARCOST	FIXCOST	ADVERT + CAP.EXP	NETCSHFLO
0						400,000	(400,000)
1	16,000	22.0	352,000	160,000.0	23,000	290,000	(121,000)
2	19,200	23.0	441,600	211,200.0	25,000	75,000	130,400
3	28,800	24.0	691,200	345,600.0	27,000	40,000	278,600
4	28,800	25.2	725,760	362,880.0	28,350	40,000	294,530
5	28,800	26.5	762,048	362,880.0	29,768	40,000	329,401
6	20,160	27.8	560,105	254,016.0	31,256	40,000	234,833
7	14,112	29.2	411,677	177,811.2	32,819	40,000	161,048
8	9,878	30.6	302,583	124,467.8	34,460	40,000	103,655
9	6,915	32.2	222,398	87,127.5	36,183	40,000	59,088
10	4,840	33.8	163,463	60,989.1	37,992	40,000	24,482

NET PRESENT VALUE   £188,469

INVESTMENT PROFILE		£
	0	1,095,037
	0.1	510,839
	0.2	188,469
	0.3	(2,895)
	0.4	(123,256)
	0.5	(202,558)
	0.6	(256,822)

INTERNAL RATE OF RETURN   29.8%

REMEMBER! DO NOT SIMULATE NPV. IT IS THEORETICALLY INCONSISTENT.
ONE SHOULD, HOWEVER, TEST NPV FOR VARIATIONS IN JUST THE DISCOUNT RATE.

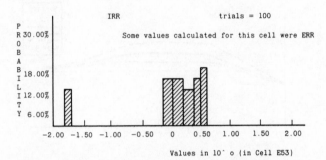

Values in 10⁻ o (in Cell E53)

Note. The graph demonstrates a problem which can arise in simulating
IRRs. While the cash flows specified in the original spreadsheet are
'normal' (i.e. only exhibit one change in sign) and therefore have a
unique IRR associated with them, upon simulation some runs may have
abnormal cash flows which led to multiple IRRs – hence the graph
above, and the difficulty the computer had in calculating an IRR in
some instances and the expected IRR of only −0.1 shown on the
following statistical print-out. The problem of multiple IRRs is, of
course, well-known, but usually thought not to be a problem if the
investment profile is graphed. When simulation is undertaken, the
analyst has to be very careful not to misinterpret the IRR output,
because the alternating signs of the cash flows may not be obvious.

Simulation statistics: IRR (in Cell E53)

Expected/mean result = −.1046568	Range of possible results =	2.276699
Maximum result = .4749121	Minimum result =	−1.801787

Probability of positive result = 79.0%
Probability of negative result = 21.0%

Standard deviation = .7180895	Skewness	= −1.781157
Variance = .5156525	Kurtosis	= 4.485719

            <Pg Up,Dn>More   <ESC>Return

[*Note.* This particular print-out is of very little value. Indeed, examined in isolation it is very
misleading with its specification of an expected IRR of −0.1. See the note on the preceding
print-out for explanation. The print-out is provided nevertheless to warn the unwary of one of the
pitfalls of this type of simulation.]

        Previous Type Statistics Zoom/Rescale Copy Overlay Reports Exit
Display Next Output Distribution

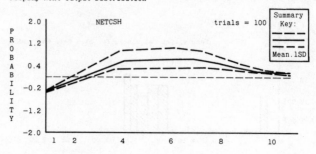

Note. This graph is useful for planning the finance needed for the
project as well as seeing the possible range of impacts on cash flow
in each year.

@RISK: B/KL.WK1
Next Previous Type   Zoom/Rescale Copy Overlay Reports Exit
Display Probabilities for Target Values

Probabilities for specified target values of NETCSH

1	0	100.00%
2	0	0.00%
3	0	97.00%
4	0	100.00%
5	0	100.00%
6	0	100.00%
7	0	100.00%
8	0	98.00%
9	0	93.00%

[*Note*. It is clear that beyond year 2 the project is most likely to have positive cash flows in
each period.]

Figure 2.5   @Risk output: KL.WK1

3

Financial Investment Appraisal in Practice and Influential Accounting Procedures

The objective of the first two chapters was to provide an up-to-date critical review of the implications of the theory of finance for investment appraisal and to extend that with the tools of financial modelling. The objective of the book as a whole, however, is to consider whether financial managers and students would not see the need to extend or modify their practices with regard to major resource allocation if they saw them within a broader context.

The book therefore commences with a view of contemporary thinking within the financial-management field, then steps outside it to see how the strategic literature and organizational-behaviour literature view major resource allocation. With this broader perspective, we shall be able to return to financial management to see if it can be brought into greater harmony with other management disciplines. An analogy can be drawn with the traveller who spends some time abroad and then returns home to see his country in a different way and better appreciate its strengths and weaknesses. Having done this, some travellers prefer just to return abroad! It remains to be seen which sort of traveller I am.

The argument has not yet reached a position where we can step outside financial management. This is because chapters 1 and 2 are essentially a critique of the *theory* of finance and this has to be distinguished quite sharply from the financial-management *function* in a large company. The former is a set of analyses all based upon a particular way of seeing the world, and is not necessarily coincident with the viewpoint of all practising financial directors and managers. The theory of finance stems from the work of financially oriented economists and their efforts to understand behaviour in financial markets. It is, for example, often said that real rigour only began to be introduced into the finance field when Modigliani and Miller (1958 and 1961) began to explore the implications of perfect-market assumptions for capital structure, the cost of capital, dividend policy, and so on. The foundations of the capital asset pricing model (CAPM) were provided by the economist Tobin (1958) when he formulated the 'separation theorum' – that investors did not need to consider their own attitudes towards risk in order to decide their portfolio of risky assets, provided that they then combined that investment with either risk-free borrowing or risk-free lending in a way which did reflect their risk attitudes.

In contrast, corporate-finance functions were not designed primarily with regard to the economic laws of financial markets. Of course, all businesses must take heed of economic pressures and seek a better understanding than their rivals possess of the markets in which they operate, but that was not the main reason why the corporate-finance functions developed. Corporate financial-management practice is derived much more from the need to exercise organizational control over financial aspects of the business: namely, to keep records by which to analyse transactions and performance. It owes its heritage more to accounting than to the theory of finance. Of course, one cannot draw a simple distinction. Accounting is concerned with planning and *ex ante* analysis as well as *ex post* monitoring, but its reliance upon theoretical economics is minimal in comparison with the theory of finance.

It must nevertheless be recognized that many companies have set up largely separate treasury functions to deal with sources of finance, foreign-exchange management, and so on. These tend to be staffed more by economists and MBA students than those with only an accounting background. But the main point is that one cannot achieve the main purpose of this book simply by comparing and contrasting the theory of finance and strategic and organizational literature. Accounting practices, though normally left aside by texts on the theory of finance, are very much part of the corporate financial-management function. One must therefore also examine how accounting practices affect corporate resource allocation and see whether an examination of the theory of finance, corporate strategy and organizational behaviour suggests any changes for accounting.

Investment appraisal in management accounting practice and the theory of finance

It is evident from various empirical studies on firms' investment-appraisal practices that net present value (NPV), or its derivative adjusted present value (APV), is not the universally accepted criterion by which to measure the worth of an investment project. Some (e.g. Petty, Scott and Bird, 1975; Francis, 1980; Bavishi, 1981; Pike, 1982;

Pike and Dobbins, 1986) argue that firms prefer to use shorter-term measures of return such as payback or short-term accounting-based profit measures. Others (e.g. Marris, 1963; Grinyer, 1986) suggest that NPV is inappropriate because it deals only with maximization of shareholder wealth and managers have multiple interests in mind when considering investment projects. Not only is there variety in practice with regard to the use of **discounted cash flow** (DCF) techniques, but there is no clear relationship between their use and firm performance (Haka, Gordon and Pinches, 1985; Pike and Dobbins, 1986). A range of other authors have also suggested when it might be more appropriate to use sophisticated capital-budgeting techniques (see Gordon, 1989, for a list of these authors).

Even when companies do use NPV (or more broadly DCF) procedures, it is not at all clear that they recognize the theoretical traps indicated in chapters 1 and 2. Even tax effects are often not properly calculated (Morgan, 1986). It is doubtful whether most firms use the CAPM properly to determine required rates of return for *projects*. This may be partly due to a lack of knowledge of the theory, but that cannot be the whole answer.

Various businessmen discussing these matters (see Weaver et al., 1989) indicate quite clearly that they are aware of the CAPM approach to determining project hurdle rates. On the other hand, it is doubtful whether many companies take into account some of the more subtle points regarding the determination of required yields and modelling discussed in chapters 1 and 2. Many companies' reactions to these points may simply be that they are too subtle for practical needs. If, furthermore, they feel that it is unnecessary to apply the CAPM generally, the more subtle points will not even be considered. This may be unfortunate, since, as argued earlier, errors in specifying the discount rate can have a *major* effect on profitability.

But is it so unfortunate? If companies needed this more precise analysis to survive, would they not have discovered this? Would not at least one major competitor have discovered the secret of identifying increased profitability and forced the others to follow suit in order to compete? From the evidence to date, it appears that this has not occurred. The refinements to NPV calculations along the lines of a good grasp of the CAPM may still prove to be desirable, but it is clearly only one factor leading to successful investment and the other factors may be more critical.

The panel discussions led by Weaver (1989), and my own private discussions with companies, suggest that a major element of investment decision-making now depends upon the place of investments in a total strategic plan for the company. Finance theorists tend to disregard such arguments and say quite simply that all positive NPV projects should be accepted.

The trouble with the finance theorists' argument is not that it is wrong, but that it overlooks the actions the company needs to take to ensure that it is examining projects in which it does have a good chance of strongly positive cash flows. The financial theorists' position tends to assume that projects are available with given cash flows. Those who argue for a 'strategic fit' for investments imply, in contrast, that projects are more likely to have good cash flow if they fit strategically, because, presumably, there is some synergy between projects through focusing effects upon things the company can do well.

At this point the argument must be left aside until an examination of what is meant by 'strategic fit' has been undertaken (see chapter 4). Then, in chapter 6, this issue will be taken up again to explore relationships and differences between the theory of finance, investment appraisal in accounting practice, and strategic analysis. At least it is clear at this point that investment-appraisal routines are widely practised and do not normally follow exact principles derived from an understanding of the CAPM.

The influence of divisional-performance measurement on resource allocation

It would be a naïve interpretation of human behaviour to think that it is only the *ex ante* analytical tools which determine which investments should be undertaken. Of prime importance in persuading people what to do will be the basis upon which their performance is evaluated and rewarded. It has been recognized in the accounting literature (Dearden, 1969; Solomons, 1968; Tomkins, 1973) that divisional-performance measures are usually not consistent with the 'correct' *ex ante* appraisal technique of DCF. Consequently, there is technical inconsistency between the theory of finance and accounting matters.

Let us leave aside, for the moment, the extra complexities of CAPM application and also whether, in the light of strategic analyses, DCF really is the correct approach. Instead let us focus explicitly on efforts made by accountants to make divisional performance, as measured by accounting **rate of return on investment** (ROI), consistent with DCF methods.

A problem of inconsistency arises because accounting ROI is not based upon compound-interest principles and also employs an accounting depreciation concept – usually on a straight-line basis. This leads to major discrepancies between the DCF concept of the **internal rate of return** (IRR) and the *ex post* accounting measure of ROI. The discussion is here framed in terms of the IRR as it is, like the ROI, expressed in terms of a percentage rate of return and so facilitates a more direct comparison of DCF and ROI.

To illustrate, table 3.1 shows a project with an IRR of 10 per cent. If the cost of capital is 9 per cent, the project is clearly profitable. If, however, a divisional manager's performance were evaluated by accounting ROI, would he not consider, before accepting the project, how acceptance of the project would affect his measured performance? The accounting ROIs anticipated for this project are also shown in table 3.1, and it can be seen that the ROI starts less than the required yield of 9 per cent but increases dramatically above it in later years. It is not at all clear what the manager would do if he decided whether to invest on the basis of the ROI. Of course, divisions do not undertake just single investments and may well have continued investment through time, but rarely will a company have an even age distribution of assets and the fact that this type of deficiency of ROI is hidden within the aggregate picture is no excuse for not addressing the problem.

Table 3.1 IRR versus ROI

Year	0	1	2	3	4	5
Cash flow (£)	−10,000	+1,200	+2,300	+5,000	+3,000	+2,001
Calculations of ROI (£)						
Inflow		1,200	2,300	5,000	3,000	2,001
Less depreciation		2,000	2,000	2,000	2,000	2,000
Net profit before interest		−800	300	3,000	1,000	1
Book value of investment (£)		8,000	6,000	4,000	2,000	0
ROI (%)		−10	+5	+75	+50	∞

It is possible, *under specific conditions*, to use the **annuity-depreciation method** to obtain a set of projected accounts which show the same ROI as the IRR. The specific conditions are that the cash flows from the project are constant each year, and the IRR is used as the interest rate for calculating the annuity depreciation. For example, suppose that one has the project shown in Table 3.2, which has an IRR of 10 per cent. The table also shows that the accounts using annuity depreciation at 10 per cent yield an ROI of 10 per cent per annum. This result is inevitable because the annuity-depreciation charge is calculated by deducting 10 per cent interest on the written-down value of the asset

Table 3.2   Making accounting ROI consistent with IRR: constant cash flows

Year	Project cash flow (£)	Annuity depreciation at 10% (£)	Profit (£)	Asset cost less depreciation (£)	ROI on opening asset balance (%)
0	–	–	–	1,000.0	–
1	315.5	215.5	100.0	784.5	10
2	315.5	237.0	78.5	547.0	10
3	315.5	260.8	54.7	286.2	10
4	315.5	286.9	28.6	0	10

from the project cash flow. Hence it would seem possible for accountants to set out a depreciation schedule using the IRR of the project. It would follow that the accounting ROI projected would not motivate managers to act other than they would by reference to the IRR.

This conclusion is invalid, however, when one allows the cash flows from the project to be uneven through time. For example, if a project with an outlay of £1,000 has cash inflows projected as follows,

	Year 1	Year 2	Year 3	Year 4
	£200	£300	£500	£285

that project still has an IRR of 10 per cent, but the projected profits and ROI would be

	Year 1	Year 2	Year 3	Year 4
Profit (£)	−15.5	+63.0	+239.2	−1.5
ROI (%)	−15.5	+8.0	+43.7	−0.5

We are back in the dilemma posed in table 3.1.

It would be possible to form a 'depreciation schedule' to ensure ROIs of 10 per cent even where cash flows are uneven through time. Table 3.3 demonstrates this for the same project. The 'depreciation' figure,

Table 3.3   Making accounting ROI consistent with IRR: uneven cash flows

Year	Project cash flow (£)	Depreciation (£)	Profit (£)	Asset cost less depreciation (£)	ROI on opening balance (%)
0	–	–	–	1,000	–
1	200	100	100	900	10
2	300	210	90	690	10
3	500	431	69	259	10
4	285	259	26	0	10

however, is nothing more than a balancing figure to enable the ROIs to become 10 per cent, although the sum of the depreciation figures do equal the initial capital expenditure. There is no theoretical reason why this could not be done, but it would be a significant change in accounting practice and so is unlikely to gain widespread acceptance. Meanwhile, there may well be dysfunctional motivational pressures on managers not to invest when they should as illustrated above.

There may be further difficulties if managers are urged to increase ROI. If a division is earning, say, 20 per cent and it is contemplating a project with an IRR of 15 per cent, with a required hurdle rate of 10 per cent, even the methodology of table 3.3 would not prevent the divisional ROI from falling below 20 per cent and so, possibly, dissuading the manager from investing when he should.

It is sometimes said that this problem can be solved by switching from the use of ROI as a divisional performance measure to the use of **residual income**. 'Residual income' is defined as profit after the deduction of both depreciation and an imputed interest charge which is normally defined as the *divisional* cost of capital. With residual income, the argument is that any project which has a unique IRR in excess of the cost of capital will bring about an increase in divisional residual income and, hence, through accounting measurement, motivate managers to undertake investment in a way which is consistent with the theory of finance. With a divisional ROI calculation, the cost of capital does not enter the analysis (unless, in exceptional circumstances, part of it is included in the form of allocated interest on debt) and so a manager urged to increase ROI may reject positive NPV projects if their IRRs are below the current *divisional* ROI. Managers can be urged to increase residual income and no problem arises.

The use of residual income is not, however, a complete solution. Difficulties arise where project net cash inflows are not constant over time. Examine the project in table 3.3 but now suppose that the divisional cost of capital is 10 per cent. Then clearly (assuming for the moment that 10 per cent is the correct discount rate) the company will be indifferent about whether the project should be accepted or not, as it has an IRR of 10 per cent. This means that a residual-income measure would need to register a zero income for each year of the project if it is to be consistent with the correct decision as·indicated by DCF. By examining table 3.3 again, it is obvious that such a resulting series of zero residual-income figures could be obtained, but only if the same 'rigged depreciation' schedule were adopted as shown in table 3.3. Then a 10 per cent cost of capital charge on the opening written-down value of assets each year would equal the profit figures shown in table 3.3. The objection to doing this is, therefore, the same as that offered for ROI: it is most unlikely that this concept of depreciation would gain widespread acceptance.

The above argument also still oversimplifies, because it assumes that the *divisional* cost of capital is the appropriate discount rate for projects. It was shown in chapter 1 that this is not so (unless the project beta happens to be the same as the divisional beta). Hence, to be consistent with the theory of finance, each project added to the divisional portfolio should have its imputed interest charge fixed at the *project* discount rate. In fact, this could be achieved under the residual-income approach without too much difficulty and so, on that score, residual income does appear to be preferable. The problem caused by non-constant cash-flow patterns remains, but recently a different suggestion has been made to overcome it

Grinyer (1986, 1987) and Gregory (1987) have independently derived an alternative divisional-performance measure. They have both developed a profit number which is quite consistent with NPV. Gregory explains his profit measure as the periodic cash flow less interest on working capital and the lease payments made to head office for the fixed assets. If the cash-flow payments are constant, his measure of income will simply be the residual-income concept derived after deducting annuity depreciation. His method, however, defines lease payments as the initial investment adjusted by interest, allocated to periods by the ratio of the present value of each period's cash flow to the present value of the cash flows for all periods. Hence the lease payments for year n are

$$I(1 + i)^n . \frac{C_n}{(1 + i)^n} \bigg/ PV$$

$$= \frac{C_n}{\text{Profitability index}}$$

Where I is the initial investment, C_n is the cash flow in period n, PV is the present value of the whole series of cash flows derived from the project, and the profitability index is PV/I.

Gregory illustrates his method with the example shown in table 3.4, where the profitability index is 1.069 with a cost of capital of 10 per cent. Hence, for example, depreciation in year 1 is $3,000/1.069 = 2,806$. This form of income measure uses the cost of capital (rather than the IRR used in table 3.2) and has the property of providing projected positive profit figures wherever the NPV is positive, whatever the projected time pattern of cash flows. It should also be noted that, while the relevant project hurdle rate is used in the derivation of the lease payments, the

Table 3.4 Gregory's divisional-income measure

Year	Project cash flows (£)	Lease payments	Profit
0	−10,000	–	–
1	3,000	2,806	194
2	6,000	5,613	387
3	4,000	3,742	258

results cannot be expressed as an ROI because the division has no fixed assets – it leases them from corporate headquarters. This, however, means that Gregory's measure is not subject to the defect of ROI in encouraging contraction of investment to increase reported ROI.

There is no theoretical reason why companies should not use Gregory's (and Grinyer's) method of income measurement, and of the proposals made to date it comes closest to providing an acceptable measure of periodic performance which is consistent with the DCF. But will companies use it? Would they consider it any more desirable than the rather more obscure income measure in table 3.3? The answer, in my view, is that they probably would if it was thought to be really necessary to use periodic income statements to motivate and assess divisional or SBU (strategic business unit) managers' *investment* performance. Consider, however, the practical difficulties even with Gregory's measure.

Investment projects on any major scale require several years lead time before the project begins to generate cash inflows. In a joint study with the CBI, Tomkins et al. (1978) showed that in UK industry the average lead time (from completion of basic research to the time products come on stream) was about two years; seven or eight years was not unusual in some industries. Then allow even longer for products to reach the more mature stage of their life-cycles. The question then arises of how many divisional or SBU managers hold their posts that long. Would the manager considering the project illustrated in table 3.4 be very interested in the actual profits earned in years 2 and 3 rather than just year 1? Most projects, however, have rather longer life-cycles, and so the relevant question is whether managers will be much concerned with the profitability of projects four, five or more years ahead if they are *only* evaluated on the basis of shorter-term improvements in accounting results.

If this is a reasonable representation of the real world situation, it follows that the manager's performance at selecting the right *invest-ments* is not going to be judged (or, at least, should not be judged) on the basis of periodic profit figures which accrue to the organization during the (relatively) short time for which he holds that position. A considerable part of those profits will be determined by *post*-investment performance management of his predecessor's projects, and the benefits of 'his' investment may well accrue after he moves on. He may well remain in the same corporate group, but it would be unusual to base his direct rewards on the profits of a division he has left – though, of course, his general reputation may be enhanced by the basis for success laid in other parts of the group. It follows, therefore, that a manager's performance in *influencing worthwhile investment* ought to be assessed by other means. The key to determining what those are, in any particular case, lies in considering why investment is undertaken. If, as suggested above, 'strategic fit' is of prime performance, perhaps we shall be in a better position to answer this question when we have examined the strategy literature. It may then transpire that the theoretical defects of ROI are not so serious in practice. If so, it may be unnecessary to move to a residual-income concept, which is obviously still far from perfect, or to the newer Grinyer/Gregory measure. There is, however, quite a different argument at the end of the next section of this chapter, which may suggest that residual income is preferable after all.

Cost-behaviour analysis, product-costing and resource allocation

Another broad area in which management accounting practices may influence resource allocation is in the analysis of cost behaviour and product-costing: accounting practices here may substantially affect the perception of a project's incremental cash flows. Readers will have covered the conventional cost-accounting practices in basic texts. They may therefore be summarized very briefly, as follows.

Cost accountants distinguish between fixed costs and variable costs. Hence, when estimating the costs associated with a project operating at different levels of activity, they will usually make a separate assessment of fixed costs and then allow variable costs to vary in proportion to output. It is also usual in product-costing to estimate the direct product costs (mainly direct materials and labour) and then add a percentage or amount per labour hour (or machine hour) for indirect costs. Basic texts show a variety of ways of doing this and, in principle, state that different types of overheads can be 'charged out' to products on different bases. In practice, however, it seems that blanket rates or departmental rates covering a broad range of support activities and based on labour hours are most often used. Moreover, the position is complicated by the assignment of service-department costs first to production departments in order to provide an addition to the production-department overheads to be 'recovered' at the blanket or departmental rate.

Cooper and Kaplan (1987) raise several questions about the appropriateness of such practices for deciding the best product mix and also, by implication, in which products to invest. The basis of the argument is that it is important to understand why costs are incurred and why they vary. While some indrect costs will vary with the number of labour hours (or machine hours or some other general measure of activity), other indirect costs will vary according to other factors – for example, the number of set-up times. A conventional (statistical or otherwise) analysis of costs into fixed and variable, using aggregated output or labour hours as an explanatory variable, may well assign some of these set-up costs into a fixed category, misleading managers into thinking that they will not vary over larger ranges of production levels and particularly product mix.

More seriously, traditional product-costing procedures may distort costs as between products. If a significant part of indirect costs concern set-up costs, the product line which has small runs, with high variety of specification between runs, will be subsidized by product lines with large runs and low variety of specification. Hence the products which are really more expensive to produce will seem cheaper than they are and the cheaper products will seem more costly. This could lead the company into disastrous product-mix or investment strategies, especially if its rivals more accurately recognize the true product costs. Despite the gibes of many strategists and finance people about the value of accounting in making key decisions, it is fundamental to good decision-making to understand Kaplan's argument (Kaplan and Atkinson, 1989). In order to arrive at relevant costs for *product-mix* and *investment* decisions, one *must* understand in depth the appropriate production and distribution processes and identify the relevant cost-drivers for each major element of cost. As Kaplan says, these primary cost-drivers include set-ups, inspections, receipts of materials, payments, number of parts, number of supplies, and engineering change orders. To assume that only costs change with labour or machine hours is not good enough. A number of manufacturing companies are therefore re-examining their practices with a view to getting more accurate analyses of product costs and cost behaviour. However, one must be careful not to push the argument too far.

Activity-based costing, as the new approach is called, is not an automatic panacea for age-old cost allocation problems. Bromwich and Bhimani (1989) argue that activity-based costing does not resolve the problems of allocating general manufacturing overheads, or indicate how set-up costs should be allocated between products when production is switched back and forth between them. Nevertheless, if accountants take the trouble to understand their production and distribution processes in more depth, and how the main cost elements of those processes are driven, they are likely to have a better appreciation of product costs and avoid the product-mix errors identified by Kaplan and Cooper. That, surely, is the main message of the advocates of activity-based costing.

When Bromwich and Bhimani argue that 'In many ways, this problem can be solved more easily by looking towards market prices than by reforming accounting systems in complex ways' (1989, p. 70), they miss the main point. If one does not know the product cost, one does not know the relative profitability of different products even if one does know their target prices. Hence the wrong product lines may be closed down as unprofitable. Bromwich and Bhimani suggest also that this need not occur if businesses focus on a few product lines with high volume. They say that the problem belongs to US companies who commit the managerial error of running too large a product range, and this is not something that can be resolved by reforming accounting. This again does not appear to be a conclusive argument. Why have these US firms maintained such a range? Perhaps because the accounting system showed, incorrectly, most products to be profitable. Also, in some industries it is not unusual to find UK companies with extensive product ranges. A subsidiary of a well-known corporate group has 1,400 types of assembly and 25,000 part numbers. That subsidiary, which I am well acquainted with, came very close to collapse partly due to erroneous product-profitability signals from a traditional costing system. The phenomenon is not confined to a few US companies identified in Harvard case studies. Once a company is in such a situation, reforming its accounting systems will not, by itself, save the day. But an accurate analysis of product profitability will be needed to show where change is needed. Moreover, if accurate product costs had been available beforehand, a crisis might well have been prevented. Bromwich and Bhimani are right to emphasize that activity-based costing must not be taken up blindly, without careful regard for need, but they do seem to overstate their case.

Of course, one does not want over-complex accounting systems for their own sake. Bromwich and Bhimani remind us of Hiromoto's argument that there may be good motivational reasons for sticking with the direct-labour basis for overhead allocation – thereby encouraging managers to cut labour costs and make further moves towards automation (Hiromoto, 1988). But the decision to adopt or reject activity-based costing (or move to a somewhat more refined product-costing system) must not be taken on such arguments alone. The need for activity-based costing will depend on the features of each company (division or plant), its technology, its product range and market strategies and, possibly, its need for a 'turn-around strategy' involving a rationalized product range. Management accountants ought not to reject activity-based costing by default; careful assessment is needed. Otherwise, the resource-allocation process can indeed be adversely affected by poor accounting systems.

Before moving on, in chapter 4, to discuss the corporate-strategy literature, we need to consider one more key point relating to product-costing. This point also links product-costing with the residual-income debate.

It was argued above that, if managers' *investment* behaviour is evaluated without close reference to short-term ROI or residual-income performance, there does not seem to be a strong case for introducing the latter in preference to ROI, even though it may *appear* that the use of residual income would bring the theory of finance and accounting reports into closer harmony. Other authors, principally Anthony (1975) but more recently Staubus (1988), argue, however, that the full cost of capital should be charged in accounts. (Staubus, in 1988, notes very interestingly that Norton, 1889, insisted that capital costs should be included in product costs, so this is hardly a new argument. Neverthe-less, it still needs advocates 100 years later!) While Staubus argues that this would help reconcile finance theory and accounting, his book also deals with activity-costing and he supports the development in costing recently highlighted by Kaplan. If one recognizes the argument that it is becoming necessary to have more accurate product costs for planning which products to produce, then it follows that such product costs should include all costs, including the cost of capital, and that differing costs of capital should be traced clearly to each product according to its own use of capital (fixed-asset and working capital) and its own risk characteristics (i.e. discount rate). Consequently, there may well be a case for using residual income *in product profitability calculations* and this may lead to better product choice and, hence, better investment decisions. But note: this is quite a different argument from the one usually presented in support of residual income – that it would over-come the faults of divisional ROI on an investment-performance measure. While the argument for residual income as an investment-performance measure may not be conclusive, the residual-income concept may be vital to improved product-costing. This latter point has not been prominent in the literature.

It is perhaps worth just a short digression to provide a simple illustration of how many basic costing texts *may* lead students into getting the make-or-buy decision wrong by not recognizing the point just made. For example, consider the treatment of this subject by

Morse, Davis and Hartgraves (1988). (This is one of the best current introductory texts and many lesser texts might equally have been selected to make the point.) Morse et al. make the usual comparison between the cost of buying a component and the differential cost of manufacture. They also are very careful to specify other factors which may affect the decision, such as alternative uses of fixed assets. They do not, however, *explicitly* note that inventory levels may change quite significantly according to whether one manufactures or purchases the finished component – especially with regard to stocks of new materials and work-in-progress. If this is so, the cost of financing those different asset levels should be included in the calculation. Of course, Morse et al. and most other texts could argue that it is assumed that inventory levels will be no different or that the inventory holding costs have been *assumed* to be included in the differential costs. But the point needs *explicit* recognition; asset financing costs may well be critical to a make-or-buy decision. I recently became aware of a large and well-known UK company that had made wrong make-or-buy decisions by ignoring the financing cost of assets released on buying in parts. It has now recognized its error and moved to considerable contracting-out and savings. The use of a residual-income approach to product-costing might have made the 'true' costs more obvious.

Chapters 1–3 have presented outline descriptions of the theory of finance, financial modelling and financial-management practice, with reference to investment-appraisal procedures, measuring performance by accounting numbers, and product-costing. The elements emphasized in these descriptions are those most closely related to corporate resource allocation. It is now time to step outside an exclusively financial perspective. The next chapter will examine a body of literature which may be broadly termed the corporate-strategy area – although it will confine itself largely to the economics-based/rational-deduction segment of that literature. We shall then go on to consider links between this literature and accounting (chapter 5) and finance (chapter 6). Finally, in chapters 7–9, we shall try to link up the literature in organization behaviour with accounting, finance and corporate strategy, to explore the development of a more complete understanding of corporate resource allocation.

References

Anthony, R. 1975: *Accounting for the Cost of Interest*. Lexington, Mass.: Lexington Books.

Bavishi, V. 1981: Capital budgeting practices of multinationals. *Management Accounting* (USA), August.

Bromwich, M. and Bhimani, A. 1989: *Management Accounting: evolution not revolution*. London: Chartered Institute of Management Accounting.

Cooper, R. and Kaplan, R. 1987: How cost accounting systematically distorts product costs. In W. J. Bruns and R. Kaplan, *Accounting and Management: field study perspectives*, Cambridge, Mass.: Harvard Business School.

Dearden, J. 1969: The case against ROI control. *Harvard Business Review*, May–June.

Francis, A. 1980: Company objectives, managerial motivations and the behaviour of large firms: an empirical test of the theory of 'managerial' capitalism. *Cambridge Journal of Economics*, 4.

Gordon, L. 1989: Benefit cost analysis and resource allocation decisions. *Accounting, Organizations and Society*, 14, no. 3.

Gregory, A. 1987: Divisional performance measurement with divisions as lessees of Head Office assets. *Accounting and Business Research*, 17, no. 67 (Summer).

Grinyer, J. 1986: An alternative to maximization of shareholders' wealth in capital budgeting decisions. *Accounting and Business Research*, 16, no. 64 (Autumn).

Grinyer, J. 1987: A new approach to depreciation. *Abacus*, 23, no. 1 (March).

Haka, S., Gordon, L. and Pinches, G. 1985: Sophisticated capital budgeting selection techniques and firm performance. *Accounting Review*, October.

Hiromoto, T. 1988: Another hidden edge – Japanese managment accountancy. *Harvard Business Review*, July–August.

Kaplan, R. and Atkinson, A. 1989: *Advanced Management Accounting*, 2nd edn. Englewood Cliffs, NJ: Prentice-Hall.

Marris, R. 1963: A model of the managerial enterprise. *Quarterly Journal of Economics*, 77, no. 2.

Miller, M. and Modigliani, F. 1961: Dividend policy, growth and the valuation of shares. *Journal of Business*, October.

Modigliani, F. and Miller, M. 1958: The cost of capital, corporation finance and the theory of investment. *American Economic Review*, June.

Morgan, E. 1986: *Corporate Taxation and Investment*. Aldershot: Gower.

Morse, W., Davis, J. and Hartgraves, A. 1988: *Management Accounting*, 2nd edn. Reading, Mass.: Addison-Wesley.

Norton, G. 1889: *Textile Manufacturer's Book-Keeping*. London: Simplin. (Reference derived from Staubus, 1988.)

Petty, J., Scott, D. and Bird, M. 1975: The capital expenditure decision-making process of large corporations. *Engineering Economist*, Spring.

Pike, R. 1982: *Capital Budgeting in the 1980s: a major survey of investment practices in large companies*. London: Institute of Cost and Management Accountants.

Pike, R. and Dobbins, R. 1986: *Investment Decisions and Financial Strategy*. Deddington, Oxon: Philip Allan.

Solomons, D. 1968: *Divisional Performance: management and control*. Homewood, Ill.: R. D. Irwin.

Staubus, G. J. 1988: *Activity Costing for Decisions*, New York and London: Garland.

Tobin, J. 1958: Liquidity preference as behaviour towards risk. *Review of Economic Studies*, February.

Tomkins, C. 1973: *Financial Planning in Divisionalized Companies*. London: Haymarket (now Prentice-Hall).

Tomkins, C., Edwards, J., Thomas, R. and Butler, C. 1978: *Investment Lead Times in British Manufacturing Industry*. London: Confederation of British Industry.

Weaver, S. C. et al. 1989: Panel discussions on corporate investment. *Financial Management* (USA), Spring.

Discussion questions

3.1   How does the use of ROI as a performance measure influence managers to make incorrect investment decisions? Is this problem solved if the residual-income measure is used instead of ROI? What if Gregory's 'lease-payments method' is used?

3.2   How, according to the advocates of activity-based costing, do traditional costing methods distort product costs? Under what circumstances is their argument likely to carry more weight or less weight?

3.3   Why might it be argued that the residual-income concept has an important role to play in make-or-buy decisions?

4

Strategic Analysis and Corporate Investment: An Economic and Marketing Emphasis

The approaches to investment appraisal discussed in chapters 1 and 2 took an individual-project perspective. It was assumed that projects exist either with easily specified cash flows or with easily specified underlying factors which give rise to those cash flows. Some uncertainty was admitted in relation to those factors, and ways of studying the impact of such uncertainties were shown, but then it was assumed that the uncertainties themselves were reasonably structured such that rough probabilities of outcomes could be assigned. This is in general accordance with the state of corporate-finance literature.

While this may be a reasonable stance for finance academics to adopt, even though the problems in analysing cash flows and given probabilities have been shown to be far from trivial, the practising manager has to recognize the limited scope of the 'investment problem' addressed by the current theory of finance. He (or she) needs to realize that considerable analysis needs to be conducted in order to form sound judgements of cash flows and underlying uncertainties for large projects, and that too ready a move into discounted cash flow (DCF) calculations may give the impression of sophisticated analysis which disguises the inadequacy of the underlying assumptions. It may indeed be far more important to get the underlying analysis right than to spend time and effort on refining financial calculations, although the dangers of using incorrect discount rates need to be remembered.

It also seems important to recognize that projects are not all the same. There are differences both in the scale of projects (the replacement of a boiler versus a large-scale merger) and in their economic profile (large companies usually operate in a range of different markets, countries, industries, and so on). It may be appropriate to end up with a net present value (NPV) calculation for all types of investment, but obtaining the correct decision may depend far more on recognizing the differences, in nature and importance, of the underlying factors which will affect the projected cash flows.

The current financial-management approach to the investment decision not only lacks insight into how the underlying factors should be analysed, but also fails to recognize the different stages of developing projects. Back in 1975, King identified six stages in the development of a major project:

1 triggering the search for an appropriate project
2 screening investment proposals, because it is impossible to conduct an extensive analysis on all possible projects and alternative versions of projects
3 definition of the project alternatives
4 evaluation of the alternatives
5 transmission of project information
6 making the decision

He then pointed out that the financial-managment literature concentrated exclusively on stage 4, and with a few exceptions this is still the situation today. Some will want to argue that King is simplifying reality in assuming a single decision-taking point at the end of the project and a neat sequential series of steps, but his message about the limited scope of finance theory is just as important now as it was in 1975.

While few finance theorists have addressed stages other than stage 4, other disciplines have been active in researching what may be appropriate in other stages. In particular, writers in the fields of corporate strategy and industrial economics have made considerable progress in areas which contribute to the types of analysis needed in stages 1–3, and others with a more behavioural perspective to their research have advanced understanding of the organizational and human processes by which these stages are acted out in companies. There have not yet, however, been any far-reaching attempts to tie together the insights of the different disciplines and perspectives. Some limited progress has been made relatively recently in linking up the analysis of corporate strategy and some of the behavioural insights of strategy formulation and implementation (see Quinn, Mintzberg and James, 1988, for a text which refers to many of these ideas but which presents little in the way of synthesis), but not much has yet been done to tie that in with financial management.

In case the reader should think that this small book is about to offer the solution to this problem, let it be stated immediately that a complete integration of all these different disciplinary approaches to the investment decision will probably take a considerable time and much research effort by a range of researchers. Moreover, the volume of literature in these other areas is such that only an outline can be presented here. What will be attempted in the remainder of this book is to provide, for accountants and financial-management students, an appreciation of developments in these other fields, together with discussion of some issues which relate to the problem of trying to integrate these different disciplinary views. Consequently, it is recognized that what is offered can only be a highly personal and limited selection of developments in disciplines other than financial management, with a few isolated ideas on linkages between them. It is hoped, nevertheless, that this will encourage students of accounting and finance to be bold in pursuing connections between their own subject and others involved in the study of management.

In this chapter we shall look at corporate resource allocation from the point of view of corporate strategy and industrial economics, summarizing their major contributions in this area over recent years. The discussion will be confined to rational-deductive strategic and economic analysis. The key ideas of those in the corporate strategy field who have focused more on understanding what companies actually do will be summarized in chapter 7.

Strategic portfolio analysis

During the 1960s most of the Western world enjoyed steady economic growth and it became increasingly evident that companies' main accounting apparatus (financial reports in the form of income statements and balance sheets and annual budgets) provided an inadequate basis for thinking ahead. It was recognized that there was a need for longer-term planning. This generally resulted in processes by which companies tried

- to identify long-run broad objectives
- to identify gaps between objectives and likely achievement under current policies
- to formulate strategy to achieve objectives
- to select investments to achieve the strategic goals
- to draw up long-term plans
- to ensure that the shorter-term budgets and plans were consistent with where the company wanted to go in the longer run

While the process did not necessarily proceed without negotiation and iteration between stages, the planning literature emphasized the general logic of the need to integrate short-term budgets with long-term planning.

With the economic recession of 1970–1, corporate managers came to realize that the form of long-term planning that they were conducting, based often on relatively straightforward projections of past growth, did not ensure corporate success. In fact, many corporate planning departments were significantly reduced in size or even abandoned around this time. Those companies that persevered with longer-term planning realized that a mechanism was needed to manage changing emphases in their multiple business interests. It was recognized more clearly than before that most large companies actually held a portfolio of businesses, and that long-term growth, or indeed survival, might depend more on managing that portfolio rather than assuming continued growth on all fronts. In 1970 the **Boston Consulting Group** (BCG) published its product-portfolio matrix, which had and still has, though now through derivatives of that early model, a major influence on strategic thinking in many companies.

The origins of the BCG matrix lie before the 1970–1 recession. That consulting group came to realize earlier than others how important market share was to corporate profitability. This was due not only to economies of scale but also to what came to be known as the **experience curve**. The experience curve itself was developed from the concept of the learning curve, which had been used for many years in industries where it was observed that labour time fell as the workforce accumulated experience in producing more of a particular type of unit. The BCG accumulated evidence that costs of all factor inputs could be reduced with an accumulation of experience if companies were conscious of the possibility and managed to make savings in labour, develop standardized products, improve equipment and processes, and so on.

The BCG then coupled the importance of market share with the rate of growth in the market to produce a growth–share matrix upon which all a corporate group's main product groups would be plotted (see figure 4.1). Each product group would be represented as a circle on the portfolio grid, where the size of each circle relative to those for other product groups indicated the proportion of group profits earned by that product group. The growth axis was said to approximate the product life-cycle, with the rate of growth slowing down as the product market entered a more mature state.

The BCG divided its matrix into four quadrants as shown in figure 4.1 and gave each quadrant a name to signify how the products in it should be treated. BCG also argued that a company with a balanced portfolio of products would use cash flows generated from the **cash cows** to invest in selected **problem children**, which would be built up to become the **stars** of the future. The current stars are generators of profits which may need investment to sustain their position. A star may or may not be able to generate its own cash to provide for its own investment. It was also pointed out that nothing in this picture is static. Stars will eventually become cash cows as they reach maturity. Cash cows will be deprived of any further major investment. **Dogs** are those cows which have further deteriorated such that they provide no cash throw-off, due to the effect of a small market share in a very mature market. Companies were advised to get out of dogs as soon as possible.

The BCG matrix, with its implications of a rigid policy for each product quadrant, has been much criticized, and some of the relevant criticisms will be examined later in this chapter. For the moment it suffices to say that the BCG-matrix approach was a critical step in emphasizing (1) the need for a balanced portfolio of products within a corporate group in order to sustain longer-run success, and (2) the dynamic nature of managing large corporations. The BCG approach provided the basis for further developments.

Various derivatives of the BCG matrix have been developed both by other consultancy firms and by large companies such as Shell, but a description of just one of these will suffice. Probably the most widely known alternative matrix is that developed by **McKinsey and Co.**, apparently in liaison with **General Electric Inc.** (USA).

The McKinsey–GE portfolio matrix is shown in figure 4.2. The fundamental logic of that matrix is essentially the same as that developed by BCG: namely, that corporate groups can be divided up into sub-categories such that appropriate expansion, hold or contraction policies can be identified for each sub-category. The matrix in figure 4.2 merely uses a 3 × 3 system of classification, rather than BCG's 2 × 2, to split out the three different policy categories more clearly.

At this time the idea of simply dividing up the group into product groups was also broadened. The relevant units of the matrix came to be called **strategic business units** (SBUs). An SBU was taken to be any subsidiary business interest of the group which could be said to be largely separable and could be treated as having a commercial life of its own. An SBU might, therefore, be a product group, a geographical region, a customer group or whatever form of classification seemed appropriate. It was critical, however, that existing organizational units, i.e. corporate divisions, should not automatically be considered the appropriate SBU units. Corporate divisions can incorporate more than one or, indeed, less than one separate economic entity. Divisions may have been formed for administrative or historical reasons, which do not necessarily produce organizational units which are identical with SBUs. This is an absolutely fundamental point. If SBUs with largely separate commercial lives cannot be identified, or are misidentified, the first basic requirement of this type of analysis is not met and there is little

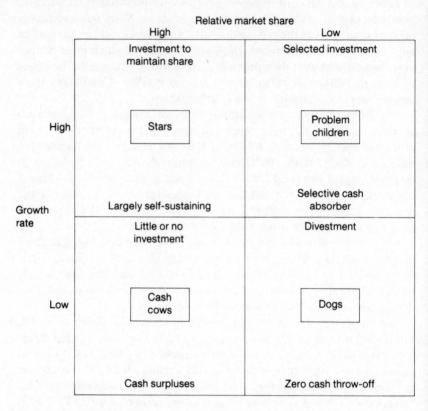

Figure 4.1   The Boston Consulting Group portfolio matrix

point continuing with the technique. The point will be taken up again later within an evaluation of these matrix methods.

The McKinsey–GE matrix also recognizes that in many businesses investment decisions cannot be made simply upon information about market growth and the current share held. Consequently, it redefined the axes as follows. 'Market growth' was replaced by **Industry attractiveness** – a term that in practice was used loosely, to refer to the attractiveness of being in that area of activity in which the SBU operated. (This area could be a particular part of an industry, a geographical area, and so on.) Also 'Market share' was replaced by **Competitive strengths**, i.e. competitive strengths within the SBU's area of activity. For good measure, McKinsey also decided to exchange the axes.

With these redefined axes, McKinsey concluded that investments should be made in attractive industries where a group was in a strong competitive position and not in less attractive industries, especially where the group's competitive position was weak. It was recognized also that selective investments might be made in unattractive industries if the SBU was the dominant operator in that industry, and similarly where attractiveness was high and the SBU's position weak.

Like the BCG, McKinsey saw the inclusion in its matrix of the industry or product life-cycle concept as appropriate for the way SBUs were defined. With figure 4.2, however, the cycle is seen as going diagonally across the matrix rather than running along one axis. McKinsey also drew up an analysis showing how different facets of financial management should vary according to the stage of the life-cycle. It follows that its 3 × 3 matrix can also be used as a basis for developing a complete range of differentiated financial policies throughout the group as well as just investment and divestment advice. The relationships that McKinsey posited between areas of its matrix, the

| | | Industry attractiveness | | |
		High	Medium	Low
	High	Invest and grow	Invest and grow	Selective investments
Competitive strengths	Medium	Invest and grow	Selective investments	Harvest or divest
	Low	Selective investments	Harvest or divest	Harvest or divest

Figure 4.2 McKinsey–GE portfolio matrix

life-cycle and financial-management policies are summarized in figure 4.3.

It is at once apparent that the McKinsey–GE matrix has much less definite measurements for its axes. Indeed, I have found that students and businessmen who are using this technique for the first time tend to get confused between the two axes. It is very easy when analysing industry attractiveness to argue that the industry is attractive because the company holds a patent or some other competitive advantage. That is obviously confusing the two axes. A useful piece of advice to avoid this is to tell users that they should be trying to decide how attractive the industry is for some SBU *that is strong in that industry*. Moreover, attractiveness must be defined in terms of looking ahead at the likely state of the industry over the usual sort of investment time horizon for that industry.

In comparison with the BCG matrix, the McKinsey–GE matrix seems at first to be less explicit about building some 'problem children' into 'stars' and identifying 'cash cows' and 'dogs', but the implications are present, as indicated by figure 4.3. The McKinsey–GE model does, however, seem inconsistent with the BCG matrix in two respects, and these seem to have been largely overlooked in the literature.

The first point of inconsistency concerns the investment policy indicated in the top left-hand corner of the grid. BCG does not say 'invest and grow' here, but implies that investment should be made in so far as it is needed to maintain a favourable position; BCG seems to be ambivalent here about the need to invest to increase market share. In contrast, McKinsey says categorically, invest where the market is attractive and where the company is strong. Also, BCG is far more explicit about the need to build certain 'problem children' into 'stars', and appears to advocate investment principally in the top right quadrant, in order to increase market share *in those SBUs where investment can be a vehicle for doing that*. The BCG position seems more defensible than McKinsey's.

If the McKinsey–GE matrix is to be similarly interpreted as a guide to the movement of the group's interests through time, one must assume that a substantial amount of investment must take place in the bottom left-hand corner of the grid in order to build future 'stars'. Of course, this conclusion depends on how one interprets the 'Competitive strengths' axis. I prefer to evaluate *current* competitive strength and plot that on the grid. This then forces a consideration of whether investment can then improve the SBU's competitive stance or not. If it can, this implies the possibility of moving the SBU up the vertical axis. If, however, the vertical axis is defined as *attainable* competitive strength, then one might expect most investment to take place in the top left

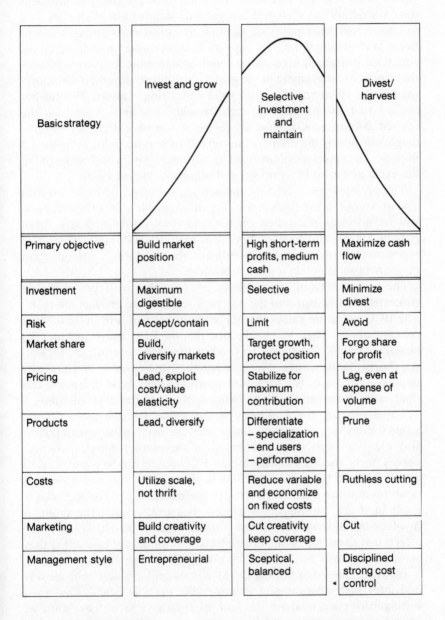

Basic strategy	Invest and grow	Selective investment and maintain	Divest/ harvest
Primary objective	Build market position	High short-term profits, medium cash	Maximize cash flow
Investment	Maximum digestible	Selective	Minimize divest
Risk	Accept/contain	Limit	Avoid
Market share	Build, diversify markets	Target growth, protect position	Forgo share for profit
Pricing	Lead, exploit cost/value elasticity	Stabilize for maximum contribution	Lag, even at expense of volume
Products	Lead, diversify	Differentiate – specialization – end users – performance	Prune
Costs	Utilize scale, not thrift	Reduce variable and economize on fixed costs	Ruthless cutting
Marketing	Build creativity and coverage	Cut creativity keep coverage	Cut
Management style	Entrepreneurial	Sceptical, balanced	Disciplined strong cost control

Figure 4.3 Financial policies for different parts of the McKinsey–GE matrix

corner. This stresses, once more, the need to be extremely careful with the basic definitions used in this apparently simple form of analysis, and to ensure that one's policy deductions are consistent with one's definitions and assumptions. To repeat, however, the interpretation of competitive strength as *current* strength is preferable, because it focuses the dynamic management of the group portfolio on the grid itself, rather than leaving it as an inference of the underlying analysis. This further implies that the product life-cycle should be seen as shown on the revised McKinsey–GE grid of figure 4.4, rather than as running diagonally across the matrix from top left to bottom right, as figure 4.3 implies. The emphasis of financial management within each stage of the life-cycle as shown in figure 4.3 still retains its logical validity.

The preference for defining competitive strength as current strength also arises out of the recognition that, if attainable status is used, there will be no clear separation on the matrix of established stars from potential stars, and this seems critical for distinguishing between two types of investment: major investment for the future and sufficient investment to maintain a market position.

The second area of inconsistency between the two types of matrix concerns another aspect of the way they relate to the product life-cycle. The BCG literature shows that the growth rate varies from 0 to 20 per cent and above. There is no indication that the BCG matrix includes the negative growth element of the product life-cycle. In contrast, McKinsey claims that its matrix covers the complete life-cycle, as illustrated by figures 4.3 and 4.4. The McKinsey position seems more defensible this time, with the negative growth being confined to the dogs' quarters.

To summarize, the McKinsey matrix seems to have more general scope for devising investment and general financial-management policy. But where industries are dominated by the market-share/experience-curve effects, the logic underlying the BCG model can be a useful aid to thinking about the policy of SBUs *in those particular industries*. It is doubtful that the BCG matrix is very useful for *total* portfolio management in many multi-business groups, because, even if the group is involved in SBUs whose business is dominated by the experience-curve effect, it is likely that some of its SBUs will not be and hence that they cannot be reliably analysed within just the BCG context.

However, one must not use the McKinsey grid in a deterministic way and infer that most investment must take place in 'stars'. One must distinguish between where the *bulk* of corporate investment must be placed and the location of SBUs on the matrix. The McKinsey investment policies shown within the matrix in figure 4.2 cannot be sustained literally. The grid states nothing about the degree to which investment is necessary to retain star position or sufficient to build competitive

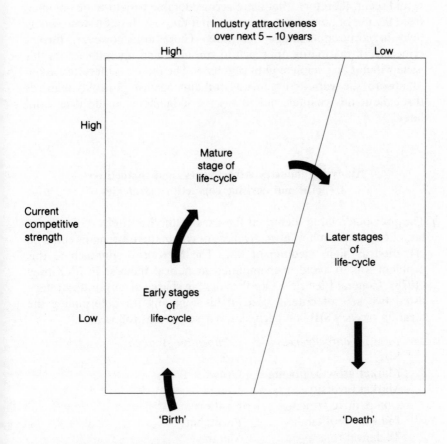

Figure 4.4 Modified McKinsey–GE matrix: natural business-unit cycle (*Note*. The cycle shown indicates the general trend; it is not meant to exclude more complex patterns as products/businesses manage to boost the height or length of their life-cycle from a mature or declining stage)

advantage. It is stressed, therefore, that a literal reading of figure 4.2 could be a path to disaster. That does not mean, however, that the McKinsey–GE grid approach has no value, especially if modified as indicated in figure 4.4. On the contrary, with intelligent and informed use, it can be a powerful tool for aiding judgement on investment and related financial-management matters. Many companies and consultants have used the approach (see Hapeslagh, 1982), and those using it will generally be intelligent people who are not going to make naïve errors through too literal an interpretation of a simple box diagram. It would seem, therefore, that there is considerable benefit to be obtained from the use of portfolio matrices, even if this view is not now so widely held in corporate-strategy literature. There are, however, further criticisms of the matrix approach to consider, and my full case on this issue will not be complete until chapter 8. The reader is therefore asked to absorb the various arguments for and against portfolio matrices throughout this chapter, but to reserve judgement on the issue until later.

Analysing industry attractiveness and competitive strengths and devising competitive strategies

The previous section identified the axes of the McKinsey–GE matrix, but did not explain how attractiveness or competitive strengths could be classified as high, medium or low. The McKinsey approach to this problem was to avoid oversimplified numerical indices. In McKinsey (1978), General Electric's Vice President in charge of corporate strategy listed two sets of criteria used in his company for determining the location of each SBU on each axis. These were as follows.

Industry attractiveness	*Competitive strength*
Size	Size
Market growth, pricing	Growth
Market diversity	Share
Competitive structure	Position
Industry profitability	Profitability
Technical role	Margins
Social	Technology position
Environmental	Strengths/weaknesses
Legal	Image
Human	Pollution
	People

Allen, the Vice President, stated that classifications as high, medium or low were then made with respect to each axis on the basis of collective judgement by corporate management. Clearly management had to decide

1 what would count as high, medium or low with respect to each criterion, and
2 what weight of importance to attach to each criterion to arrive at an overall assessment for each axis.

The emphasis was on judgement and discussion rather than precise measurement, but Allen said, 'It is surprising how little disagreement there is in positioning of our businesses on this matrix each year.' He also stressed that, as the environment changed, the emphasis was shifted to different factors, and that the approach was used to reallocate major imvestment resource amongst competing needs.

One cannot, of course, say from this description how rigorously each SBU was evaluated, or how well devised the strategies to move SBUs around the matrix were. More recent work by **Porter** (1980, 1985) has shown, however, that, from a knowledge of industrial economics, it is possible to develop a rigorous basis for solving both of these problems. In comparison with Porter's work, the lists of factors given by General Electric back in the 1970s now seem little more than a tentative beginning at an appropriate form of analysis.

In his 1980 study, Porter argues that the first thing for a firm to understand is the structure of the industry or market in which it operates. It is that structure which determines longer-run profitability. Moreover, industrial structure is not something which can be resolved merely by general debate over a general checklist of factors. There are five main factors which determine the structure of any industry. Three of these are based upon the input–output relationships affecting the production of goods or services in the industry: factors affecting inputs, their conversion into outputs, and saleability. The other two factors are the degree to which it is easy to enter the industry or market, and the degree to which there are substitutes for the products. These five factors can in turn be broken down into a number of subsidiary aspects to produce a specific number of questions to be answered in identifying the likely longer-run attractiveness of the industry. These can, following Porter, be put together as shown in figure 4.5. This makes much better sense than the General Electric list, because it places projected profitability as the major element of industrial attractiveness, rather than simply listing it as one of several factors, and provides a sound theoretical basis for determining it.

Following the implications of the McKinsey matrix, Porter states that there is usually little that the firm can do in the short run to affect industry structure and hence attractiveness. It should focus upon understanding that structure in order to develop a competitive strategy. Porter points out, nevertheless, that industry structures do change over time, perhaps due to technological or other developments, and that the firm itself may, through its competitive strategy, change the structure – either inadvertently or not. In particular, a market leader's actions may significantly affect the industry structure. One must therefore develop

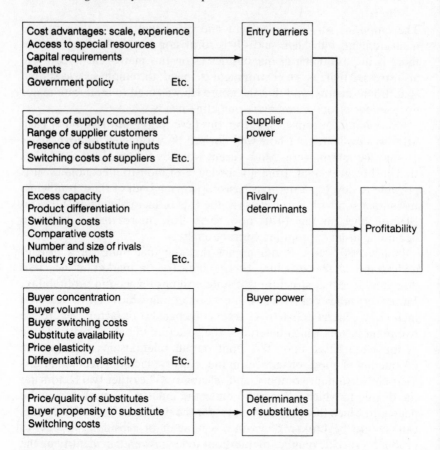

Figure 4.5 Porter's factors for analysing industrial structure (factors are illustrative; for a full list see Porter, 1985, figure 1.2)

Adapted with permission of The Free Press, a division of Macmillan, Inc. from *Competitive Advantage:Creating and Sustaining Superior Performance* by M. E. Porter, copyright © 1985 by M. E. Porter.

strategies taking into account the way in which they, and rival responses to them, may change the industry structure and its related profitability. Hence, a dynamic consideration of portfolio analysis, as applied to major investment decisions with their relatively long time horizons, does not just mean moving SBUs up or down the portfolio grid by transferring resources between them (from 'cash cows' to 'problem children' and 'stars'). It means identifying, too, how actions on the competitive-strengths axis may feed into the industry-attractiveness axis, which may then create further movement of the SBUs and challenge the relevance of the competitive strategy first devised. There must be an iterative movement between effects of each of the two axes, and a *set* of matrices, each reflecting a stage of this process, will be necessary to analyse this process.

Despite the comprehensiveness and relative complexity of Porter's analysis, he concludes that, once one has arrived at an assessment of one's competitive strengths by considering how strong an SBU is in terms of the factors in figure 4.5 which are most important for the relevant industry, there are only three generic strategies open to any SBU to become more competitive. It must

1 aim to be the lowest-cost producer with, usually, a standard 'no-frills' but serviceable product, or
2 differentiate its broad product range in some way so that it is not competing directly with lower-cost products, or
3 adopt a strategy of focusing upon a particular niche or segment of the market.

In fact Porter really offers just two possible competitive strategies (i.e. be a cost leader or differentiate your product) which can be applied over either a broad range of products in an industry or just in a special niche.

Porter also feels that firms should not get 'stuck in the middle' between differentiation and striving for cost leadership. He does not recognize that it is possible to alternate between the two according to the stage of industry development, and Gilbert and Strebel (1988) illustrate how some companies do outpace others in the industry on both cost and quality. Moreover, there seems to be no reason why economic competition should take such a dichotomous form, with a clear separation between the low-cost producers and the differentiators. Phillips, Chang and Buzzell (1983) also showed that it was quite possible for there to be several different degrees of differentiation. The main requirement is for each degree of differentiation to be clearly demarcated from others in the eyes of buyers and for each firm to be the lowest-cost producer within each category. One only has to consider the markets for restaurant meals, motor cars and clothes to realize that there are more than two successful cost–quality mixes available in a number of industries. Moreover, Miller and Friesen (1986) have tested Porter's position on this point and concluded that differentiators do also employ cost-leadership strategies and that cost leaders do employ differentiation policies. They emphasize, however, that their results relate to the consumer-durables industries, where marketing, branding and economies of scale go hand in hand. In capital-goods industries, where knowledgeable buyers are more informed about the technical attributes of different products, Porter's argument about the need to avoid getting 'stuck in the middle' may be more sustainable. This might explain the Gilbert and Strebel finding on IBM and the personal-computer market. Perhaps that was just a case where, in the early stages of the life-cycle, corporate managers acted more like private consumers than industrial purchasers of large-scale equipment.

One may also attack Porter's cost–differentiation dichotomy in terms of the logical use of language. He seems to be saying that the product must be seen to be either cheaper or different if people are to buy it. But being different can be due to a whole range of factors. Hill (1985) sets great store on identifying relevant order-winning criteria from a set including price, product quality, product reliability, and other factors. He also distinguishes clearly between criteria which qualify a firm's products to be considered and those which actually win the order. From this viewpoint, cost simply becomes one of many ways in which the product may be seen to be different from others. The simple two-way split between cost and differentiation disappears. That does not, however, detract from the value of separating out the notion of cost leadership from differentiation *conceptually* in order to work out the implications for measurement and control (see chapter 5).

All this does not, however, detract at all from Porter's basic argument about the underlying analysis needed to identify industry attractiveness, competitive strengths and competitive strategies. Moreover, he shows clearly how strategies can be grouped in terms of broad emphasis into a few types according to whether the industry is in the emergent, mature or declining phase of its life-cycle. Fundamentally this is what McKinsey tries to do, as shown in figure 4.3, although Porter's analysis is richer.

Porter also shows how identifying the precise requirements of a strategy for each SBU requires a little more thought that just a broad consideration of that SBU's position in relation to its industry structure. In his 1985 study he develops the notion of a **value chain** from earlier similar notions of complete business systems discussed and used by both McKinsey and IBM.

A value chain is simply an analysis of the totality of activities associated with adding value to some basic commodity in order to provide end consumption. An SBU should then look at all elements of the chain that it is involved in (e.g. procurement, production, transportation, marketing) in order to see exactly how it already adds value and might add value in future. This entails examining the SBU's competitive position on each of the dimensions that are shown by the industry structure analysis to be critical to longer-run profitability.

Porter also points out the importance of defining the SBU in terms of the complete network of a value chain within a corporate group irrespective of what that includes in terms of operations in different divisions. This reinforces the statement made earlier about the need to define SBUs very carefully.

Finally, attention needs to be drawn to the possible transient nature of competitive advantage. Even a dominant firm will face rivals seeking to find a window of opportunity to chip away at the dominant position. Competitive strategies therefore need regular review and modification within the realistic rate of change defined by the nature of the industry.

Porter has undoubtedly had a considerable impact upon corporate strategic thinking, and in this brief discussion it has been possible to present only the barest outlines of his ideas developed in two sizable books. Some further reference to his views will, however, be inevitable in an attempt to provide an evaluation of the portfolio-matrix approach and concepts associated with it.

An interim evaluation of the portfolio-grid approach

The evaluation presented in this section is an interim one because it is based upon viewing the matrix from a rational economic perpsective. A final review of the use of the matrix will be offered in chapter 8, once more behavioural matters have been considered.

This section is divided into two parts. In the first, reports of empirical data are reviewed to see to what extent statistical data on corporate performance support the broad policy guidelines suggested by the BCG and McKinsey–GE matrices. In the second part, some key literature which has challenged the conceptual foundations of these matrices will be examined.

Empirical findings from the PIMS studies

'PIMS' stands for 'Profit Impact of Market Strategy'. It is a large-scale data collection and analysis exercise begun back in the early 1960s by the General Electric Company. Its broad aims were to analyse large American companies in order to discover differences in return on investment (ROI), to establish par values for ROI for different industries and their segments, and to attempt to explain variations in ROI across companies and their subsidiary business units by reference to strategic factors. For example, market attractiveness was to be captured by factors such as long-run and short-run growth rates and the stage of the product life-cycle, whereas competitive strength was to be assessed by market share (both absolute and relative) relative product quality and breadth of product line, relative costs, and so on (for more details see McNamee, 1985). The PIMS exercise was subsequently taken over by Harvard University and by the mid-1980s a data base had been established including about 250 companies which have provided information on about 3,000 SBUs. More extensive reviews of the results of tests on this data base can be found in McNamee (1985), Abell and Hammond (1979), and Buzzell and Gale (1987). The present discussion will highlight just one or two main conclusions which are of relevance to the main lines of argument in this book.

A major conclusion from cross-sectional studies based on PIMS is that ROI increases significantly as market share increases. ROI as a percentage is in the low teens for market share below 30 per cent and up to the mid to high thirties for market shares above 80 per cent. The PIMS study explains this as due to economies of scale, experience effects and bargaining power. This appears to provide strong support for one of the main planks of the BCG model. It is important, however, to consider this question carefully. The study merely shows a positive relationship between market share and ROI and this is not necessarily a causal connection. A later study by Jacobson and Aaker (1985) examines this proposition and runs regressions including ROI from earlier periods as lagged independent variables as surrogates for other factors which could be giving rise to the positive association between market share and ROI. They conclude that the effect of market share upon ROI is much less than earlier studies showed and that, broadly, a 1 per cent increase in market share led to a 0.1 per cent increase in ROI rather than the 0.5 per cent earlier supposed. Consequently, they state that much of the association between ROI and market share reported earlier was spurious.

Buzzell and Gale (1987) contest the Jacobson and Aaker view by arguing that they, in effect, have related the change in ROI (not the level of it) to the level of market share. Moreover, Buzzell and Gale argue that, as larger-share businesses do not continuously increase their ROI differential over small-share businesses, one would expect a zero correlation between the *change* in ROI and market share, which is broadly what Jacobson and Aaker found. Hence, the latter underestimate the effect of market share on the level of ROI. Buzzell and Gale then regress ROI on both market share and relative quality of product and find a 4.7 per cent ROI differential per ten points of market share. (When quality is left out of the regression there is a 5.3 point ROI differential.) They stress, however, that this is just an overall industry average and that, as market share accounts for only about 14 per cent of the dispersion of ROI among businesses, other factors need to be considered. One of these factors is investment intensity.

The next major conclusion of relevance to this discussion is the PIMS finding that investment intensity, measured by investment divided by sales, is negatively correlated with ROI. For an investment-intensity ratio of below 35 per cent, it seems that one gets an ROI above 30 per cent, whereas, when investment intensity is above 70 per cent, ROI falls to about 10 per cent. A not-surprising result is that low market share coupled with high capital intensity spells disaster. The important question, however, is why high capital intensity is associated with lower ROI even when market share is high. A range of possible reasons has been put forward, stressing that it is important to get the right degree of capital intensity for the business and that many businesses may simply be misled by current profitability and push investment too far. This may have some truth, but seems unsatisfactory as a complete explanation. Part of the reason for getting such a result could well be the cross-sectional nature of the analysis. An SBU with high capital intensity could well be at an early stage of its product life-cycle, when one would expect it to be building up its investment relative to sales and also experiencing low profitability as it fights to establish itself in the market. At a more mature stage, the increase in sales volume should have resulted in a decline in investment intensity, while profit and ROI will increase if the investment is successful. This explanation would be quite consistent with a cross-sectional picture in which capital intensity is inversely related to ROI even when market share is high. It is virtually an obvious consequence of the accounting formulation used with investment as both the numerator of investment intensity and denominator of ROI, while profit in the numerator of ROI is possibly a fairly stable proportion of sales in the denominator of investment intensity. It would therefore be incredibly naïve to conclude from the PIMS data that it is erroneous for companies to increase capital intensity – when their snapshot was taken by PIMS they might still have been waiting for their day to come. This view is enforced when one remembers that investment lead times – that is, the period between basic investment in assets and the time when the product shows up as profitable in the company accounts – can be quite long. As we have already seen, it can take several years for a product to come on stream, let alone break even in reported accounts; seven or more years is possible in some industries (see Tomkins et al., 1978).

The PIMS data still give some cause for puzzlement over the question of investment intensity, however, because Buzzell and Gale show that five-year averages of ROI are highly positively related to increases in the long-term value of the business, both being closely and positively associated with initial competitive position. (The basis of their valuation of the business will be explained in chapter 6.) One might infer from this that investment intensity is therefore also negatively correlated with increases in the value of the business over a five-year period. This would be more worrying. One explanation might be that five years is still not a long enough lead time. On the other hand, the explanation might lie in the study by Wagner (1984), who stresses that researchers have usually focused upon PIMS data for an average four-year period. In contrast, he selected those companies that had data in the PIMS system for at least seven and up to thirteen years; this gave him data on 460 US companies. Then, studying changes over time, he set out to test the main conclusions derived from cross-sectional studies. His results are of considerable interest.

He found first that ROI was remarkably stable over time at the *company level*, but that it showed considerable variation over time for *individual businesses* (i.e. the SBUs). Moreover, the rich businesses do not get richer and the poor do not get poorer. In fact, the reverse is true. Those with high ROI tend to experience falls in ROI and those with low ROI tend to have increases, taken across the whole population. Ideally one needs to subdivide the original low-ROI businesses into those at the beginning of their life-cycle and those at the end, because one would expect ROI to increase in the former but to fall in the latter. Indeed, Wagner found that the position in the life-cycle explained over half the variation in ROI.

Wagner's findings on investment intensity also bring some economic sense to the question raised above. He states that businesses with the highest investment intensity have the greatest chance of improving ROI when one takes the longer run into account. He says that his data showed that those businesses with low investment intensity did indeed start off with high ROI, as the earlier cross-sectional studies discovered, but that this often led managers to over-invest. In contrast, the managers of the longer-run winners did not over-invest, but were in the upswing of the business cycle facing markets with rapid growth. While his explanations do not seem clearly to separate older arguments about managers under- or over-investing from the impact of the business-cycle stage itself, it does seem clear that investment at the right time, i.e. early in the product life-cycle, does lead to increased ROI if management is able to establish its product in the market place and control costs. Indeed, it would be contrary to basic economic laws if this were not so. Nevertheless, given the earlier findings on investment intensity, this matter did need clarification.

It is interesting that Wagner's findings also seem to support Porter. Wagner concludes that managers should strive to increase market share, lower relative costs and/or achieve high product quality, and that any investment activity must be directed at at least one of these aims if it is to prove successful. He also states that his analysis showed that it is not easy to increase market share through time. The few businesses that do manage to achieve this profit handsomely, but most do not achieve it once the market is established.

So, what can be concluded from the PIMS data base about the relationships implied in the portfolio matrices? First, that there may be a lot more to the relationship between growth and market share established by BCG than has been accepted of late. High market growth, if taken to be an indicator of an early stage in a life-cycle (or a break-point upwards in a revitalized mature-stage life-cycle; see Gilbert and Strebel, 1988), coupled with high market share should lead to high ROI if the appropriate investment is undertaken. The key words are, however, 'appropriate investment'. One needs a Porter-style analysis to discover exactly what type of investment and competitive strategy is needed to achieve or maintain market share or competitive position; one cannot just assume that any type of investment in capacity in areas of high market share will lead to future success. Nevertheless, given managerial competence in performing and acting upon that analysis, one would expect to find largest positive *NPV* (and not highest *current* ROI) projects in the regions of the BCG or McKinsey matrix that relate to high growth and high market share. Normally this would be in the region of the matrix indicating early phases of a life-cycle, where competitive advantage can be built up by investment (although where this region is on the McKinsey matrix depends upon how the axes are interpreted, i.e. whether one works with figure 4.3 or 4.4). This will be supported further by the theoretical analysis undertaken in chapter 6. From Wagner's results we would conclude, however, that building competitive position or market share is really successfully achieved by relatively few businesses. A rigorous Porter-style analysis seems to be a more important ingredient in the decision inputs. Buzzell and Gale (1987) conclude from the PIMS data that product and service quality is the most significant factor for the longer-run success of a business. The interpretation of quality is variable, however, by product and service and context. It is the economic analysis which Porter demands that determines what quality, product and service mean in each case. It is that form of analysis which indicates what Hill's order-winning criteria are in specific situations.

Conceptual pitfalls of portfolio analysis

While the limited time-series of PIMS to date seems to indicate some broad credibility for the implications of portfolio grids, other criticisms of the approach challenge its underlying assumptions on a conceptual basis. There are a number of different arguments, which will now be summarized.

Some argue that high returns are possible in declining industries and that this is inconsistent with the harvest/divest strategies indicated in the BCG and McKinsey–GE matrices. Indeed, Buzzell and Gale (1987) also point this out. First, it needs to be made clear that high returns now must be distinguished from high returns in the *long run*. In a declining market one might well expect a business that had earlier established a dominant share position to be able to trade on this position in the short run and increase prices and profits, because rivals are unlikely to come into the market or compete strongly for market share. Also, it might be able to increase revenues as rivals drop out of the market. This does not mean, however, that one should invest in that declining industry beyond the level justified by short-run returns. Declining markets are therefore not likely to be receivers of major investment even if *current* returns are high.

In response to this argument it may be observed that even the BCG itself, in a series of articles about strategic investment in the *Financial Times*, November 1981, points out that there can still be profitable niches in declining markets and that 'dogs' may be able to bite back by identifying new possibilities in their industries (see also Thietart and Vivas, 1983–4). That fact is taken into account in a proper definition of an SBU. A significant new niche is tantamount to a new SBU and should be recognized as such and brought into the matrix in its proper place. Labelling a particular SBU as a 'dog' should be seen as a challenge to the people involved with it to search out and propose new SBUs and not just a signal to give up and die. With appropriate management attitudes, the element of the group labelled 'dog' can be encouraged to seek self-renewal, i.e. as an *organizational entity*, not as a particular product line. This would seem to be an obvious recognition that nothing lasts for ever. Even personnel associated with stars will be wise to think ahead to the need for renewal. In essence, what the portfolio matrix says is, let's have the various business elements at their different stages of growth explicitly on view in the matrix and not lost from view within organizational units. The matrix does not pretend to show organizational units *within which* there may be a mixture of growing, mature and declining sub-elements.

It is also quite possible for a 'dog' to find a way of extending its life in a previously unanticipated way. All that says is that this particular product line is not following a smooth transition from youth to middle age and then old age, but that it has managed to find some rejuvenation late in life. In that case it should no longer be defined as a 'dog'. It is a nonsense to say that an SBU is a 'dog' but that it should not be treated as a 'dog' because it is not really a 'dog' at all. Rejuvenation (see Chakravarthy, 1984) does not invalidate portfolio analysis if the axes are properly formulated and researched. The linking of the life-cycle to the portfolio matrices is a general relationship that is expected to hold. Perhaps it is better to say that it is a *prima facie* relationship which can be used for prescriptive advice to hold back investment *unless* the 'dog' management can establish an exceptional case. The model (and good management) can handle exceptions. On the other hand, much of this confusion may come from loosely identifying SBUs as industries, rather than products or product groups. While there is some justification for arguing that industries never mature (or only over an extremely long time-span), there is also every justification for arguing that products often do have life-cycles short enough to make sense of this type of analysis.

Another argument sometimes put forward is that the model assumes a capital-rationing situation. Obviously, if there is not such a situation, the company should invest in every positive-NPV product available to it, subject to having the capacity to manage investment on that scale. But the portfolio-matrix approach does not offend that principle. It just says that some parts of the business will throw off cash surpluses, that it may well not be worth investing further in those businesses, and that, in that case, the funds can be used to further investment elsewhere. If the corporate group wishes to raise further funds from external sources or use some of the funds for dividends or to repurchase shares, there is nothing in portfolio-grid analysis to stop it. The portfolio approach does *not* need to assume that investment has to equal that achievable with internally generated funds, although, of course, most UK and US companies do rely extensively on retained earnings to supply funds for investment.

Others have argued that the axes are misleading because they focus on absolute profitability rather than that earnable on marginal invest-ment. Once more, however, that can be handled by a proper definition of the axes; obviously it is future profitability of incremental investment that should go into the assessment of SBU attractiveness. If companies do not recognize that they are applying the model incorrectly; it is not the model which is at fault,

Similarly, others have argued that the matrices make little allowance for risk and in their early application this was true, but, if one undertakes a Porter-type analysis to give a solid foundation to industry attractiveness and competitive strengths and the derivation of the appropriate strategies, that will take into account a risk assessment. In fact, by focusing upon the specific factors within the value chain, managers will gain a much better appreciation of the specific risks and uncertainties associated with their strategies than some less well-defined, hit-or-miss sensitivity analysis.

Derkinderen and Crum (1984) raise a rather different point about risk. They stress the need for an organization to build financial resilience, i.e. focus on the necessary financial structure and other factors needed to help it live through adverse times. This may not be covered in the initial simple descriptions of the portfolio grids, but one would expect the underlying risk analysis to include such matters. Derkinderen and Crum do well to remind us of this, but it does not really invalidate the portfolio-grid approach. This argument applies equally to Wensley (1981). He argues that portfolio matrices fail to indicate the considerable risks faced in diversification. On the face of it this is true, but that simply means that there should be a thorough assessment of competitive strengths to underpin the matrix.

A wide range of comments have also been made about the simplistic nature of the grids as specifiers of where investment should be placed. While such criticism was perfectly correct in relation to the early portfolio-grid literature, it should now be clear that, when properly supported by rigorous analyses of industry structure and the value chain, portfolio analysis survives as a valid concept. Porter seems to argree with this view, but says that the extra value obtained from putting the results of the sorts of analyses that he recommends into the matrix form is marginal compared to the value derived from the underlying analysis itself. I believe that the benefits of the portfolio concept may be greater than Porter sees from his largely industrial-economics perspective. An attempt to substantiate this point will be attempted in chapter 8 from an *internal* management perspective. Nevertheless, from the viewpoint of the necessary *external* analysis, Porter is clearly correct in seeing a rigorous and informed economic analysis of the market place as the most vital element. Simplistic or casual analysis based on little more than common sense and drawing 'portfolio boxes' is obviously totally inadequate.

All the arguments considered so far against the use of portfolio-grid analysis of the McKinsey–GE type are, in my view, better seen as warnings about simplistic use of the technique rather than as indicating fundamental flaws in it. Intelligent application of the technique can take these warnings into account and still derive considerable benefit from it. We have still, however, to consider one much more fundamental attack upon the use of a McKinsey–GE type analysis.

A range of critics (including Coate, 1983; Hamel and Prahalad, 1985; Porter, 1985; Naylor, 1982, 1986; Prahalad and Doz, 1987) have emphasized that the validity of the portfolio-matrix approach depends fundamentally on the existence of SBUs which have little or no interdependence in a corporate group's portfolio. Porter, in particular, argues that a horizontal strategy affecting a number of different SBUs must be a necessity for a diversified firm, since there is no economic reason for SBUs with distinct lives of their own to be combined into a corporate group. In fact, such separable SBUs with no possibilities of synergy with other SBUs are, he says, likely to be prime candidates for divestment when a good opportunity arises.

While Porter is obviously right to argue that there is no economic reason for *completely* separable SBUs to be combined, it does not follow that they would function any better by becoming completely independent. There is no economic reason why they should be divested unless it can be shown that they would have synergistic benefits from being combined with SBUs of a different type from those possessed by the group that currently owns them. Porter might wish to question how such groups with non-related SBUs came to be formed in the first place. They may have been formed in the interests of diversification (unnecessary though this might be from the viewpoint of the theory of finance) or for political reasons, for example. Alternatively, the corporate management might simply have wanted to acquire them. There is no reason why a professor of history, say, should not also manage a family business if he has the time and energy. Yet the two activities have no obvious relationship. Indeed, the professor's rationale may be that he wishes to be involved in two completely different activities. Similarly, shareholders who rank the capacities of their company management very highly may support expansion on the basis that they can generate larger profits even without synergistic advantages. Hence, corporate groups can continue to exist with separable SBUs and will not inevitably be broken up. At least, therefore, *for such groups*, the portfolio matrices and their separable SBUs are potentially relevant concepts.

A more important question, however, is whether portfolio matrices can be sensibly applied only to such conglomerates. At face value the answer might seem to be 'yes'. Naylor (1986), for example, notes that even General Electric itself (as well as Xerox and Texas Instruments) ran into difficulties with its portfolio-grid analysis because of the existence of interdependencies. In fact, by 1988 General Electric had reorganized into fewer key businesses in order to overcome this problem, and in so doing had become more like a conglomerate. (See the *Financial Times* of 16 May 1988 and further discussion in chapter 9.)

There are basically only two types of interdependencies between SBUs. In Porter's terminology they are **tangible** and **intangible** interdependencies. Tangible links are where SBUs have buyers, distribution channels, technology or competitors in common (Porter has three categories, but it seems that competitor interrelationships are just as much a tangible link as those he specifies under that heading). Naylor

(1986) also gives an example of a tangible link between SBUs when he cites the interdependence of the multiple car lines at General Motors, where a change in the demand for one line may well be reflected in another. Intangible connections between SBUs are defined as the transference of management know-how. There may be no direct collaboration between SBUs, but what Porter calls the same generic skills may be called upon. For example, beer and cigarettes may both be purchased as recreational products.

Porter first identifies the problem that will be encountered if one proceeds with portfolio planning without explicit management of these interdependencies. SBUs will value these interdependencies differently and this will lead to inconsistencies in the behaviour of linked SBUs. Next, he says, SBUs may well form alliances outside the corporate group to obtain the same benefits as could be obtained by internal linkages while retaining more control over their situation. It is difficult to see why external links should inevitably give rise to greater control over one's actions. Of course, you may prefer to choose outside alliances rather than restrict yourself to the family, but in times of hardship the family may be more dependable. At such times it may be easier to achieve flexibility in a contractual relationship with another SBU in the same corporate group, but there is something in what Porter says. There will be a tendency for joint customers to be ignored and for know-how transfer to be lost.

Porter then develops the argument that the presence of interrelationships between SBUs implies that strategies must be broader than simply build, hold or divest. But must they? Is it not simply the case that the underlying analysis becomes more complex because, before knowing whether it is beneficial to build or hold or divest, it is necessary to know the effects beyond the immediate SBU in question? Surely, no other fundamental policies are possible.

If the interdependencies do not involve all SBUs in a corporate group, it might be possible to form largely separable business clusters and form the portfolio-grid analysis in terms of those rather than smaller SBUs. There is a suggestion of this in both Porter and Chakravarthy, who talks in terms of business families. This may indeed be one possible solution, but it has the disadvantage that the need for analysis of the industry structure and competitive strengths of each of the smaller SBUs may be ignored. After all, when one recognizes the different types of interrelationships which can exist, the linkages may be between SBUs in quite different industries. Also, some groups may have so many interconnections that such a clustering approach is impossible. Prahalad and Doz provide, for example, a diagram showing the worldwide interconnections of different parts of IBM. The diagram looks like a closely woven spider's web.

So severe does Naylor believe this question of interdependency to be that he devotes the whole of his 1986 study to an attempt to develop an alternative to the portfolio matrix. This alternative, which he calls the **trategy matrix**, essentially requires top-level corporate management to formulate six to eight key strategies which go across the various subsidiary businesses. Each strategy will be given its own management team, which will be expected to work out all the effects over the whole company, including estimates of resource requirements for each subsidiary business. Naylor says it is important that these corporate-wide strategies should be worked out before the individual businesses commence their planning. While one can see that a certain number of strategies might be conceived at corporate level before reference to the individual businesses, in general it is very difficult to see how this can be done at corporate headquarters unless the central authority has a careful analysis of the attractiveness and competitive strengths of the major SBUs. The main point of the Porter analysis was to establish that that form of information was fundamental to any strategic analysis. At the very least, therefore, there must be some preliminary analysis at SBU level, even if that ignores the interdependencies, and this must then be transmitted to corporate level before the central teams can carry out their cross-SBU analyses of the key corporate-level strategies. In other words, some iterative process between SBUs and corporate headquarters will probably be necessary and this may prove to be the key to solving this problem. It seems clear, however, that corporate groups may have many interdependencies between SBUs. When that occurs, the ability to plan resource allocation by looking at independent SBUs becomes impossible. Some overall 'optimization' process and global strategy become necessary. Whereas the wide range of earlier criticisms of the portfolio-grid approach could be countered, this form of criticism, which strikes at the heart of the construction of the matrices and their SBUs seems devastating. Things look black for the portfolio matrix. But, just before the reader buries the portfolio matrix once and for all, he or she might remember that I said that my case would not be complete until the end of chapter 8, where more organizational and behavioural matters will be considered. It will be shown how conclusions based upon the analytical economic framework may need at least some qualification when these other matters are brought into account. Then it will be clear that a (pre-1989) 'Soviet' dirigiste planning style is not inevitable.

Meanwhile, it can be noted that both academics and businessmen largely working outside the field of corporate finance have contributed significantly to the areas that King (1974) said needed addressing. Much of the work evaluated in this chapter takes us a long way towards identifying mechanisms for triggering the need for investment, screening the proposals and defining them. Also, bases of evaluation differen from those which dominate finance theory – namely, DCF techniques have been proposed. These differences in approach to investmen evaluation will be examined in chapter 6. Some progress toward satisfying King's other requirement (the form of 'transmitting th project' through the organization) will be considered in chapter 7.

References

Abell, D. and Hammond, J. 1979: *Strategic Market Planning*. Englewood Cliff: NJ: Prentice-Hall.

Bogue, M. C. and Buffa, E. S. 1986: *Corporate Strategic Analysis*, New Yorl Collier Macmillan.

Buzzell, R. and Gale, B. 1987: *The PIMS Principles: linking strategy * performance*. New York: Collier Macmillan.

Chakravarthy, B. S. 1984: Strategic self-renewal: a planning framework fc today. *Academy of Management Review*, 9, no. 3.

Coate, M. B. 1983: Pitfalls in portfolio planning. *Long Range Planning*, 1(no. 3.

Derkinderen, F. and Crum, R. 1981: *Readings in Strategy for Corpora Investment*. London: Pitman.

Derkinderen, F. and Crum, R. 1984: Pitfalls in using portfolio techniques assessing risk and potential. *Long Range Planning*, 17, no. 2.

Gilbert, X. and Strebel, P. 1988: Developing competitive advantage. In Quinn, H. Mintzberg and R. James (eds) *The Strategy Process*, Englewoo Cliffs, NJ: Prentice-Hall.

Hamel, G. and Prahalad, C. K. 1985: Do you really have a global strategy *Harvard Business Review*, July–August.

Hapeslagh, R. 1982: Portfolio planning: uses and limits. *Harvard Busine* Review*, January–February.

Henderson, B. D. 1987: *Henderson on Corporate Strategy*. Cambridge, Mass Abt Books.

Hill, T. 1985: *Manufacturing Strategy*. London: Macmillan.

Jacobson, R. and Aaker, D. A. 1985: Is market share all that it's cracked up t be? *Journal of Marketing*, 49 (Fall).

King, P. 1974: Is the emphasis of capital budgeting theory misplaced? *Journal * Business Finance and Accounting*. 2, no. 1.

McKinsey and Co. 1978: *Strategic Leadership: the challenge to chairmei* London: McKinsey.

McNamee, P. B. 1985: *Tools and Techniques for Strategic Management*. Oxfor Pergamon.

Miller, D. and Friesen, P. 1986: Porter's (1980) generic strategies and perfo mance: an empirical examination with American data. Part 1: testing Porte *Organizational Studies*, 7, no. 1.

Naylor, T. 1982: *Corporate Strategy*. Amsterdam: North Holland.

Naylor, T. 1986: *The Corporate Strategy Matrix*. New York: Basic Books.
Phillips, L. W., Chang, D. and Buzzell, R. 1983: Product quality, cost position and business performance: a test of some key hypotheses. *Journal of Marketing* (Spring).
Porter, M. E. 1980: *Competitive strategy*. New York: Collier Macmillan.
Porter, M. E. 1985: *Competitive advantage*. New York: Collier Macmillan.
Prahalad, C. K. and Doz, Y. 1987: *The Multi-national Mission*. New York: Free Press.
Quinn, J. B., Mintzberg, H. and James, R. 1987: *The Strategic Process*. Englewood Cliffs, NJ: Prentice Hall.
Thietart, R. and Vivas, R. 1983–4: Success strategies for declining activities. *International Studies of Management and Organisations*, 3, no. 4.
Tomkins, C. R., Edwards, J. P., Thomas, R. E. and Butler, C. A. 1978: *Investment Lead Times in British Manufacturing Industry*. London: Confederation of British Industry.
Wagner, H. M. 1984: Profit wonders, investment blunders. *Harvard Business Review*, Sept–Oct.
Wensley, R. 1981: Strategic marketing: betas, boxes or basics. *Journal of Marketing*, 45 (Summer).

Discussion questions

4.1   Finance theorists tend to assume that the problem of investment decision-making begins once the project cash flows have been specified. Corporate strategists tend to assume that it ends at that point. How fair are these statements, as a representation of the viewpoints of these two different views on corporate resource allocation?

4.2   Compare and contrast the BCG and McKinsey–GE portfolio matrices. Which do you prefer and why?

4.3   It might be argued that Porter has provided an underpinning of rigorous economic theory to the McKinsey–GE portfolio matrix. Discuss fully.

4.4   To what extent do the empirical findings of the PIMS studies throw light on the importance of (1) market share and (2) investment intensity in determining increased ROI? Discuss fully and critically.

4.5   There are a number of conceptual pitfalls for the unwary analyst using portfolio grids to analyse a corporate group's strategic position. What are they?

5

Towards Integrating Accounting into Strategic Analysis

It was seen earlier in the book that there are inconsistencies between different components of what may be loosely called the finance function. These occur between the theory of finance and financial modelling practice and between the theory of finance and accounting practice. Some space was given over to discussion of these questions in chapters 2 and 3. The analysis has now reached the stage where far larger problems of integration occur. In this chapter an attempt will be made to look for possible links and conflicts between accounting and the strategic analysis of chapter 4. Chapter 6 will then conduct a similar comparison of the theory of finance and corporate-strategy concepts.

The ideas put forward are offered as a structure to enable finance theorists and accountants to widen their perspectives and also to encourage those operating in the strategy field to welcome collaboration with finance specialists. What is offered is, therefore, speculative rather than proven.

The reader is also asked to bear in mind that the strategic perspective covered is as described in chapter 4. Whether such a global rational analysis may be applied after considering studies of organizational behaviour is a question that will be discussed in chapters 7 and 8. Similarly, chapters 5 and 6 will also be largely concerned with the *analyses* that finance theorists, modellers and accountants might make. How their *roles* might be enhanced in recognition of the behavioural literature will be examined to some extent in chapter 9.

As already indicated in chapter 3, accounting practice may interact with strategy in two broad ways: either by providing analysis prior to investment, or by providing performance reports and costing statements. In the latter case the effect upon strategy may be to signal that it is time to divest rather than invest.

No attempt will be made to separate out what accounting methods might do for pre-investment as distinct from post-investment. The type of analyses that in one company may be conducted with a view to maintaining strategic control and identifying the early signals of a need to change the product mix may in other companies be conducted largely at the pre-investment stage. Much depends upon the nature of the industry and product.

For example, Kaplan's arguments for 'activity-based costing' (Kaplan, 1988) are usually expressed in terms of providing an annual review of product-costing for pricing and product-mix decisions. Yet I recently visited a hi-tech company which was fully conversant with activity-based costing yet did not do it on a regular annual basis. It was explained that this was because the company was perpetually producing new products with life-cycles of two to four years and that the product mixes over the narrow product range in current production were largely set by the available type of capacity over such periods. Nevertheless, the company's financial controller said that, if one looked at the methods used by the cost accountant at the *pre-investment* (i.e. product-design) stage, it was clear that the notions of activity-based costing *did* receive careful consideration, *before* approval of the product design and projected product prices used in the investment appraisal. In fact, once the investment was completed and operational, the accounting data were highly aggregated, designed merely to keep a more general watch on total operating costs. The real business of product-costing took place before the investment and was largely *ad hoc*. In fact, in this company division, cost-accounting had in recent years become pre-eminently a pre-investment activity, but this obviously was a function of the nature of the business.

Consequently, the subsequent discussion will focus on different analyses which may be pursued before or after the initial investment. It will be seen that various analyses proposed have both pre- and post-investment implications.

With all this in mind, this chapter will explore the links between strategic analysis and accounting, beginning with the accounting inputs to the portfolio analysis of strategic business units (SBUs), their market attractiveness and competitive strengths. Following this, we shall consider how to detect the right generic strategy. With our minds clearly on strategy formulation, we shall then pick up again the debate about return on investment (ROI) begun in chapter 3, but put aside until a better understanding of 'strategic fit' had been developed in chapter 4. In the latter part of the chapter we shall consider, at a deeper level, how accounting analyses might facilitate a cost-leadership strategy. That discussion will be broadened to take in the notion of generic strategies and the further implications for accounting. All of this will be discussed without any reference to a given state of technology of development. The chapter will therefore end by taking a look at recent and forthcoming developments in manufacturing to see how these fit in with the idea of generic strategies and their implications for accounting – i.e. not just now, but for the foreseeable future.

Accounting for portfolio analysis

The discussion of the use of the portfolio goals in chapter 4 made it quite clear that SBUs labelled 'stars' will have quite different financial profiles from 'cash cows' or 'dogs'. Accountants might therefore pay more attention to indicating the types of profiles to be expected for each category of SBU; clearly, unthinking comparisons between them with respect to their financial performance should be avoided. The most obvious trap to avoid is a stringent comparison of ROIs as an indication of what each SBU is contributing to the total group. Each type of SBU has a different business role to play and should be evaluated in terms of its role and life-cycle stage.

The precise differences in accounting numbers between the different types of SBU will depend upon the nature of the products, the length of their life-cycle, the type of technology used, and so on, but one can draw some general distinctions. SBUs being nurtured as the profit-earners of the future will have lower ROIs in the early stages of their cycle. Their cash flows may well be negative. Sales to fixed-asset ratios may be low. In contrast, 'cash cows' will be expected to have a good ROI and cash flow and higher sales-turnover ratios. Accountants should ensure that general managers know what financial profile to expect for each type of SBU.

Figure 4.3 was McKinsey and Co's attempt to spell this out in more detail. It not only considers the general financial profile, but also indicates different emphases in cost control and pricing according to stages in the life-cycle. Subsequent analyses by Porter (1985), and critics of Porter, described in chapter 4, suggest that figure 4.3 attempts to push the financial differences between different types of SBU too far. The emphasis on costs at a given stage of the life-cycle may well depend more upon the product strategy – i.e. whether it is a cost-leadership or differentiated-product strategy. Also, we have seen that critics of Porter have stressed that often the two types of strategy are used either in sequence (Gilbert and Strebel, 1987) or in combination. Certainly no manufacturer attempting to differentiate by quality *can* ignore cost control, just as the producer of the cheapest product will not be successful if quality falls below some critical level. Consequently, setting up *detailed* financial controls based *only* upon whether an SBU is considered to be a 'star', 'cash cow' or 'dog' is also simplistic.

On the other hand, there are some general differences in emphasis, as indicated, which should be highlighted by the accounting function. In particular, accountants need to note the earlier arguments that even 'dogs' can sometimes be regenerated and that SBUs must be viewed as product groups or business interests and not necessarily as corporate organizational units. Hence a prime accounting task is to ensure that for business-portfolio planning the financial details of embryo businesses being built for the future are separated from those of ongoing businesses. Furthermore, general elements of policy regarding R&D, engineering development and even management development should probably be separated out for each SBU. Otherwise, mature profitable products may be loaded with the costs of new product development and closed down too quickly. New developments must be justified on their own merits.

When SBUs reach the last phase of their life-cycle (irrespective of whether a cost-leadership or differentiated-product strategy is being employed), there are still further options available which will need to be understood by the accountant in order to ensure that all options are considered and relevant financial profiles selected. The strategy for a very mature 'cash cow' or 'dog' need not be just an exit from the industry. A change in manufacturing method or a movement to bought-in parts may remove the risk of excessive fixed assets at the end of the life-cycle, and enable further profits to be extracted. Alternatively, a decision to produce at lower levels may, with accounting pressure, be accompanied by release of capacity for other purposes. None of these things is a wonderful new panacea, but greater awareness of SBUs and life-cycles and the sort of options available at each stage will ensure that a fuller range of options is considered. Accountants need to be aware of this as much as other functional staff.

Contributing to market-attractiveness and competitive-strengths analyses

To use the portfolio grid, the key determinants of market attractiveness and competitive strength must be identified and measured. Whether a full Porter-style analysis or some less rigorous approach is used, those key determinants (or key factors) and action in response to them should be the linchpins in the corporate control system once the strategy is established. It seems possible, therefore, that financial managers should be involved in the identification and analysis of those key factors. Clearly they will not work alone, but with corporate economists as well as marketing and manufacturing experts, but financial skills should be available to the team. Much of the work of determining the attractiveness of the industry or market place will revolve around estimates of profitability, where accounting knowledge can help prevent significant errors in interpreting accounting statements.

Indeed, a business manager involved in trying to develop a portfolio analysis of SBUs recently stated to me that he knew that assessing the profitability of the different SBUs was a key step in determining market attractiveness, but he did not know which accounting concept was correct. Should it be return on investment? If so, should it be accounting ROI or the internal rate of return (IRR)? If ROI, should it be on an historic or current cost-accounting basis? Accountants may not realize how much confusion there is amongst non-financial colleagues about basic accounting concepts. The answer given to the businessman was that he should be trying to assess the stream of *future* cash surpluses to be generated by each SBU. Accounting statements from the past were relevant only in so far as they provided some clue to future cash surpluses. In particular, he was warned of the errors likely to be associated with naïve projections of past accounting profit calculations, whether based upon historic or upon current costs. Nevertheless, past accounting statements will be one prime source of information used to project future cash flows, and the accountant should be on hand to avoid misinterpretation of those data. Otherwise it is likely that strategic analysis will rest on very shaky foundations.

In addition, if one takes Porter's analysis in figure 4.5 as a guide, considerable financial and cost-accounting data are needed as an input for analysing market structure. While none of the calculations is necessarily wholly new, financial managers should consider clearly whether they and their financial information systems can adequately provide analysis of economies of scale, experience cost reductions, switching costs, competitive operating costs among members of the industry or market, and so on, all of which help to determine the power of different market participants and the resulting market profitability. Accountants weaned only on traditional accounting and finance texts may tend to see their financial information from a more restricted and mainly internal perspective, leading to the conventional income statements and balance sheets. Such accountants may then find that they have shrinking roles and power within the corporation.

Testing for generic strategies

Financial analysts have a role to play in testing the validity of generic strategies, too. Porter (1985), for example, concludes from his extensive economic analysis that there are just three forms of strategy: cost leadership, product differentiation or a market-focused strategy. On the other hand, this conclusion is not universally accepted (Gilbert and Strebel, 1987; Buzzell and Gale, 1987) and so a company would be wise to study the extent to which separate or continued 'generic' market strategies determine profitability in its particular industry. Accounting texts are silent on this issue. Accountants should have some estimates of how much profitability will vary with such differences in strategy.

Bogue and Buffa (1986, pp. 169–70) provide an indication of how one might proceed with such tests. In a study of the US agricultural equipment and chemical industries they show how a V-curve may be

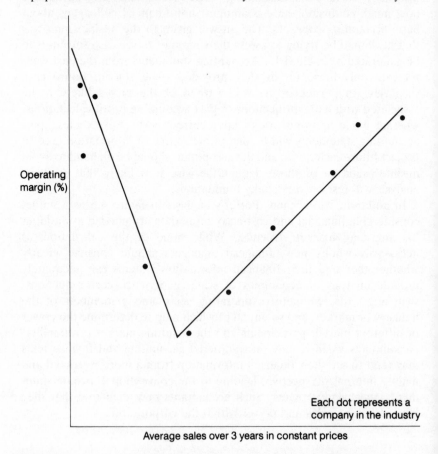

Figure 5.1   V-curve for an industry (based on Bogue and Buffa, 1986)

Adapted with permission from The Free Press, a division of Macmillan, Inc. from *Corporate Strategic Analysis* by M. C. Bogue and E. S. Buffa. Copyright © 1986 The Free Press.

derived as illustrated in figure 5.1. They plot operating margins against average sales in order to illustrate that there are two preferred positions: (1) high sales with cost competitiveness to yield high margins, or (2) lower sales with a differentiated product (or niche) policy, which also produces high margins. This supports Porter's generic-strategies hypothesis. Those firms which get caught in the middle appear not to do so well. It is not certain, however, that such a V will always be found, or what the 'depth' of the V will be. Moreover, if one found that one's company was at its nadir, the slopes of the V-curve might be revealing of the magnitude of the task in shifting to a better level of profitability. Financial analysis of this type could assist considerably in providing a preliminary understanding of strategic requirements within an industry. The accounting implications of generic strategies, however, go far beyond this, but, before addressing them, it is appropriate here to pick up again the ROI debate left uncompleted in chapter 3.

Does widespread use of ROI lead to poor corporate strategies?

In chapter 3 we saw that accountants and finance theorists have for years debated the inconsistencies between accounting ROI and discounted cash flow (DCF) calculations. In more recent years specialists from other areas have also criticized ROI (see Hayes and Garvin, 1982; Hill, 1985). It is now appropriate to review this problem again in the light of the strategic analysis discussed in chapter 4.

With major investments, a study of the corporate-strategy literature suggests that a company will indulge in investment in order either to maintain or to improve its competitive position. It has also been shown how to analyse the significant factors relevant to competitive position in each SBU. It may therefore be assumed that a manager is maintaining an adequate policy if the competitive position is being maintained and projections indicate that it is likely to be maintained in future. Furthermore, if investment has been undertaken to improve the competitive position, then it may be desirable, during the manager's stay in the SBU, to assess the likely performance of that investment by reference to *early signals* of a change in the competitive position. The relevant factors will vary from company to company, from SBU to SBU, and perhaps from investment to investment, so they must be determined by reference to specifically relevant competitive-strengths criteria. The signals of changes in competitive strengths begin *before* any increase in sales and profits is seen.

They will also depend upon the generic strategies being adopted for the SBU or even the product line. For example, early indicators of investment success under a cost-leadership strategy might be the proof, at an embryonic stage of the life-cycle, that the product matches its rivals in quality but is being produced at lower cost. If, at the same stage, the cost-leadership policy is being coupled with an aggressive pricing policy in order to gain market share, the benefits of that investment would not show up in ROI or accounting profit for some time. In fact, the high ROI, in accounting terms, may not appear until late in the product life-cycle.

Alternatively, an SBU may be following a product-differentiation policy, in which case, depending on the type of industry, progress in product development and field tests, success in taking out patents, the results of early market-research tests and various other indicators provide early signals of whether the investment policy is likely to be successful.

An SBU or divisional manager will be motivated to seek appropriate investments if he knows clearly what the generic strategy for his SBU is (he would presumably have participated in determining it), is aware of what is expected of him in terms of building or maintaining competitive strengths, and knows that early-warning indicators will be set up to monitor how his investments are contributing to the improvement or maintenance of those specific strengths. This does *not* mean that his investment proposals need no longer be quantified in financial DCF terms. That is needed where possible to make the strategic analysis more rigorous before final approvals are given. It is just that the type of early-warning signals just discussed will indicate whether the expected improvement in competitive strength and the projected cash flows are likely to be achievable. Both SBU managers and their superiors ought also to be aware of the time pattern of likely ROI development in each part of the group.

The conclusion suggested by this line of argument is that accounting academics have, perhaps, been worrying too much about trying to find a short-term measure of income which is consistent with DCF. Performance evaluation by short-term income measures is for short-term control purposes and not for motivating appropriate *investment* behaviour. This type of argument is not new. Parker (1979) argued similarly in calling for measures other than short-term profit calculations in order to reflect a balance between short-term and long-term responsibilities. Daniel (1961), Anthony, Dearden and Vancil (1966), Dermer (1977), Rockhart (1979), Bullen and Rockhart (1981), and Leidecker and Bruno (1984) have all also stressed that, while it is important to identify key result areas (which may or may not be financial), it is far more vital to identify the critical success factors which lead to the desired results. Furthermore, Daniel, Bullen and Rockhart, and the student dissertations produced under Rockhart's supervision at MIT show, in particular, that the really critical factors in any one period are usually relatively few, so that it should not be necessary to establish a massive information bank which can be interpreted in a wide variety of ways. Bullen and Rockhart also show how the critical-success-factor approach can be applied equally at either the strategic or the operational activity level, and offer advice on how to ascertain from managers in fairly short interviews what these factors are. What the analysis of the corporate-strategy literature suggests is that, while it may be possible to ascertain the relevant factors in this way, the findings will be more reliable if those managers have been involved in a careful strategic analysis of competitive strengths. The corporate-strategy literature now offers a more systematic approach to the precise definition of what the critical success factors need to be in each *specific* business setting and especially how they relate to each other within a model of success. The specificity also assists in the construction of parsimonious, but relevant, information systems for control purposes. Rockhart says that the critical-success-factor approach aims to unlock the manager's implicitly held model of success. It would be even better if that model were made explicit and tested for validity against a more complete analysis of the firm's competitive position – the manager may, after all, be wrong.

It has been argued that building systems to motivate and evaluate appropriate investment behaviour is better achieved when based upon a careful strategic analysis and critical success factors. Does this at least then mean a reprieve for ROI in terms of short-run performance measurement? Much will depend upon the degree to which divisional/ SBU ROI figures are important in the managers' reward system. If ROI is a relatively unimportant part of this reward system, it may then be used as a very useful *diagnostic* tool by which to assess operating performance. ROI has a long-established pedigree of use through the familiar Du Pont pyramid. As an accounting-based measure it can be decomposed through the asset-turnover or profit-margin ratios to pinpoint exactly where problems arise (or progress has been achieved) in short-term financial performance. ROI is here at its most valuable – as a familiar, easily understood diagnostic tool for appraising the short-term economic performance of an *organizational unit* such as an SBU or division, decoupled from the evaluation of *managers*' performance.

If a company does wish to use ROI to evaluate managers' shorter-term performance and those managers are in a position to influence significant investment decisions, then, where the manager's short-term performance is stressed at the expense of his investment performance, there is a danger that he will restrict investment to increase his ROI. This can, however, be largely avoided by insisting that his ROI targets are reset each year in the knowledge of assets held and investments to be undertaken during the year. Short-term performance is then to be judged by a comparison of budgeted and actual ROI for that year.

Through these arguments one arrives at the position that the use of ROI need not be so harmful as academic accountants (including me in the early 1970s!) and more recently academics from other fields have argued it to be. It must be stressed, however, that, if the potential dysfunctional effects of ROI use are to be avoided, financial controllers must make it very clear throughout the organization exactly how supervisors are using ROI for evaluation and exactly how it is to be used by SBU and divisional managers. If this is not done, the considerable dangers inherent in the indiscriminant use of ROI remain.

It is very difficult to ascertain whether the many companies which use ROI do use it in the way proposed. Older surveys such as those by Mauriel and Anthony (1966), Tomkins (1973), and Reece and Cool (1978), and more recent studies such as those of Pike (1983), Scapens and Sale (1985) and Cornwell (1987), do not get close enough to behaviour in specific contexts to reveal whether companies are suffering from a misuse of ROI. Meanwhile, while Reece and Cool feel that on balance they are not, Anthony, Dearden and Bedford (1984, p. 362) continue to insist that their experience tells them that they are, and Hayes and Garvin (1982) obviously agree. Practising financial controllers need to consider the position in their own organizations, while academics might undertake more detailed case studies of the matter. In fact a new study, by Merchant (1989), was published as I was drafting this section. Merchant takes a useful step forward. In his analysis of fifty-four profit centres in twelve major corporations, he discovered considerable variation in the overemphasis on short-run ROI performance. He argues that the problem is most severe in 'growing corporations'. This squares with the contention earlier in this chapter that the ROI targets set for embryo 'star' SBUs should be different from those for 'cash cows', and so on. Merchant also discovered that some corporations do try to reduce the potentially dysfunctional effects of ROI by various methods:

1 by using leading indicators, and not just ROI, to determine managers' rewards
2 by basing rewards on long-term profit performance (either written or unwritten)
3 by simply not putting so much emphasis on increasing ROI

Method (2), as discussed in chapter 3, may not be of much value if managers do not stay long enough in one position. Method (3) has also been discussed, and it has been suggested that it would be enhanced by resetting ROI targets each year. Method (1) comes close to the view, argued above, that critical success factors could be a better basis for measuring investment performance. Merchant does not, however, push his argument far enough. He qualifies advocacy of leading indicators by saying that they may duplicate each other (market share and sales, for instance) or may not give additional lead time over conventional measures (he cites bookings as an indicator of sales) or do not yield reliable measures. He further argues that with multiple measures there is a danger of losing focus, and that it is difficult to set targets for some indicators because there are no historical data on them. He is right to warn of such dangers, but they are more likely where leading indicators are set in some general, non-rigorous way without carefully developing a model of *what* is needed, and by *when*, to improve or maintain *each* SBU's competitive strengths. Merchant's companies do not seem to distinguish between key result areas and critical success factors. Also, he does not adequately discuss how to relate those critical success factors in a logically connected way through a model for improving competitive strength in a *specific* situation, and fails to recognize that it is essential for a strategic analysis to indicate *who* is responsible for which central success factor. A careful strategic analysis as described in chapter 4 will help to lessen the disadvantages of using leading indicators. Even so, Merchant's study, which also covers many other topics, provides more depth than previous empirical work on this question and is most valuable from that standpoint. It should be used as a platform from which to explore the different modes that he suggests of lessening the short-run myopia.

Accounting and cost-leadership strategies

It has just been argued that detailed financial and managerial controls need to be based on specific product and/or SBU categories. It has also been recognized that Porter may not be correct in supposing that cost-leadership and differentiation policies should always be mutually exclusive. Whether they should be or not, accountants need to give careful consideration to the impact that a cost-leadership strategy would have on their practices. The separation of strategies into generic versions is a useful conceptual device, even if such strategies become intertwined in practice.

Where the aim is to sustain cost leadership over the longer term, rather than to gain a short-term advantage through temporarily having, say, more modern equipment, one must look ahead over the life-cycle of the market (however narrowly or broadly defined). The experience curve briefly mentioned in chapter 4 as the basis of the BCG matrix is soon invoked where cost leadership is the goal, and we now need to discuss it more fully.

Recall that the experience-curve theory says that the ability to learn is directly related to the accumulated production experience and that it is possible for a company to reduce total costs over time by a careful introduction of new management and production processes (see Abernathy and Wayne, 1974, and Dutton and Thomas, 1984, for careful assessments of this claim). Since the experience-curve concept was developed by BCG, it has been shown that there is much more to dominating markets than simple mastery of the experience curve – even where cost leadership is the strategy. It is still, however, *potentially* a very important *part* of the strategic analysis required. In some industries and markets, it is still a major factor in market economics. I have visited an electronics manufacturer where the notion of continual cost reduction is an important feature of operating policy. There are charts displayed in the factory recording manufacturing costs by month and the planned and actual reduction over time. The firm works to relatively short product life-cycles, but still expects some learning to occur. In response to questioning, the production director stated that the firm is in an industry where a highly intelligent workforce is necessary, and that, if encouraged to do so, such a group of people working together can always find improvements. This company, incidentally, had been strongly influenced by the Japanese way of doing things and had introduced just-in-time and kanban methods.

It is also worth bearing in mind that the experience curve does not apply only to single products. Even where products have short life-cycles and the strategy is to keep ahead of rivals by product development and modification at frequent intervals, as indicated in figure 5.2, such new products are rarely *totally* different from their predecessors. Hence there can be experienced-based cost reductions over a generic class of products through time, even though the products differ in some respects. In fact, the intention of product redesign may be partly cost reduction and partly product differentiation. Also, if one thinks in terms of longer-run generic experience curves, the argument put forward by Pogue (1985) that more effort on pre-planning reduces the scope for learning has less weight. It is less easy to pre-plan a future series of *design* changes. It is also less easy to forecast their cost consequences. But design changes can be a key determinant of the experience curve for a generic group of products. The point is just that some basic concepts relating to the experience curve may still be valuable if used with intelligence and discretion.

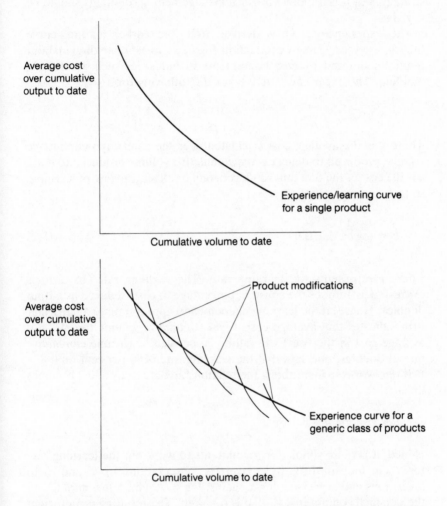

Figure 5.2 Experience-based cost reductions for a single product and a generic class of products

Ghemawat (1985) argues that the debunking of the experience curve has gone too far. It is, he stresses, neither a panacea nor a Pandora's box. He also sets out clearly the conditions under which the experience curve *can* be the basis of effective strategy. In such situations, accountants need to be familiar with full life-cycle costing based on the experience-curve concept. Such an analysis may not totally determine strategy, but it is a tool with which management accountants should be familiar.

The experience curve is derived from the earlier learning-curve theory, used for years by production engineers to estimate direct labour requirements and by cost accountants in industries such as aircraft-building. The experience curve takes the following form:

$$y = ax^{-b} \tag{5.1}$$

where y is the average cost calculated over the company's cumulative volume produced to date, x is the cumulative volume produced to date, a is the cost of the first unit produced, and b reflects the rate of learning. In fact

$$b = \log \frac{1}{r} . \log 2.0 \tag{5.2}$$

where r represents the learning rate. The learning rate, in turn, is expressed as 1 minus the constant percentage of costs reduced as output doubles. Hence, if the learning phenomenon appropriate to a particular firm indicates that average costs (over *cumulative* volume to date, not average cost in the year) will fall by 20 per cent each time *cumulative* output doubles, one says that the learning rate is 80 per cent on 0.8

If one works in logarithms, the relationship between y and x becomes linear:

$$\log y = \log a - b . \log x$$

Hence, it is quite simple for accountants to work out the learning rate for their industry/firm by converting observations of y and x to logarithms and regressing $\log x$ against $\log y$. Again, a few minutes on the personal computer is all that is required. The resulting b coefficient from the regression is the value of b needed to determine the learning rate, which, by rearrangement of formula 5.2 is

$$r = \frac{1}{\text{antilog} (b . \log 2.0)}$$

Traditionally, cost-accounting texts have described learning curves, but have not adequately emphasized their strategic importance. Moreover, one recent major text (Kaplan and Atkinson, 1989) deletes learning curves because it is misleading to extrapolate cost reductions based literally on experience alone. Perhaps so, but it seems to me that, if the experience curve is understood as reflecting the continued, planned desire for cost leadership as more is produced, the expression of the curve and the learning rate provide a useful way of monitoring cost-reduction possibilities and helping to formulate strategy. Perhaps we should put the words 'experience curve' in quotes to indicate that the reduction in cost is not automatic. However, if a cost-leadership policy is being planned, it is useful to have some projections based on assumptions about learning rates. How might knowledge of the experience curve be used strategically? The answer, as implied earlier in this chapter, is through a policy of strategic pricing.

Suppose that a company and its potential rivals in a market for a new product are in agreement that the rate at which it could drive costs down is as illustrated in figure 5.3. Then the first company might decide to introduce the product at a price level below initial cost, such as P_1, in order to frighten rivals off and gain the maximum possible accumulated production experience. The benefit of doing this comes later as, through continued effort, costs are reduced. Having gained the initial advantage, the company can then price at a level to give itself a profit but still deter rivals, who face higher costs from entering. It might be argued that rivals would be aware of this possibility and therefore move in quickly, bearing initial losses in the same way as the initial company does. But

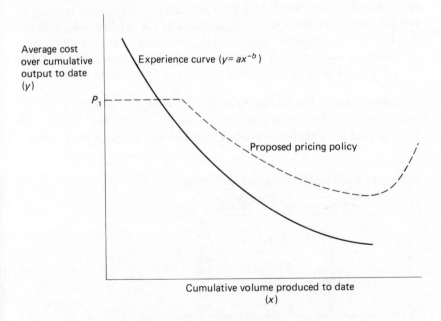

Figure 5.3 An experience curve and related pricing policy

that depends on whether rivals *can* move in so quickly. We are discussing strategic new developments – someone has to be the first to develop the product or technology. If the potential for cost reduction through learning more about the product and its manufacturing processes is significant, the experience-curve theory shows how cost analysis and pricing can be used to protect that strategic advantage. Furthermore, rivals may, owing to the different combination of activities in their groups, not be able to bear initial losses, which would cause financial distress rather than lead to balanced growth. (The need to consider such matters, despite the theory-of-finance arguments in chapter 1, is addressed in chapter 9.)

Table 5.1 shows in simplified form the type of strategic calculations needed. The remainder of the analysis in this section, and in the third section of chapter 6, rests on work initiated by Marshall (1985) and reported in Marshall and Tomkins (1988).

Suppose, first, that a company has just developed a new product with an estimated life-cycle as shown in table 5.1. Suppose also that the company estimates that it will cost £200,000 to produce the first unit and that, by watchful management, an 80 per cent learning rate will be achieved. It then decides to set its market price at such a level that the one possible rival in the market can, at best, only earn a zero net present value (NPV). Assume, purely for ease of calculation and exposition here, that the rival can achieve the same learning rate, that demand is not price-sensitive and that, if the rival enters the market, sales will be divided equally between the two rival companies. These assumptions can easily be relaxed for more realistic modelling. Assume also that the rival will need to spend £7 million on capital expenditure to enter the market.

With this scenario, assume next that the company decides to set its price initially at £56,700 and lets it be known generally that it will hold price at that level until the average cost per unit of *cumulative* output

Table 5.1 Estimated life-cycle for new product

Year	Quantity to be sold	Cumulative quantity
1	100	100
2	200	300
3	300	600
4	350	950
5	380	1,330
6	350	1,680
7	300	1,980
8	100	2,080

falls below that figure, whereupon the company will set its price at 20 per cent above the falling average cost per cumulative unit.

The next key question is whether such a strategic pricing policy will deter the rival from entering the market by offering it at most a zero NPV. Table 5.2 shows the necessary calculations and the fact that, if its cost of capital is 15 per cent, the rival can only earn a negative NPV of £252,497. This might indicate, in turn, that the initial company could afford to price a little above 20 per cent over average cost and still prevent the rival from entering the market.

Table 5.2 Calculations showing that the rival will face a negative NPV

Year	Cumulative quantity for each firm	Average cost (£) based on (2)	Price (£)	Rival's annual cash flows (£)
(1)	(2)	(3)	(4)	(5)
1	50	56,765	56,700	−3,250
2	150	39,855	47,826	1,642,605
3	300	31,884	38,261	2,152,166
4	475	27,499	32,999	2,277,825
5	665	24,676	29,611	2,278,661
6	840	22,888	27,466	1,989,965
7	990	21,709	26,051	1,641,809
8	1,040	21,368	25,641	551,892
		Present value of cash inflow		6,747,503
		Less capital outlay		7,000,000
		Rival's NPV at 15 per cent		−252,497

To construct table 5.2 the first step the cost accountant has to take is to construct the rival's experience curve which reflects the learning rate of 80 per cent. The observations for plotting the experience curve are shown in columns 2 and 3 of table 5.2, where column 2 shows one half of the total market demand shown in table 5.1 and column 3 is calculated as

$$y = ax^{-b} = 200,000 \cdot \text{column } 2^{-0.32193}$$

$b = 0.32193$ is found by equation 5.2. The price in column 4 is simply 20 per cent on the corresponding average cost from year 2 onwards. A little care is needed to calculate the cash flows for column 5. For example,

Year 5 cash flow = revenues less costs for year 5
= revenue for year 5
less cumulative costs to end of year 5
less cumulative costs to end of year 4
= 29,611(665 − 475) − (665 × 24.676) − (475 × 27,499)
= 2,278,661 (allowing for rounding)

With a spreadsheet set up on a personal computer, this requires very little time to calculate and provides a direct guide to strategies concerned with cost leadership. Obviously, a number of simplifying assumptions have been made here, but the model can be elaborated to allow for price elasticity of demand, differences in learning rates, differences in cost of capital, and so on. Of course, the rival may fight back, but the point is not that this type of calculation ensures a successful barrier to entry, but that it provides a way of assessing what it will cost the rival to surmount the barrier to attain cost leadership. This must be a useful input into strategic thinking.

There are a number of derivatives of this type of model. For example, suppose that your company has a two-year lead into this market. It would be possible to deduce what will happen to this market if the rival builds a larger plant to try to catch up with your experience and at what level you need to price to try to prevent that. In fact, you do not actually need to price at that level; the rival just has to believe that you will if it enters the market.

There is also the implication in the model that, if you successfully prevent entry up till the mature stage of the life-cycle, you will then, subject to the price elasticity of demand, be able to increase prices in the way illustrated in figure 5.3. This would be quite consistent with seeing the product as a high-yielding 'cash cow' in the mature stage of its life-cycle. The type of calculation in table 5.2, therefore, may provide a financial basis for assessing *how soon* one can begin to manage an SBU or product group as a 'cash cow'. It offers the promise of much more precision to the vague categories of the BCG and McKinsey–GE matrices, while attempting to incorporate the valuable insights of those matrices into the capital-budgeting decision.

It was also argued earlier in the book that there is always some point at which customers will turn from a differentiated product to yours because your price is so much lower. If possible price levels to achieve this can be hypothesized, the model of table 5.2 can be used to inquire whether the experience-curve effect is adequate to sustain a positive NPV at such price levels.

This type of calculation may also be helpful in assessing trade-offs between alternative strategies open to one firm. The problem in gearing up investment to shoot off down the experience curve and become the cost leader is that you may be overtaken by technology. You may produce the cheapest typewriters, but everyone is moving to word-processors. One needs a projection of life-cycle costs in order to see the benefits of adopting a risky cost-leadership policy if technological change does not occur. One needs a calculation like table 5.2 to assess how long the delay in the next technological leap needs to be to make one's cost-leadership policy worthwhile. With an increasing emphasis on high technology, life-cycles in some industries rarely achieve the mature, 'flatter' stage. In such situations an assessment of the slope of the experience curve is vital in determining the likely profitability of new investments.

Bogue and Buffa (1986) also show how an understanding of the experience curve can give one a quite different perception of what is happening in the market. They describe two companies, one of which is experiencing a rapidly decreasing profit margin and is therefore loath to invest. The other company, a more recent entrant into the market, is investing on a considerable scale. The first company cannot understand why, given that it almost certainly has lower costs. Figure 5.4 illustrates

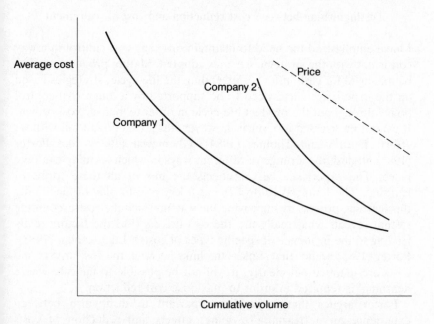

Figure 5.4   Experience curves can make it easier to understand a market (based on Bogue and Buffa, 1986)

Adapted with permission of The Free Press, a Division of Macmillan, Inc. from *Corporate Strategic Analysis* by M. C. Bogue and E. S. Buffa. Copyright © 1986 by The Free Press.

how such a situation might arise. Company 1 does have lower costs but has a flatter experience curve than the declining price schedule. Company 2 has a much more rapidly declining experience curve and is increasing its margins. The crucial point is that company 2 will be 'bullish' about the increasing margins. It may, however, be in trouble if it does not project the whole life-cycle to ascertain how long the increasing margins can continue. Also, company 1, by focusing on decreasing margins through time, rather than the fact that it is still earning better margins than a rival, may be 'bearish' and let company 2 get established in the market too easily. Company 1 still has a cost margin on which to fight, and, if it chooses to do so, it could later reap the 'cash cow' benefits.

On occasions accounting has received a 'bad press' from rival disciplines for focusing too much on detailed costs and not on the key strategic issues. If a company adopts a definite cost-leadership strategy, and many do, detailed cost analysis and subsequent control on a life-cycle basis is absolutely critical for success. Accountants should not be backward at pointing this out.

Distinguishing between cost reduction and cost measurement

I have emphasized the need to maintain on-going cost control in a way consistent with the strategic schemes adopted. Mature products need to be managed for cash inflow or extending the life-cycle; strategies based on the experience curve need to be supported by a tough cost-control policy throughout the product life-cycle in order to manage costs down. It cannot be stressed too much, however, that costs do not fall without effort. Dutton and Thomas (1984), Ghemawat (1985), and Porter (1985) all describe a range of different ways in which learning can take place. The experience curve reflects the mix of all these forms of learning. The financial controller has a key role to play in facilitating this learning process by improving the way in which the cost-accounting system reveals what really are the cost-drivers (i.e. the factors really leading to the incidence of specific types of costs). Like Kaplan (1988), Porter (1985) argues that, unless the links between the cost-drivers and costs are mapped out clearly, it will not be possible to indicate where 'learning' is required in order to maximize cost reduction.

Porter argues that it is also important to distinguish between experience-curve (learning-by-doing) effects and reduction of costs through economies of scale, i.e. the reduction achievable in any one period by increasing efficiency through the use of larger production plants, thereby spreading infrastructure costs over more units of output. Such economies of scale must be distinguished from savings through fuller utilization of existing capacity, which spreads the fixed costs of a *specific* existing piece of plant over more units. In addition, as Porter shows through extended discussion, the phrase 'economies of scale' itself hides many subtleties. What is the appropriate measure of scale difference between industrial activities? Sometimes it is global scale and sometimes local market scale. Only by a careful understanding of the market place can one be sure that one is thinking in the appropriate dimension and take full advantage of scale economies.

Cost-leadership policies do not, therefore, depend for their success upon some crude belief in the experience curve. There may not even be a marked learning process based on accumulated experience. Cost leadership may come more through capturing a large-enough share to enable the company to take better advantage of economies of scale than its rivals. The important point is to monitor pressure for cost reductions from all sources and to take such possibilities into account in strategic analysis. Even if one thinks one's own company will not reduce costs further, it is dangerous to make the same assumption for one's rivals.

It is important to make a clear distinction between Porter's use of the term 'cost-drivers' and that of Kaplan (1988). Porter lists ten factors, including learning, economies of scale, interrelationships with suppliers, and discretionary policies, that should be examined with a view to reducing costs. In contrast, Kaplan, in developing activity-based costing, is more concerned with an accurate measurement of current product costs and product profitability. The similarity of the 'cost-driver' terminology may disguise the different underlying purpose of each writer. In product-costing Kaplan tends to emphasize cost-drivers in terms of outputs from activities, e.g. number of set-ups. Costs may be driven down by reducing the need for activities, but one should not overlook the reduction of costs in terms of both what causes activities to take place and the efficiency of conducting the activity itself.

This difference is emphasized when one examines how Porter proposes to go about cost reduction. He and Rappaport (1987), extending Porter's approach, offer suggestions for an outline analysis of costs by strategic categories of action. Porter refers to his basic value-chain analysis, which was briefly described in chapter 4 and now needs closer examination. He argues that the value-creating activities may be summarized in nine categories as below; each of the support activities may support any of the primary activities. Remember, the firm can add value to its products and services by improving its performance in any of the primary or support activities.

Primary activities

1 *In-bound logistics*: receiving, storing and issuing materials
2 *Operations*: transferring inputs into outputs
3 *Out-bound logistics*: distribution activities
4 *Marketing and sales*
5 *Servicing*

Support activities

6 *Procurement*: the function of purchasing
7 *Technology development*
8 *Human-resource management*
9 *Firm infrastructure*: planning, legal, financial, accounting, general management, etc.

To commence a cost analysis from a strategic viewpoint one first needs an analysis like that shown in figure 5.5, derived from Rappaport. Rappaport shows how the cost of support activities must first be carefully allocated over primary-activity categories. Then the costs, working capital and capital expenditure associated with each type of primary activity need separate identification in order to produce a net cash flow by primary activity. One has then begun to develop the figures needed to show how the cash flows and costs will be affected by actions taken to restructure the value chain.

This analysis is, however, merely a first step. One presumes that Rappaport's cost framework relates to the accounts of the whole company. It is obviously necessary to analyse each product (or product group) in this way.

Porter argues that one should look at the areas of the value chain which contain the largest proportion of costs and then consider what cost-drivers of the ten he identifies cause those costs. Rappaport's diagram can obviously be used as a basis for commencing this analysis. One should not overlook the possibility, however, that some activities are not adding value at all, and these need to be removed completely. There is no need for sophisticated cost-behaviour analyses on those.

Now the differences between Porter's and Kaplan's proposals become more clear. On the one hand, it is difficult to see how some of Porter's ten cost-drivers can be used to assign costs to products in an activity-based costing sense. Of course, he never meant them to be used like this. He was concerned with focusing quickly on the areas most amenable to cost reduction. Nevertheless, he could learn from Kaplan. It would seem that the primary activity of operations needs to be split into direct and indirect costs, with the latter analysed into major

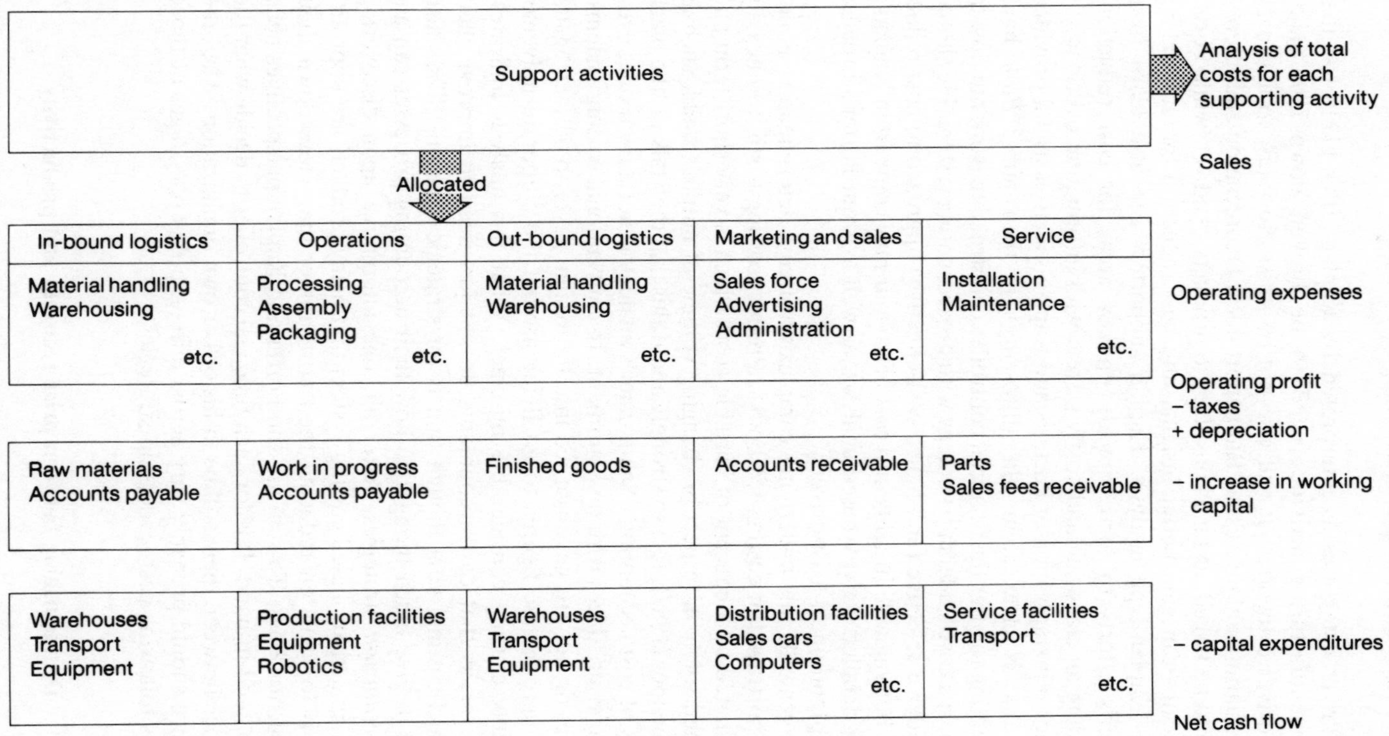

Figure 5.5 The value chain and cash-flow analysis (based on Rappaport, 1987)
Adapted with permission of The Free Press, a Division of Macmillan, Inc., from *Creating Shareholder Value: The New Standard for Business Performance* by A. Rappaport. Copyright © 1986 by A. Rappaport.

cost-driver categories as interpreted by Kaplan. It is likely too that non-manufacturing activities need to be broken down into major cost-driver categories. It will also not be satisfactory just to add back depreciation and interest as Rappaport does. Depreciation and interest need to be traced, as far as possible, to products. And yet, while Porter advocates can gain better insights into cost reduction by undertaking some Kaplan-type analysis, Kaplan supporters can also learn from Porter's efforts to focus quickly on key areas for cost reduction, avoiding an elaborate and costly system with information overload.

Such a juxtaposition of Porter's and Kaplan's ideas is useful provided that one is clear about the differences in their aims. *Both* have something to offer the financial controller concerned to work out how to support a cost-leadership strategy with his accounting system. He should consider a selective (and hence cost-effective) approach to cost reduction, but valuable insights into cost behaviour may come from Kaplan's more detailed activity-based analysis, as well as from Porter's broader interpretation of 'cost-drivers.'

In general, this underlying complexity of cost determination is not well portrayed in costing textbooks. Product-costing is still too heavily dominated by a concept of variable costs which is very short-term and defined solely in respect of changing volume of output. Some, such as Schmenner (1987), feel so strongly about this that they talk of 'the black holes of cost accounting'. Schmenner's analogy is not a good one, even if one sympathizes with his sentiment. In conventional costing systems, figures do not just get absorbed into the system never to be seen again; they may release figures to go flying around the corporate universe, possibly causing considerable mischief. What this analysis indicates, however, is that cost accountants do not just need to improve their product-costing, vital though that is for strategic decisions. They also need to give much thought to how their accounting processes can aid cost-*reduction* strategies. After all, one alternative upon discovering from an activity-based costing system that many products are unprofitable is to focus on reducing their costs rather than close down their production lines. To sum up, the Porter and Kaplan perspectives need to go hand-in-hand. It is for each financial controller to decide what the balance between them will be in his or her own organization. Also, the balance should probably vary across different life-cycle stages of those SBUs following cost-leadership strategies.

Distinguishing between price recovery and productivity

The discussion in this chapter so far has addressed cost reduction in general without trying to distinguish between the ability to become more efficient through productivity increases and the ability to improve the relationship between input and output prices. Clearly, either can help a cost-leadership strategy. Relatively recently, van Loggerenberg (1988) and his associate Hayzen (1989) have developed an alternative to conventional standard costing based upon this distinction. (See also Kaplan and Atkinson, 1989, for a slightly modified version.)

The essentials of productivity accounting are described in figure 5.6, where it can be seen that changes in profits through time are decomposed into two major elements, changes in productivity and changes in price recovery, which are defined as follows:

$$\text{profitability} = \text{productivity} \times \text{price recovery}$$

i.e.

$$\frac{\text{product value}}{\text{resource value}} = \frac{\text{product quantity}}{\text{resource quantity}} \times \frac{\text{product price}}{\text{resource price}}$$

Where there are multiple products and resources there will be a productivity measure for each pair of resource and product. Similarly, there will be a price-recovery calculation for each. Changes in profits

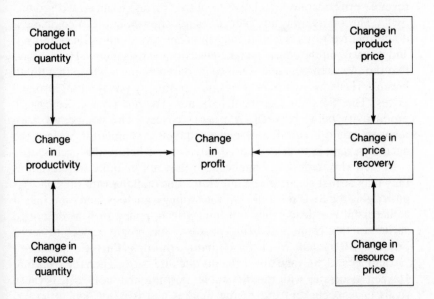

Figure 5.6 The essentials of productivity accounting (*Note*. This form of profit decomposition contrasts with normal cost-accounting decomposition, which explains profit changes in terms of changes in revenue and costs)

can therefore be analysed by a set of productivity and price-recovery changes. One of the advantages claimed for this approach to separating off productivity measurement is that it can be done from conventional accounting statements, thereby providing, as Hayzen says, the link between productivity and profit calculations. Numerical examples are provided in Hayzen (1989) and, for a slightly different system, in Kaplan and Atkinson (1989). Hayzen has also produced a computer package for commercial application.

Without going into detailed calculations which readers can obtain for themselves, the concept has been introduced here to provide a clear distinction between internal operating efficiency and action on relative prices. In many competitive markets the company may not be able to do much about price recovery, but, by separating out those effects, it can focus more accurately on cost reduction and internal efficiency. If the company feels that it can largely pass changes in input prices on, it will be more appropriate to focus on productivity changes than on absolute cost changes. Hayzen also shows how a series of 2 × 2 matrices can be developed in order to give more specific insights into the company's competitive position. Figure 5.7 presents just the basic grid. Readers are urged to consult Hayzen's small booklet for supplementary charts.

Hayzen's preferred position is the 'Pursue' segment, which he interprets as the situation where prices are kept keen through absorbing revenue price increases (relative to output prices) in increased productivity. This on its own, however, does not show how well a company is doing relative to its rivals. Ideally the company should plot both itself and its rivals on the chart. To take just two other segments, Hayzen says that the 'Awaken' segment is not so favoured as one might at first think, because rivals may chip away at one's profits by undercutting product prices. The 'Scramble' segment indicates, Hayzen says, a decrease in productivity being covered by price recovery. The company's price recovery could be eroded by more productive competitors, hence the need to scramble to achieve productivity gains before this occurs.

In fact, Hayzen's policy implications may not be quite so relevant as they may at first seem. If one integrates this thinking with the concepts underlying the SBU portfolio grids in strategic analysis, and especially if a successful cost-leadership and limit-pricing policy such as described earlier in this chapter is being pursued, one might expect to see a product (SBU) shift from 'Fine tuning', through 'Pursue', 'Awaken', 'Scramble' and 'Salvage', over the product life-cycle. Then the risks that Hayzen associates with the 'Scramble' position may not exist, because rivals have been kept out of the market and it is too late to enter. 'Scramble' might then be a better position to hold than 'Pursue'.

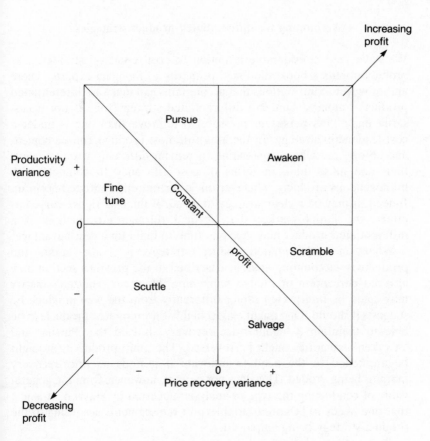

Figure 5.7 Hayzen's productivity–profit grid (from Hayzen, 1989)

The main point, however, is that this alternative way of analysing profit seems to lend itself more naturally to business thinking and can be linked in with conceptual thinking about strategy. In terms of *detailed* variance analysis, it does not, it seems to me, have much of an advantage over conventional standard costing in most situations, but it does help considerably in focusing on the key competitive issues. By developing the chart analysis as Hayzen does, one can avoid getting bogged down in detailed variances and concentrate on strategy. The system relates much more readily than standard costing to the concept of productivity lying at the heart of cost reduction in competitive markets.

Accounting for differentiated-product strategies

We have paid considerable attention to cost-reduction strategies, as probably befits a book addressed primarily to financial experts. There are, however, contributions that accountants can make to differentiated product strategies. Under a differentiated strategy, one is not necessarily under less persistent pressure to improve than one is under a cost-leadership strategy. In the long run most products can be copied, and so one must keep innovating to remain different. If one cannot, then one must think in terms of cost efficiency to compete with homogeneous products, whatever one's current differentiated position. Indeed, it may be a clear strategy to do so. If the experience curve has effect, the initial market share gained through introduction of a differentiated product may give one time to build up a cost advantage.

Where a differentiated-product strategy is being used, the productivity-accounting analysis described in the previous section may also aid perception of what is happening. However, Hayzen's matrix may again be interpreted rather differently from the way in which he suggests it should. One might expect highly differentiated products to be able to maintain a higher price recovery. Indeed the 'Pursue' and 'Awaken' categories might be reversed. The multi-product firm might be awakened to the need to innovate if it finds its price-recovery margins being eroded. This does not detract, however, from the general value of conducting the type of analysis suggested by Hayzen. It is just that one needs to be careful to interpret the segments according to the product strategy being employed.

Great care is also needed in considering the concept of differentiation. What is referred to in this book as 'differentiation' is often referred to rather vaguely as 'quality improvement'. The increased competitive pressure experienced by many US and UK companies as a result of the Japanese emphasis on reliability and the inclusion of 'extras' in basic models has made them much more aware of the need to pay attention to quality. In fact Buzzell and Gale (1987) say that the PIMS data establish that quality is *the* most important factor in success. But what does 'quality' mean? Is it just to do with production quality control or does it also embrace marketing, accounting and other functions?

The term 'differentiation' is preferable, because it throws the emphasis on the need to be 'better' than rival products not just in some general way, but in precisely specified ways. Hill's notions of order-winning criteria (Hill, 1985) encourage attention to the *precise* needs of the potential customer. That is surely what quality is. It concerns the effectiveness with which products and services meet customer requirements, and affects *all* aspects of the interaction between the customer and the company or its agents: the initial inquiry about products, the information provided, product design, reliability, availability, speed of delivery, after-sales service, and so on. Ascertaining what a company's order-winning criteria are should, it seems, be primarily a marketing task, although, depending upon the nature of the product and industry, there may also be a significant role for manufacturing-development engineers. Accountants, too, need to understand these criteria if they are to be able to help management reach decisions about product effectiveness. Delivery of such criteria is not costless, and competitiveness may depend upon the ability to provide such criteria at a specified cost.

Some commentators, such as Berliner and Brimson (1988) and Buzzell and Gale (1987), argue that the idea of a trade-off between quality and cost is outdated. For example, Berliner and Brimson say,

> In the past, it was common practice to work toward economically balanced levels of inventory, quality and other critical factors of prediction. . . . However, strong competition from quality-minded foreign competitors forces manufacturers to work towards absolute quality and to realize that quality and cost are complementary – raising quality decreases cost. (1988, p. 44)

The main foreign competitors are, of course, the Japanese. They, we are told, identify exactly what the customer wants and at what target price (as one of the order-winning criteria) and then attempt to produce the highest-quality product possible at that price. Pressure is continually applied to encourage the search for higher production quality in the sense of zero defects, minimum delays and minimal scrap. One must, however, be precise over the use of the word 'quality'. The term, when being used to justify the statement that increased quality reduces costs, really refers to *reliability* of the product and its delivery according to *pre-specified attributes* (i.e. order-winning criteria). If one is at the design stage, there is an obvious trade-off between cost and the attributes one can provide. It is a fundamental law of economics in a world of scarce resources and could not be otherwise. Even the Japanese do not try to make a profit selling Rolls-Royce equivalents at £15,000. To avoid confusion, the advocates of cost reduction through pursuing quality ought to make it clear that this applies *after* the product design has been set. In the process of product design itself (or deciding what degree of product differentiation to go for) trade-offs *are* inevitable. Where trade-offs are inevitable, the cost accountant needs to be present to advise on whether the given attributes can be supplied at the target price.

Let it now be assumed, however, that the product design has been set. There is still a task for the accountant in analysing the cost of quality, now interpreted as product and delivery reliability.

A number of companies, recognizing the need for quality, are experimenting with the notion of the 'cost of quality', but, as far as I am aware, most such schemes to date are fairly rudimentary. One scheme of which I have received some details is being developed by a well-known engineering company. Like many other companies, it has recently instituted a 'total quality management' drive with a view to 'getting it right first time'. Before this, it was realized that quality had an impact on the bottom line, but there had been little analysis of its effects.

The company began its financial appraisal of such questions by trying to assess the actual 'cost of quality' across all activities. In order to quantify relevant costs, it identified a number of cost categories, for which costs were collected over a ten-month period. These categories were selected to represent the costs of exercising or of *not* exercising quality control. The former included the costs of full inspection of products, training and certain engineering operations, while the latter (costs of not exercising quality control) included the costs of rework, warranty claims, defect investigation after transmission of the funded product, obsolete stock, scrap, and so on. In addition, each cost area examined was subjected to a causal analysis. For example, costs in the area 'scrap and rectification' were shown to derive from these factors:

- management control
- production methods
- machines used
- people
- supplies and material
- design and customer management

Each one of these causes was further analysed into five or six sub-factors. For example, 'people' was analysed into

- inability to read drawings
- excessive overtime
- poor training
- 'booze factor' (after lunch hour)
- carelessness
- rush job

Having built its model, the company then made rough calculations of costs and an approximate indication of their causes. It was shown that the cost of not exercising quality control was far in excess of the cost of operating such a system.

The company in question would be the first to admit that the analysis was a pioneering effort and that the estimates obtained were, in some cases, quite crude, as the accounting system could not readily provide all the relevant data. Also, there were clearly large gaps in the analysis as an 'assessment' of the total 'cost of quality' in relation to all order-winning criteria. For example, no attempt was made to assess the cost of a poor delivery performance in terms of lost sales, or the extra costs necessary to ensure a delivery performance consistent with a desired sales level. Clearly, in industries with a wide customer base, estimating the costs of not satisfying each specific order-winning criterion, and of any portfolio effect where several criteria are not satisfied, will be a complex task. Nevertheless, the approach described does indicate an area in which there might be considerable expansion of the accounting function. No single function can carry out such an analysis reliably.

It should be pointed out, however, that a company need only carry out such a 'cost of quality' calculation where it is unsure whether the extra effort required to improve quality (i.e. reliability) is worthwhile – that is, where it *is* contemplating a trade-off in the area where Berliner and Brimson say a trade-off should *not* be contemplated. The Japanese, in pursuit of 100 per cent reliability, do not seem to undertake much in the way of quality-costing investigations. They pursue reliability just because they *know* it leads to lower costs and increased market share. Perhaps, in the West, it is still necessary for accountants to demonstrate that fact by calculations in order to get general managers and the workforce to take it to heart. This would especially be the case, it would seem, if a company were contemplating a move to total quality control for the first time.

The impact of new manufacturing methods

The discussion in this chapter has so far not explicitly recognized the changes that have been taking place and will continue to take place in manufacturing methods. Such changes are likely to have fundamental effects upon the way companies operate, and so consideration must be given to the impact of developments upon product-costing, cost control and investment appraisal – concepts already discussed as central to the corporate resource-allocation process. The impact upon investment appraisal will be left until chapter 6, but it is appropriate to look at the effect upon costing here.

These production developments are loosely termed 'advanced manu-facturing techniques' but, in fact, cover a variety of developments (see Berliner and Brimson, 1988, and Lee, 1987, for reviews of them). One way of classifying such developments is as follows:

- **just-in-time** methods (JIT);
- **islands of automation**, incorporating **computer-aided design** (CAD), **computer-aided engineering** (CAE) and **computer-aided manufacturing** (CAM), and **flexible manufacturing systems** (FMS);
- **computer-integrated manufacturing** (CIM).

Despite the impression given by some authors (e.g. Brimson, 1987), a company does not necessarily develop its production methods along a continuum from JIT to CIM systems. JIT and FMS developments, for example, may go hand in hand or in sequence, and either development may stand alone or precede the other. It is important, however, to consider the main distinguishing features of each system in order to understand how product-cost analysis and cost control may be affected, which will in turn influence how resources are allocated within the company.

Just-in-time methods

JIT systems are now generally known to encourage considerable reductions in stock-holding. This is achieved by arranging efficient delivery systems, both within the firm and for goods from outside suppliers, so that the time between receipt of a sales order and delivery of the product is kept to a minimum, and the flow of deliveries and production proceeds so smoothly that there is no need to produce for stock. JIT is not, therefore, just a way of reducing stock, but implies a commitment to total waste avoidance, removal of bottlenecks and total quality control – i.e. getting the product out as soon as possible and right first time. Adoption of such methods implies significant changes for accounting, beyond those discussed in the previous section for 'cost of quality' calculations.

First, this manufacturing approach facilitates a drastic simplification of accounting systems. 'Backflush' accounting methods (see Lee, 1987; Foster and Horngren, 1988; or Bromwich and Bhimani, 1989) in their more radical versions may involve the complete elimination of stock accounts, including finished-goods accounts. This not only simplifies accounting systems, but also has an important behavioural effect. Under a system without work-in-progress and finished-goods stock accounts all costs become period costs – thereby overcoming the age-old incentive, under absorption costing, to produce for stock to increase current profit without full regard for the impact on future reported profits. Hence, just the introduction of backflush accounting may have a significant effect in reinforcing the JIT (low stockholding) philosophy.

Another feature of JIT methods is the organization of the production process into cells within which operatives have group responsibility over the whole operation. Production cells may carry out their own machine maintenance, set-ups, and even packing and labelling. Usually, too, with the abandonment of work-in-progress, control over production progress is maintained by physical counts of products demanded and produced, along with measures of defects, stock levels, and so on. This is often described as establishing a reduced need for cost-accounting, and this is obvious from the viewpoint of regular routine control. It does not follow, however, that the *principles* of activity-based costing are redundant. Decisions still have to be made based on product profitability. There will normally be a need at least for *ad hoc* estimates of product costs, and, failing this, it will still be necessary to *understand* the *logical relationship* between variations in physical processes and variations in costs incurred, even if this is not measured precisely. Moreover, JIT may make it easier to understand these relationships, as more activities will be directly traceable to production cells. Whether this makes individual product costs less ambiguous will still, however, depend upon the nature of the product flow through those cells and the joint-cost problem within cells. Furthermore, JIT may reduce the number of cost pools which need to be allocated to products under a conventional manufacturing system. Stock controls and warehousing costs, quality checking on goods received, and materials-handling costs will be significantly reduced. Under well-developed JIT systems, the principles of activity-based systems may, therefore, be more easily and fruitfully applied when making product-mix decisions of the strategic kind.

As already indicated, JIT stemmed from the general Japanese philosophy of continual improvement. This implies continual cost reduction. The Japanese are famed for their 'quality circles', but many of their companies also have 'cost-reduction circles'. See, for example, the discoveries made by Ford Europe on examining the role of the finance function for Japanese motor manufacturers (IMEDE case study, 1984). These cost-reduction circles may operate on an informal basis and focus on the removal of obvious bottlenecks rather than looking where the company's cost system directs, but, as business becomes more and more competitive, it may be necessary to track cost-reduction progress. At least the Japanese show conclusively that the notion of continual cost reduction is not redundant, as some critics of the learning-experience-curve phenomenon seem to suggest. Accountants should take the lead in establishing cost-reduction circles.

The JIT approach developed by the Japanese also reinforced their concept of total quality control. The accounting implications of this have already been discussed in the previous section.

In more advanced applications of JIT, companies have been very active in restructuring their value chains particularly in relation to their procurement activities. Many firms now buy in rather than make components themselves, and overcome the problems of controlling quality and delivery by forming very close relationships with suppliers – sometimes in return for single-supplier status. Some major companies build this relationship by offering engineering and manufacturing guidance on modern manufacturing methods to smaller suppliers. In return, these suppliers are sometimes required to operate an 'open book' policy in relation to the purchaser. It then becomes appropriate to wonder whether the analysis proposed by Rappaport in figure 5.5 for a single entity might not, in such situations, be expanded to encompass the partnership. Accountants could play a key part in analysing the joint situation of the two firms in order to propose areas in the 'partner organization' where value-chain reconfigurations might be of benefit to both firms.

'Islands of automation'

Here we need to consider the impact of CAD, CAE, CAM and FMS.

With more sophisticated design procedures under CAD, the balance of costs is clearly being shifted from manufacture to design and it becomes more important for cost accountants to use their cost analysis at the design phase (i.e. the *ex ante* use of activity-based principles discussed earlier).

Similarly, as more attention is paid to CAE, engineering and testing costs become more significant and need to be incorporated into product costs rather than left floating around as a general charge 'below the line'. In one case that I know of, a subsidiary of a major UK company got itself into difficulty through totally misunderstanding its product costs as engineering costs, written off as a lump-sum period cost, increased with the production of more advanced products. On almost any basis of cost allocation, this would have resulted in the wrong product costs and a wrong emphasis on product mix (long-term, not just short-term).

Moving to CAM and FMS, one expects to see a significant decrease in direct labour costs. If companies stick with on-cost rates on direct labour, percentages in the hundreds or thousands are not unusual. This in fact was one of the driving forces behind the development of activity-based costing – the labour-hour basis was no longer applicable. CAM developments therefore give greater credence to the ideas behind activity-based costing, though not necessarily to its application in complex routine costing systems providing regular monthly reports on an activity basis.

Computer-integrated manufacturing

One will also expect to see more physical controls, rather than routine cost-accounting controls, on production performance as the degree of automation in manufacturing increases. This is clearly seen if one jumps to the 'ideal' world of CIM, with its notions of 'ghost factories' operating with minimal human interference. Under such automated systems and automated quality controls, the production line will be stopped if performance is not up to standard. One will not need an accounting report to generate this. It also follows that in such an advanced mechanized world the scope for cost reduction will be limited once manufacturing has commenced. Cost analyses will then become almost wholly *ex ante*. The long-term cost reductions will be achieved mainly by the redesign of both the product and the process, rather than through the refinement of operations alone. Further cost pools may disappear: set-up costs will become minimal as machines switch from product to product. The 'costs of increased variety' argument will lose much of its force, chipping away at the need for a complex form of activity-based costing as conceived by Kaplan. Also, with a stark division of costs into direct (variable) material costs and largely fixed machine costs, it may become impossible to use detailed activity-based logic to allocate these fixed costs. All that may be needed is a classification of machines and a measurement of time spent on each machine by each product. Moreover, the depreciation debate will be 'dusted off' after years of shelf-life and revisited in more depth as depreciation becomes *the* major cost. Perhaps that is where the Gregory/Grinyer model of leasing charges described in chapter 3 will come into its own. However, before getting too carried away and concluding that detailed activity-based accounting may soon be outdated, and replaced by more simple machine-time analyses, it must be remembered that the extremes of CIM are still a long way off for most industries. In the meantime, I would argue, the logic of activity-based product-costing has a vital part to play in ensuring proper corporate resource allocation. At least, this would seem to be the case for companies that have many product lines and are no further ahead than the 'islands of automation' stage. Also, most companies and other organizations can still benefit from applying activity accounting in pursuit of cost reduction, even if their product range is well focused.

Summary

The chapter began with a discussion of the contribution that accountants might make to financial profiles for different locations on portfolio matrices, and the use and abuse of ROI. The main argument then turned largely to cost-accounting and cost reduction. In the process many challenges to cost accountants were identified. Schmenner (1987) says that traditional cost-accounting has been a 'star' for years and is now collapsing in a black hole from which managers must escape. This is eloquent, but misleading. One needs to build upon the foundations of cost-accounting, not escape from it. With the increasing scale of international competition, it will become vital to know exactly what product costs are where price is an important order-winning criterion. New, more refined forms of cost-accounting, such as activity-based costing, will be needed and become more feasible with added computing power. They will become indispensable strategic tools for both product-costing and cost reduction. Though still far from perfect, as Bromwich and Bhimani (1989) indicate, they are an improvement on older practices. Moreover, with improved internal-management accounting practices, it is likely that external disclosure practices will also improve, to help combat concerns about the short-term biases of current accounting practices and stock-market pressures. However, I believe that in the longer run, as production processes become more automated, Kaplan's activity-based costing concepts will find their main application at the stage of product design and investment selection, although they might have a wider application in service industries, such as the Health Service, and in the control of non-manufacturing costs. These developments in cost-accounting are likely to be of central importance in resource-allocation decisions for the foreseeable future. Cost-accounting can regain its rightful place alongside, and integrated with, business policy and strategic analyses. They should never have been developed separately in the first place. At least the up-to-date cost accountant has plenty of ammunition to fire at the chief executive who insists that accounting has little to do with strategy.

References

Abernathy, W. and Wayne, K. 1974: Limits of the learning curve. *Harvard Business Review*, September–October.

Anthony, R., Dearden, J. and Vancil, R. 1966: *Management Control Systems*. Homewood, Ill.: R. D. Irwin.

Anthony, R., Dearden, J. and Bedford, N. 1984: *Management Control Systems*. Homewood, Ill.: R. D. Irwin.

Berliner, C. and Brimson, J. 1988: *Cost Management for Today's Advanced Manufacturing*. Cambridge, Mass.: Harvard Business School Press.

Bogue, M., and Buffa, E. 1986: *Corporate Strategic Analysis*. New York: Collier Macmillan.

Brimson, J. 1987: CAM-I cost accounting systems project. In R. Capettini and D. Clancy (eds), *Cost Accounting, Robotics and the New Manufacturing Environment*, Sarasota, Fla: American Accounting Association.

Bromwich, M. and Bhimani, A. 1989: *Management Accounting: Evolution not Revolution*, London: Chartered Institute of Management Accounting.

Bullen, C. and Rockhart, J. 1981: *A Primer on Critical Success Factors*, CISR, no. 69, Sloan Working Paper no. 1220–81. Boston, Mass.: MIT.

Buzzell, R. and Gale, B. 1987: *The PIMS Principles: linking strategy to performance*. New York: Collier Macmillan.

Cornwell, D. 1987: An examination of the Gap between the Theory and Practice of Capital Budgeting. MSc dissertation, University of Bath.

Daniel, J. 1961: Management information crisis. *Harvard Business Review*, September–October.

Dermer, J. 1977: *Management Planning and Control Systems*. Homewood, Ill.: R. D. Irwin.

Dutton, J. and Thomas, A. 1984: Treating progress functions as a managerial opportunity. *Academy of Management Review*, 9, no. 2.

Foster, G. and Horngren, C. 1988: Cost accounting and cost management in a JIT environment. *Journal of Cost Management*, Winter.

Ghemawat, P. 1985: Building strategy on the experience curve. *Harvard Business Review*, March–April.

Gilbert, X. and Strebel, P. Developing competitive advantage. In J. Quinn, H. Mintzberg and R. James, *The Strategy Process*, Englewood Cliffs, NJ: Prentice-Hall.

Hayes, R. and Garvin, D. 1982: Managing as if tomorrow mattered. *Harvard Business Review*, May–June.

Hayzen, A. J. 1989: *Productivity Accounting*. Buckingham: FMP Associates (in liaison with B. van Loggerenberg).

Hill, T. 1985: *Manufacturing Strategy*. London: Macmillan.

IMEDE, *Ford Europe (A) and (B)*. Cranfield: IMEDE.

Kaplan, R. 1988: One cost system isn't enough. *Harvard Business Review*, February.

Kaplan, R. and Atkinson, A. 1989: *Advanced Management Accounting*, 2nd edn. Englewood Cliffs, NJ: Prentice-Hall.

Lee, J. Y. 1987: *Management Accounting Changes for the 1990's*. Reading, Mass.: Addison-Wesley.

Leidecker, J. and Bruno, A. 1984: Identifying and using critical success factors. *Long Range Planning*, 17, no. 1.

Marshall, P. 1985: The Experience Curve and Limit Pricing as a means of Integrating Portfolio Matrices into Capital Budgeting. PhD dissertation, University of Bath.

Marshall, P. and Tomkins, C. 1988: Incorporating DCF contours onto a BCG portfolio matrix using limit pricing. *Managerial and Decision Economics*, 9.

Mauriel, J. and Anthony, R. 1966: Misevaluation of investment center performance. *Harvard Business Review*, March–April.

Merchant, K. A., *Rewarding Results – Motivating Profit Center Managers*. Cambridge, Mass.: Harvard Business School.

Parker, L. 1979: Divisional performance measurement: beyond an exclusive profit test. *Accounting and Business Research*, Autumn.

Pike, R. 1983: A review of recent trends on formal capital budgeting processes. *Accounting and Business Research*, Summer.

Pogue, G. 1985: Some applications of the learning curve. *Management Accounting*, May.

Porter, M. 1985: *Competitive Advantage*. New York: Collier Macmillan.

Rappaport, A. 1987: Linking competitive strategy and shareholder value analysis. *Journal of Business Strategy*, Spring.

Reece, J. and Cool, W. 1978: Measuring investment center performance. *Harvard Business Review*, May–June.

Rockhart, J. 1979: Chief executives define their own data needs. *Harvard Business Review*, March–April.

Scapens, R. and Sale, T. 1985: An international study of accounting practice in divisionalised companies and their associations with organizational variables. *Accounting Review*, April.

Schmenner, R. 1987: *The Black Holes of Cost Accounting*. Cranfield: IMEDE.

Tomkins, C. 1973: *Financial Planning in Divisionalized Companies*. Englewood Cliffs, NJ: Prentice-Hall.

van Loggerenberg, B. J. 1988: *Productivity Decoding of Financial Signals: a primer for managers on deterministic productivity accounting*. PMA monograph (no place indicated).

Discussion questions

5.1   In what ways can the management accountant contribute to the specification of market attractiveness and competitive strengths for a McKinsey–GE portfolio analysis?

5.2   Most of the problems raised by the use of ROI can be overcome through a sensible policy of investment motivation based upon a careful strategic analysis, with ROI retained for short-run performance evaluation. Discuss.

5.3   There is more to strategy than simple mastery of the experience curve, even where cost leadership is critical to the domination of an industry, and yet it is still important to project cost reductions and make sure that they happen. Discuss.

5.4   Assuming that you operate in an industry where the experience-curve effect is significant, how might you vary pricing policy through the product-life cycle? What are the dangers of the policy you propose?

5.5   How can cost-reduction advantages be used to formulate a policy to block entry to your market? What are the dangers of such a policy?

5.6   Why might changing gross margins be very deceptive as regards the attractiveness of a product market where the experience-curve effect exists?

5.7   How might a management accounting structure be created around Porter's value chain?

5.8   Instead of focusing on revenue variances and cost variances, we ought to address the issues of price recovery and productivity. How can the latter be integrated into management accounting reports? Is this accounting approach more easily integrated into strategic analysis?

5.9   Do management accountants have any role to play when a company is following a generic strategy of differentiation? Discuss fully.

5.10   Changes in accounting necessary to accommodate changes in manufacturing will have such an impact on product-costing and cost control that one must consider what impact they will have on the corporate resource-allocation process. Discuss.

5.11   While CIM is not yet widespread in UK industry, when it comes accountants will have to sharpen up their treatment of depreciation. Discuss.

5.12   UK accounting in its product-costing and cost-control dimensions must be integrated into strategic analysis. Discuss.

5.13   Distinguish between critical success factors and key result areas. How would you set about the construction of a *parsimonious* set of critical success factors to serve as part of the corporate control system?

5.14   Even if a company does not need an activity-based costing system for product-costing, it needs it for establishing a cost-reduction programme. Discuss.

6

Towards Integrating the Theory
of Finance and Strategic Analysis

It should have become apparent to the observant reader that there are
marked inconsistencies between the theory of finance as described in
chapter 1 and the basis of strategic analysis as described in chapter 4. It
is now time to identify these issues more clearly and see whether it is
possible to integrate these different perspectives.

The relevance of discounted cash flow calculations

It is quite clear that the theory of finance adopts net present value
(NPV) as the proven and accepted valuation criterion for any asset. In
contrast, the portfolio-management analysis of corporate strategy may
take some account of discounted cash flow (DCF), but it does not figure
as a central concept. The emphasis is upon detailed analyses of
competitive positions; the financial benefits are evaluated in very
general terms by reference to rates of return and profitability. The
exception is the Boston Consulting Group (BCG) matrix with its precise
'Growth'/'Share' axes, but it still does not use DCF. It is appropriate,
therefore, to ask a very basic question first. Is DCF as desirable a form
of analysis as the theory of finance implies – especially given criticisms
of the technique voiced by some academics in the corporate-strategy
area?

Hayes and Garvin (1982), for example, went so far as to blame the
growing use of DCF for the relative decline in the performance of
Western businesses. Such views are often picked up and repeated by
non-finance specialists (e.g. Hill, 1985). In addition, criticism of DCF is
often not separated clearly enough from criticism of accounting return
on investment (ROI). While accountants are criticized for producing
excess 'short-termism' through stressing ROI, they are also accused of
'devaluing the future' by discounting its importance using DCF. If such
obvious confusion exists in management literature without a financial
orientation, it is high time financial analysts devoted more attention to

it. In fact confusion can also be found in the accounting literature. Even Berliner and Brimson (1988, p. 186) in their valuable report on the CAM-I study, tend towards such confusion when they say companies have focused on *short-term* investment benefits using quantitative financial information such as ROI and *NPV*! As was made clear in chapter 3, the question of the appropriateness of DCF obviously needs to be separated from that of the appropriateness of using ROI. The latter has already been addressed in earlier chapters. Here the focus will be on DCF.

It is fashionable among some general business academics to attack DCF by stating that the Japanese do not get caught up in 'DCF number games' but place more emphasis on corporate discussion and the generation of a consensus about whether the development being considered should go ahead or not. The argument runs that the Japanese take a long-run perspective in building market share and that this has paid off; hence, if they do not use DCF, it is probably dysfunctional. The argument is then reinforced by reference to studies which say that the Japanese rarely use the concepts of NPV or the internal rate of return (Tsurumi and Tsurumi, 1985).

Hodder (1986) has showed that it is dangerous to rely upon casual observations of that sort. He says that, while it is true that few Japanese companies use NPV and IRR, 'the *vast majority* of Japanese firms' do incorporate an imputed interest charge based on the capital outstanding in their cash flow projections.

Hodder offers an 'idealized' example of a company evaluating a project with an outflow of 1,000 million yen followed by an inflow of 200 million yen per annum for ten years. The annual cash flow of 200 million yen is then split into an imputed return of interest on the investment outstanding at the beginning of the period and a recovery of the initial investment. Hodder then suggests that the decision is based upon the ability of the project to recover the initial outlay plus imputed interest and yield a surplus. Hodder's example is shown in table 6.1: the project hypothesized recovers imputed interest and capital outlay in just over seven years.

Of course, Hodder's table reflects a concept very close to the familiar annuity-depreciation method – the only difference being that the latter method would spread depreciation over the full ten years of the asset's life. Also, what Hodder calls 'adjusted cash flow' is a form of residual income – a concept used by accountants for many years and discussed in chapter 1. Indeed, this issue was addressed in an earlier study (Tomkins, 1973, pp. 115–21), where it was illustrated how it was possible to devise an investment-appraisal rule (just like that above) consistent with NPV but based on residual income even when the project cash flows were

Table 6.1   Project cash flows with imputed interest (million yen)

Year	Project cash flow	Imputed interest	Adjusted cash flow	Residual investment
0	−10,000			1,000
1	200	100	100	900
2	200	90	110	790
3	200	79	121	669
4	200	67	133	536
5	200	54	146	390
6	200	39	161	229
7	200	23	177	52
8	200	5	195	−143
9	200	0	200	−343
10	200	0	200	−543

Source: Hodder (1986).

uneven through time – although it was felt that NPV was more straight-forward. The important point here, however, is that, while Hodder stresses that the example he gives is 'idealized' and that the interest charge is often based on the undepreciated investment balance, he shows that imputed interest *does* enter the investment decision-making process of many Japanese companies.

The DCF calculation is therefore one way in which recognition of the cost of funds can be incorporated into corporate investment calculations. It would be absurd if, following the Hayes and Garvin criticism of DCF, companies were to drop it and then assume that funds had a zero cost. Even Japanese companies do nothing of the sort! If DCF is not used, account has to be taken of the cost of funds in another way. This may be an explicit allowance for imputed interest as a deduction from revenues in periodic income calculations to arrive at a residual income figure, or there may be no deduction for required equity yields in the income calculations at all. In the latter case the net income attributable to shareholders will have to be assessed on the basis of whether it is reasonable compared with desired yields. Moreover, if conducted rigorously, all these different approaches should be consistent with each other and lead to the same investment decisions. So, why does finance theory tend to stress the use of DCF rather than other approaches? The answer is just that it simplifies interpretation of the figures by reducing uneven streams of benefits and costs to a single index of NPV (or IRR). It is easier to work in terms of one number (or valuation) instead of trying to assess a whole stream of different figures. The cost of funds *must* be incorporated into investment analysis in one way or another, and DCF is probably the simplest technique for summarizing its impact.

It follows that, if the Japanese do incorporate imputed interest charges, they are obviously trying to assess whether the cash inflows are sufficient to meet all claims upon them, including the yields required by shareholders. The relative success of the Japanese is, therefore, not based upon disregarding the risk-related cost of funds, which is what the DCF mechanism is designed to address. In so far as cost-of-funds matters lead to Japanese competitive advantage, it is more likely to be due to their willingness to take greater risks because of the low relative cost reported by Prowse (1986) and confirmed by Hodder (1986), rather than a propensity to disregard DCF.

It is also possible that, through the process of developing consensus, the Japanese arrive at better estimates of cash flows and obtain more general commitment to their projects among management and work-force. That, however, cannot be blamed upon the DCF technique. As Hodder and Riggs (1985) say, in response to Hayes and Garvin, the fault, if any, in US business lies with the way the DCF technique is often based on inadequate data (i.e. inadequate consideration of the factors affecting cash flows) or incorrectly applied (i.e. incorrectly using discount rates, or adjusting for inflation as discussed in chapter 1).

The essential point, then, is that the NPV approach to evaluating alternative cash streams is a generally correct valuation model where the discount rate is the opportunity cost of committing resources to one course of action rather than another. In particular, it is the basis for estimating how shareholders, who can more easily conceive of their investment problem as one of switching funds between alternative projects, will evaluate projects. If companies wish to see the impact of their decisions on shareholder wealth, the DCF apparatus and associated cost of capital formulation are vital. Companies may not go ahead with every investment with a positive NPV because other stakeholder positions may have to be considered, but that does not mean that there is a theoretical defect in DCF as a market-valuation mechanism. Finnie (1988) also provides recent support for this view.

Before leaving the discussion of whether DCF is relevant, a brief reference should be made to the possible use of option-pricing theory as a basis for valuing corporate strategies (see Logue, 1981). This is relevant to the debate because no *explicit* estimate of the cost of funds is incorporated into this type of analysis. Brennan and Schwartz (1986) demonstrate this by an interesting application of option-pricing to the valuation of a mine. It must be stressed, however, that an option-pricing approach implicitly takes into account the cost of funds and that it should, in theory, arrive at the same current valuation figure as the DCF method. This will not be pursued further here, as it is still uncertain whether option-pricing analysis can fulfil its promise in the valuation of a broad set of corporate strategies. Developments in the area need to be watched by those with interests in corporate finance and strategy.

Difficulties in measuring net cash benefits from investment projects

The conclusion that DCF is correct conceptually and, contrary to the arguments of Hayes and Garvin, Hill, and others, does not have a short-run bias may not be very useful practically if it is very difficult to estimate the future benefits to be derived from the project in cash-flow terms. There are at least two situations where this is likely to occur: (1) where the aim in making the investment is to be ready to take advantage of a development if it occurs, and (2) where the investment is in the latest technology.

In the first situation, the ideal, as suggested at the end of the previous section, is to produce a valuation of the chance of taking up a strategic option. Without a general market in such options, this is difficult. Nevertheless, the recognition that one is investing in a strategic option may help focus attention upon relevant matters. In particular, in this type of assessment it is important not just to think in terms of incremental cash flows above those *currently* being received, but also to bear in mind what the problems will be if no investment is undertaken. Declining the chance to invest may result in considerable losses through lack of maintaining competitive strengths in the industry. The base from which to measure incremental cash flows is then that position and not the current benefits being received. In such a situation an investment may be more in the nature of an insurance policy to protect existing business: a step to reduce uncertainty. Of course, not all strategic options are of that type, but, where they are, this approach may at least get one into the right position for estimating the cash benefits to compare with the investment outlay.

Investment in new technology has similar characteristics and the above approach may again be worth contemplating, but there are also other matters to watch for. First, the selection criterion should be NPV and not some arbitrary and very short payback period. Many companies still use incredibly short payback periods, often set by financial directors playing a very risk-averse game. Bearing in mind the notion of a portfolio spread of risk, directors do not have to be so risk-averse to all types of investment – especially where, with new technology, it may indicate the creation of an option to stay in business. Also, the discussion in chapters 1 and 2 about the nature of project betas is relevant. To the extent that the technological success is not highly correlated with the returns on the market portfolio, the project is not so risky for a well-diversified shareholder. Hence, the requirement for very large rates of return is not justified from a shareholder-wealth viewpoint. If DCF is to be criticized, it is not the technique which is wrong, but the setting of discount rates which over-discount the future. But this can only be put right by changing attitudes to risk aversion. The solution is more far-reaching than just changing a technique.

Investment in new technology has often been directed to achieving fairly tangible benefits: reductions in inventories, savings in space and production time, and improved reliability of the product. It should not be underestimated how important it still is to seek such benefits from investment in new methods. A chief executive of a major UK company who in a public speech stressed how far companies in his industry lagged behind the Japanese found, upon analysis, that the shortfall was almost all due to excessive holdings of assets. In comparison with the Japanese, UK companies often have somewhat larger profit margins, but then ROI is substantially less due to excessive fixed assets and work-in-progress and excessive investment lead times leading to more idle assets. This same executive said that he was against incrementalism in the sense that *major* reductions in assets (or increases in asset turnover) had to be achieved. Where new technology can be used in such a way to reduce assets and lead times, it should be possible to establish reliable measures of investment benefits.

Increasingly, however, the benefits of new technology are more related to providing a flexible manufaturing base – i.e. where product mixes can be rapidly changed with little human intervention and set-up costs are low. I recently visited a factory that produces heavy engineering goods. A flexible engineering system had been introduced after considerable debate about the worthwhileness of the investment. The investment was eventually approved on the basis that it would be possible to vary products quickly over six different types. Within two years of the investment the company, realizing that it could now offer customers more custom-built specifications, was producing a considerable range of products from the new machines. It believes that this has added greatly to its competitive position in the market. It is this last comment which provides the clue to the better definition (though not necessarily precise specification) of project cash flows. Large-scale investments should be supported if they have positive NPVs. They will be likely to have positive NPVs if they enhance product order-winning criteria which are related to a thorough analysis of competitive strengths and industry attractiveness – preferably using a clear model of the industry such as Porter (1985) proposes.

Kaplan and Atkinson (1989) address the problem of new-technology investment and suggest that benefits are split between the tangible and the difficult to define. If, they say, projects are not found acceptable purely on the basis of the tangible benefits, then it may be useful to turn around the investment question to ask what the present value of the benefits must be to justify the investment. This may, indeed, have some merit, but by itself it is not likely to help with decisions about major investments to keep up with the technological race. It is *vital* to set the estimated present value of the benefits within a carefully structured model of the likely changing scenarios of order-winning criteria as identified through a strategic analysis.

Simmonds (1987) and Bromwich and Bhimani (1989) also consider the problem of strategic-investment appraisal. Both recognize the need to trace the benefits of such investments on a range of market factors. It must be realized, however, that there are many factors which could be incorporated into most major investments of a strategic nature. A broad assessment of increased market share without an analysis of order-winning criteria is not good enough. General statements that investment appraisals should include data on, for example, product enhancement, diversification, risk reduction and increased internal benefits do little more than say that something new is needed. While the 'manufacturing critique' of DCF presented by Hill (1985) may be resisted as argued above, he is nevertheless correct in his fundamental message that assessment (of the cash flows) needs to be based on the degree to which order-winning criteria are enhanced. A checklist of *some* strategic factors which *may* be relevant is not good enough – the *appropriate* factors and their relative weights can only be determined through a conceptual model of the market place. The relevant factors to consider in investment appraisal are likely to be different for each product and can be determined only through a thorough understanding of the company's and industry's actual and specific situation. This can only be acquired through detailed knowledge of the technical nature of the product and the manufacturing process, knowledge of the economics of the relevant markets, and awareness of the complete value chain for the company's products and how investment will enhance each part. Without a conceptual model of the market place and the organization's possible place within it, general checklists of factors lack rigour and may simply make it easy for interested parties to emphasize different factors at different times, depending on their interests. As we shall see later, this may happen anyway, but, in so far as the financial analysis is meant to estimate the increase in value of the corporation to the shareholder, the system surely should do its best to meet that objective and to narrow the scope for obfuscating the effect upon shareholder wealth. If there are viewpoints to consider other than that of shareholders, they should be considered separately and with like rigour.

Similar criticism can be levied at the Multiple Attribute Decision Model (MADM) highlighted by Berliner and Brimson (1988, pp. 189–96). Examination of the model shows that managers are asked to form an objective function with numerical weights attached to critical success factors (there is no clear distinction between critical success factors and key result areas). Two projects are compared by means of weighting the following specific factors.

	Weights
Financial – qualitative	
NPV	20
Operating profit margin	25
Level of investment	5
Level of savings	5
Non-financial – quantitative	
Throughput time	7
Process yield	15
Schedule attainment	3
Lead time	5
Qualitative	
Process	5
Basic R&D	2
Technology obsolescence	5
Product obsolescence	3
	100

The values attached to these factors for the two projects are weighted and summed, with an adjustment reflecting the level of confidence in the estimates. The projects end up with scores of 250 and 215 respectively, and, hey presto, the project with the higher score is deemed the better. The pertinent question is what *theoretical* basis there is to such a model. It could be argued that the weights reflect the decision-makers' theory of investment desirability, but what theory could rate NPV $33\frac{1}{3}$ per cent more important than process yield and ten times as important as basic R&D? To estimate the effect upon shareholder wealth the criterion *is* NPV. One will probably need to consider many critical factors in order to develop cash-flow estimates to calculate an NPV, but those critical factors themselves will only be identifiable by developing an understanding of the market place. For this one needs to consider industry attractiveness and competitive strengths, taking into account short- and long-run customer needs, marketing strategies, *appropriately linked* technologies and R&D activities. The development of relevant critical factors needs to be based on a *properly sequenced series* of requirements leading logically to success in the market place and hence NPV. Moreover, the closer a company moves towards computer-integrated manufacture (CIM), the less possible will it find it to look at investments in isolation. Their position in the whole network of assets will need to be considered and how the total capacity contributes to strategic success. The company needs to know what the investment *must* achieve to produce goods which can be sold profitably. Vague weighting is inadequate! Models *can* be useful and have a part to play, *if* built on a sound theoretical basis. If reliable evaluations of strategic investments are required, there is no substitute for a thorough understanding of how to enhance the company's competitive situation in the market place. *General* checklists or weighting systems not based on such an understanding are likely to do more harm than good. Similarly, if investment appraisal is to rely upon more non-financial data, the logical link between those data and improved financial performance in the longer run should still be implicit and may well benefit from being made explicit. Such factors stand as *surrogate* factors for NPV in view of estimation difficulties. They are not *alternatives* to be balanced off against it.

Can more financial rigour be incorporated into portfolio-grid analysis?

The discussion in the preceding section has emphasized how insights from the corporate-strategy literature may help in arriving at a sensible assessment of individual project cash flows, and that models need to be based upon theories about market success. While fully believing in this, Marshall (1985) and Marshall and Tomkins (1988) have also explored the possibility of building a more direct link between corporate finance and strategic portfolio grids. Marshall raised the question of how one could go about drawing financial-value contours on a portfolio grid. Is it possible to make the policy advice derived from a portfolio grid more specific by incorporating into the grid increases in value?

It is very important to realise *exactly* what was intended in the analysis about to be described. We were *not* drawing DCF contours to represent a range of *different* strategic business units (SBUs) located on a portfolio grid. We were attempting to model the NPV effects of investment in *one* product (or one SBU) in *one* type of market situation at different stages of its life-cycle *as that one product/SBU moves around the matrix*. If this could be done for one product, it could be done for others with their own market strategies and situations. In due course, perhaps, these might be combined to provide a 'harder' quantification of a multi-SBU portfolio grid, although we have not progressed that far. Indeed, we fully recognize that the model about to be discussed is only suggestive of one avenue of development and is not conclusive.

A hypothetical product for which a cost-leadership strategy is being employed was assumed. While the exercise about to be described was a theoretical model, not an empirical test, its results indicate that positive NPV opportunities probably do exist in some 'cash cows' and that an integration of DCF and portfolio-grid analyses may lead to a more careful and sophisticated use of portfolio grids. The model offered is *not* a general model. It essentially takes one of the simplest situations possible. It is intended to illustrate the broad direction in which modelling *might* be developed to build bridges between financial and strategic analysis. Much more sophisticated models will be needed in the more complex situations met in practice.

Marshall wondered, first, whether NPVs for investment *to increase market share* would always be positive or negative as might be inferred from the BCG matrix. Note that the focus was on investment to *increase* market share, not just to retain a market position. The inferences for NPV taken from the BCG literature are as shown in figure 6.1. (See Marshall and Tomkins, 1988, for a justification of this inferred BCG pattern in relation to investment to improve market share). The BCG matrix was chosen because it had clearly measurable axes for hypothetical examples, which is not the case for the McKinsey–GE matrix. The simplicity of the BCG assumptions was recognized, without forgetting the need for a more rigorously derived conceptual model of the market. The analysis simply took the BCG framework as given to see what results would be obtained. The framework may be simple with its emphasis on market share and the experience curve, but it is a model with a logical basis related to what is needed in order to be successful.

It was then decided to hypothesize a particular market situation *for a single product line* and ascertain whether investment to increase market share at different stages of that product's life would have positive or negative NPVs. The BCG matrix has a vertical axis labelled 'Market rate of growth' which never goes negative (i.e. never moves into the declining phase of the life-cycle), as noted in chapter 4. Hence, Marshall pointed out that one could simply use years from 1 upwards in the ascending part of the life-cycle as an index of a falling growth rate. (See, for example, the vertical axis of Figure 6.2.) In addition it was decided to calculate NPVs for further investment in the hypothetical product for

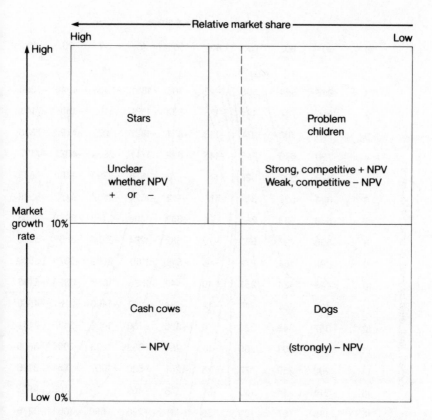

Figure 6.1 NPV by quadrant with respect to investment in increased market share (*Note.* Quadrant NPVs are only those related to investment in *increased* market share)

each year according to a range of assumptions about the initial market share held – shares from 10 to 90 per cent, with separate calculations for each 10 per cent. (See the horizontal axis of Figure 6.2.)

The market situation posited was similar to that described in the example of table 5.2: a company was attempting complete market dominance through a cost-leadership strategy. That strategy would be enforced by a limit-pricing procedure which would only allow the rival a zero NPV. On the assumption of a two-firm market and that a rival would not enter the market if it faced zero NPV, NPVs were calculated for investment by the price-setting firm based on the limit prices needed to prevent the rival from entering the market and the cost levels that could be achieved by moving down the experience curve. The main

N	90	80	70	60	50	40	30	20	10
			Star				'?'		
1	947	884	538	-23	-795	-1801	-3105	-4840	-7360
2	845	767	424	-125	-882	-1874	-3168	-4904	-7443
3	776	700	374	-148	-871	-1827	-3087	-4798	-7336
4	720	649	346	-145	-829	-1741	-2954	-4621	-7137
5	670	607	327	-171	-773	-1636	-2796	-4408	-6883
6	624	529	312	-112	-712	-1524	-2624	-4173	-6589
7	579	533	298	-91	-647	-1406	-2443	-3920	-6263
8	536	497	285	-70	-582	-1284	-2254	-3652	-5908
9	492	461	272	-60	-512	-1160	-2059	-3370	-5523
10	448	424	257	-40	-449	-1035	-1857	-3073	-5108
11	403	385	240	-12	-384	-907	-1450	-2761	-4660
12	357	345	222	3	-320	-780	-1438	-2436	-4181
13	310	303	200	16	-259	-653	-1223	-2099	-3669
14	262	259	177	25	201	-529	-1007	-1754	-3126
15	214	214	150	31	-148	-409	-794	-1405	-2558
16	165	167	121	33	-101	-298	-590	-1061	-1976
17	118	121	90	30	-62	-197	-401	-732	-1397
18	72	75	58	23	-31	-112	-234	-434	-848
19	32	34	27	12	10	-45	-97	-184	-367
			Cow				Dog		

Market share

Growth (indicated by years of product life-cycle)

Experience curve 75 per cent: discount rate 15 per cent

Figure 6.2   Illustration of imposing DCF contours on the BCG matrix

table produced from Marshall's study showed NPVs as in figure 6.2. These were calculated with both companies facing 75 per cent experience curves and discount rates of 15 per cent. Interestingly, the dividing line between positive and negative NPV in figure 6.2 coincides exactly with the BCG division between 'stars' and '?s' ('problem children'), and between 'cash cows' and 'dogs' (see Hedley, 1977). More importantly, however, there is, in figure 6.2, no natural dividing line between 'stars' and 'cash cows' or between '?s' and 'dogs'. Certainly positive NPVs are larger in 'stars' than in 'cash cows', but there is a gradual shading-down. There is some profitable investment for increasing market share in 'cash cows'. This is consistent with some critiques of the use of portfolio grids as discussed in chapter 4.

Of course, the NPVs obtained derive from the assumptions made. Given the market position posited, successfully excluding rivals early in the life-cycle obviously gives a longer-term prospect of profits and a higher NPV. But, despite the few years remaining, there is still some positive NPV for investment late in the cycle (strictly at the end of the upward stage of the life-cycle), because prices can be increased given the cost advantage over rivals gained through accumulated experience.

Now consider the right-hand side of figure 6.2. A firm with a lower market share than its rival would be foolish to try to play the game of cost leadership through the experience-curve effect. With its low market share it has higher costs than the rival, and so, by pricing to give its rival a zero NPV, it can only earn a negative NPV itself. With the example described in figure 6.2, a company needs to achieve a 60 per cent market share before the cost-leadership strategy proves advantageous. The '?s' have more negative NPVs than 'dogs', because they bear negative profits for more years.

Also, it is clear that the results of the situation modelled in figure 6.2 challenge the BCG's interpretations from an application of the very tests and logic (the experience curve) underlying the development of the BCG matrix itself. The BCG is only partly right, even on *its own* assumptions. Market situations can arise where the inferred investment directives of the BCG matrix are misleading. The results do not mean that the bottom left quadrants are not cash cows. But, while they are cash cows, some further investment in them is worthwhile (in the example tested).

The finding about '?s' also raises problems for the BCG. How can investment be encouraged there with such negative NPVs? The answer is simple: investment in '?s' may be justified if a generic strategy of *differentiation* is pursued. In the type of market situation examined here, it cannot be justified if a cost-leadership policy *based on a belief in the experience curve* is pursued. That, however, leaves the BCG with a problem, because the logic of its matrix is based on cost leadership through the experience curve. On these grounds, it should not have identified '?s' as possibilities for investment. Our analysis therefore suggests that portfolio grids might yield different strategic advice for specific locations on the grid according to the market situation and the type of generic strategy to be followed.

The reader may justifiably feel uneasy with all this. It is obvious to ask whether these results are not simply those obtained in this particular numerical example. The answer is partly 'yes', but that does not invalidate what we were trying to do. Marshall (1985) had already carried out a range of sensitivity tests, and had found, for example, that varying the discount rate from 0 to 30 per cent only shifted the break-even market share at time $N = 1$ from 50 to 70 per cent. The major shift was caused when the two rivals were allowed to have *markedly* different experience curves, but this is unlikely in practice unless one has discovered markedly better practices for continual cost reduction. These tests indicated no reason to doubt our basic conclusion: that the BCG is only partly correct even on its own assumptions. Moreover, our 1988 study shows that these results using NPV bear some similarity to empirical findings from PIMS studies (see chapter 4) where profitability has been related to market share.

Despite all this, it is obviously necessary to avoid a naïve interpretation of figure 6.2. Reference to the original work with its full specification of assumptions is essential. Also, it needs to be stressed that the McKinsey–GE matrix or a Porter analysis allows for *different* key characteristics to represent market attractiveness and competitive strengths according to the nature of the SBU and the market in which it is located. A test based on a *single* product at different stages of its life-cycle does not attempt to deal with that situation. Nevertheless, this test does demonstrate how one particular market situation can be modelled on the basis of prescribed strategic assumptions and DCF contours placed on the portfolio grid. This is a tentative, *very tentative* step towards injecting more rigour into strategic portfolio analysis, using modelling to integrate financial analysis and concepts from one of the generic competitive strategies. If other, more complex situations can be modelled, it may be possible to gain insights into how financial, strategic and industrial-economics concepts may be fitted together, not just to explain general market tendencies, as the PIMS studies do, but to provide direct advice to business managers in *specific* markets with *specific* competitive strengths. Such analyses might indicate, for example, which competitive weaknesses, if removed, are likely to bring about the largest increase in NPV; how much market share needs to be increased in different SBU locations to provide an adequate NPV; whether this is easier in some locations than in others; and the degree to which some markets are more attractive than others in terms of potential NPV.

All we really claim is that such models may be useful in helping managers assess *how much* the value of the firm might be increased through investment in alternative locations on the portfolio grid. The inputs to the model would need extensive debate in practice. Similarly, its relationship and relative priority to models for other SBUs would need debate. In this test, the portfolio grid was not used to model the whole of a corporate group. Furthermore, I have long borne this in mind:

> The major strategic decisions in a corporation are seldom taken by its directors or senior executives referring to a mathematical algorithm to suppress judgement. Rather they rely not only to some extent upon judgement and intuition about the future, but also upon personal negotiations and bargaining between the executives, who may be competing with each other for scarce resources and may each be supporting their case with OR and economic models. A planning process which fails to accept this . . . is unlikely to be of much use in the realities of business life.
>
> (Wagle and Jenkins, 1971, p. 39)

Accordingly, we would see our modelling approach as an input to corporate debates over resource allocation, not as a provider of prescriptive advice. This theme is developed further in chapter 8.

A further point of interest arises from this analysis in respect of the use of DCF. Earlier in this chapter it was argued that the use of DCF was justified on pragmatic as well as theoretical grounds because it provides a single index of value and avoids the necessity for comparing streams of cash flows. Imagine the complexity of trying to produce an analysis like that in figure 6.2 if one had no calculus for reducing projected streams to single-value indices. If it proves possible to develop useful modelling links between financial and strategic analyses, DCF will be a device for simplifying and summarizing – quite apart from its theoretical justification.

The cost of capital in strategic analysis

Another role for the finance specialist in relation to strategy has to do with the cost of funds. Corporate-strategy literature rarely works through such issues carefully and this can be especially important when considering global strategies. For example, Prowse (1986) provides a comparison of the cost of funds in Japan, West Germany, the United Kingdom and the United States. He demonstrates that funds are unusually cheap in Japan. Understanding international competitors' behaviour may depend crucially on understanding the way they finance their business.

We saw in chapter 1 how single projects should be evaluated using the adjusted present value (APV) method when sources of finance are linked with specific projects. Such finance and investment interdependencies are also important at the more general strategic level. It will not be very helpful to designate a foreign division a 'cash cow' if it is located in a part of the world from which it is impossible to remit funds. Similarly foreign-exchange and political risks and their relationship to required returns on investment need a proper evaluation as determinants of market attractiveness. Too often finance texts see such finance analyses as separate activities related more to individual project appraisal and not integrated into broader strategic analysis. Finance experts have a clear role to play, along with accountants, in improving the specification of market attractiveness and competitive strengths.

It was made very clear in chapter 1 that, in determining the yields required on investment, it is possible to formulate the required rate of return according to the level of the corporate group addressed. That is, it is possible to use the capital asset pricing model (CAPM) to determine the rate of return that shareholders require on the whole corporate group, or from specific divisions or individual projects. The relevant level of focus for strategic portfolio analysis is the yield required by different SBUs.

For the moment assume that one may treat SBUs and divisions as identical; this assumption will be relaxed shortly. Chapter 1 showed that the required return for any SBU depends upon the covariance of that SBU's projected returns with projected movements in the market index. Note that the required yield should depend upon the *projected* covariance and that the finance literature usually uses historic data as the only available data upon which to base an assessment of the future covariance. It was also stated that, even at the level of explaining security returns, CAPM tests using historic data have not been terribly successful.

Some well-informed practitioners are highly sceptical of the reliability of corporate betas based on historical data. Weaver (1989) says, 'When you plot Hershey's excess return versus the market's excess returns, our betas are not necessarily statistically significant from zero and the correlation factors are anywhere from 0.2 to 0.3. . . . I'm not willing to bet my career on that type of correlation' (p. 24). It seems appropriate, therefore, to search for a way of specifying required yields which does not rely exclusively upon historic data.

When attempting to specify the market attractiveness of *strategic* options, the finance theorist may find it even more difficult to use his conventional CAPM approach for determining a particular divisional beta and cost of capital using historic relationships. The nature of the strategic movement itself may render the company's past experience of little relevance. Of course, there may be historic data available from outside the corporate group which can be used to help formulate the required yield for a new area that the group is entering, but suppose that this is not the situation. Suppose that the strategy involves real innovation – not only for the group but for the whole industry. Isn't this what the core of strategic thinking is all about? How does one arrive at the required covariance then? An approach described by Gup and Norwood (1982) may offer the basis of the method needed, even though they were not attempting to push their analysis as far as that implied here. It is interesting to note that Weaver's company (1989) also used a version of this method.

Gup and Norwood (1982) describe an approach for developing the divisional cost of capital used in Fuqua Industries Inc. This method attempted to combine CAPM principles with other forms of business-risk information. Fuqua Industries first estimated the cost of capital for the corporate group using CAPM principles and then modified it for a division by reference to fourteen key risk elements. Each division was assessed on each of these fourteen risk elements and compared, element by element, with the corresponding assessments made for the group as a whole. In this way a risk index was formed showing whether the division was relatively more or less risky than the corporate group as a whole, and the group CAPM-based yield was modified on a divisional basis. Several comments are in order.

To begin with, it is clear from chapter 1 that the CAPM does *not* require any comparison between the divisional risks and the risk of the corporate group as a whole. The divisional cost-of-capital risk premium depends upon the covariance between divisional returns and market-index returns. On that score the Fuqua approach may be criticized. Nevertheless, it is interesting to note that the risk elements used by Fuqua are very similar to some of the elements one might expect to see in a strategic analysis of market attractiveness and competitive strengths. By incorporating such strategic factors into the cost of capital calculation for a division, Fuqua Industries might at least suggest a more theoretically sound way of assessing the required divisional rate of return. What is required is a divisional risk premium based upon a clear specification of the key strategic factors which will determine how the *projected* returns for this division are likely to vary with movements in the economy as a whole. These key strategic factors ought to be observable from a thorough analysis of market attractiveness and competitive strengths. It will be extremely difficult to determine this statistically, and a judgemental basis for assessment of the required yield will be necessary. At least, however, the judgement will be based on the relevant *future* covariance, which seems vital where innovative strategic activity is involved. In any case, as we saw in chapter 1, considerable judgement is involved in assessing sub-group betas even where a more conventional statistical approach is employed.

In the Fuqua case there does not appear to have been any problem of divisional interdependence, but this will not always be the case. The problem may not, however, be as difficult as it seems. Once major strategies have been set, they are likely to be held for some time. Hence, one may be able to work out the broad effect of interdependencies once and for all when the strategy is set. The required yield from the division may then be stable for long periods, apart from variations in the level of interest rates generally.

The interdependence problem may also be less severe when one reintroduces the distinction between the cost of capital for a division and the cost for an SBU. It is the latter one really needs for strategic analysis. Given that a very precise and reliable estimate of a required yield is unattainable anyway, the problems of both interdependence and estimation of covariances from key factors may be less severe if financial analysts work with the more homogeneous SBU as the unit of classification, rather than with a division which may contribute to various corporate business activities. Perhaps companies should never seek *divisional* costs of capital but should have several different rates to apply to different *businesses*. Finance theorists may be able to develop more reliable costs of capital by using the strategic concept of an SBU. Research is also needed in this area.

It has just been argued that a thorough analysis of the market attractiveness and competitive strengths of an SBU (possibly based upon a Porter analysis), should provide more insight into the future covariability of the SBU and total market returns. This would be essential information for a CAPM approach to estimating the cost of capital for an SBU. It may, however, just be worth recalling the Arbitrage Pricing Theory (APT) model. If Roll and Ross (1984) are right that there are only four basic economic forces, and that these are the four forces listed in chapter 1, then estimation of an SBU's required yield could be attempted by examining the likely sensitivity of the projected SBU returns with just these factors (inflation, aggregate production, risk premia and the term structure of interest rates). This may be easier than using the CAPM approach. It would, however, be hazardous to rely upon these four factors while the theory remains unproven.

The conclusion reached on the relationship between the cost of capital and strategic portfolio analysis is, therefore, that there is a need to incorporate far more rigorous financial knowledge into the assessment of an SBU's position in respect of both market attractiveness and competitive position. It is equally important, however, to use the basic analysis underlying the location of an SBU on the matrix in order to improve subjective assessments of required SBU yields. Wensley (1981) says that management must decide how much effort should be exerted on CAPM compared to the strategic analysis of competitive advantage, but the position adopted here is that the two concepts are related and that effort on one ought to improve understanding of the other, even if little research on such matters has yet been performed. Wensley also raises issues about the level of focus in resource allocation – project versus SBU analysis. These will be addressed in chapter 8.

Diversification and capital-rationing

In addition to the matter of required rates of return for shareholders and the relevance of DCF, the earlier strategic analysis gives finance theorists a number of other points to ponder.

It will be recalled first that the theory-of-finance specification of how to maximize shareholders' wealth does not refer to any need for *corporate* diversification. The shareholder takes care of his (or her) own risk-spreading needs by investing in a mix of different securities. He will need to be informed about new strategic departures and their effects upon the covariance between corporate and market-index returns so that he can alter the portfolio held if the risk–return mix is not the one desired; but *corporate* diversification to manage total risk is not required by the shareholder.

It has sometimes been suggested to me that the portfolio-matrix approach is inconsistent with finance theory because it balances investment over different businesses and this is inconsistent with the finance-theory view of the irrelevance of corporate diversification. This is a puzzling argument. The portfolio matrix *could* be used to focus on different risk–return combinations and to develop a corporate mixed risk–return portfolio, but there is absolutely nothing inherent in the McKinsey–GE model which says that this is what a portfolio grid is meant to achieve. The concept of a portfolio contained in SBU analysis is quite different from that used in finance or investment theory. It is *not* the corporate equivalent of an individual's investment portfolio. The only connection between SBUs, assuming largely separate SBUs can be defined, is that the cash flows from some are used to finance investment in others. There is no attempt in strategic portfolio grids to measure covariances of returns between different SBUs. If corporate diversification were relevant, it might be a good idea to try to do this, but corporate strategic portfolio analysis does *not* consider it. Consequently, there is no unavoidable contradiction between strategic portfolio-grid analysis and finance theory due to corporate diversification.

There is, in contrast, a potential conflict between strategic matrices and finance theory if the former are assumed to imply a fairly rigid capital-rationing situation such that the only funds available for investment are the cash throw-offs from SBUs in the matrix. It was argued in chapter 4, however, that there is no reason why portfolio matrices should be interpreted in that way. A looser interpretation in terms of those SBUs to be managed for future growth, perhaps with the help of external finance, and those managed for cash surpluses now, perhaps to service debt repayment or dividends, is quite consistent with both the strategic grids and financial theory. Nevertheless, as Wensley (1981) argues, the portfolio grids must not be used to suggest to non-financial experts that the company must be a cash recycling machine ignoring the external market as a source of funds.

On the other hand, the standard position of finance theorists that hard capital-rationing doesn't really exist, because funds can always be raised where prospects are good, needs to be softened. It will be impractical, for example, to go to the market too often for new equity or to get the debt–equity ratio too far out of line. Similarly, changing dividend policy to yield more cash for investment needs to be handled with care. Thus, many companies commonly face a short-run form of 'soft rationing'. In such a situation it may be appropriate to think of restricting development of some SBUs – not to a specific amount of investment each year, but to a projected rate of development consistent with internal funds generated by the whole company over a period of years. The strategic matrices may well be seen to represent this looser form of capital-rationing and balanced development, but, interpreted in this way, there seems to be no violent conflict with practical corporate finance. Indeed, Bromiley's results (Bromiley, 1986) suggest that soft rationing and the need to manage a well-balanced programme of growth is a predominant mangement concern in practice. Weaver (1989) also provides some support for this view.

Just as companies must not overlook the market as a source of funds, so they should avoid getting locked into the idea that they must invest their own cash surpluses. Corporate diversification may often be due to a sense of needing to use up cash surpluses, rather than risk-spreading. Given the very patchy record of companies that have diversified into areas not related to their existing businesses or not requiring similar managment skills, corporate managers ought always to bear in mind the option of planned divestment of inevitable dinosaurs with a view to returning cash to shareholders (see Lorenz, 1988). To repeat, portfolio matrices imply nothing to contradict this, but, if they are viewed by non-financially oriented people as models of cash-balancing having nothing to do wtih the financial market, they will be used in a way that the theory of finance would judge inappropriate.

There is obviously a marked difference between the strategic and finance approaches, but they are not mutually exclusive: the one is strong where the other is weak. Hence, there is real scope for integrating the two forms of analysis. Corporate-strategy models are strong at specifying the cash flows by reference to key strategic factors, but weak at assessing the impact upon the valuation of the firm. The finance approach is weak at assessing future cash flows, but says 'give me the cash estimates and I will tell you how that affects the shareholders' risk positions and hence the market value of the company'. The two approaches not only can, but *should*, be brought together. (Peavy, 1984, arrives at similar conclusions, though his arguments have a different emphasis.)

Market valuation and strategic analysis

Earlier in this chapter a tentative attempt was made to integrate DCF, the notion of generic strategies, and interpretations of portfolio-grid locations. The objective was, however, to search for ways of modelling to improve the rigour of strategic analysis. There is also a role for the finance specialists in trying to test relationships between strategic data and corporate performance. PIMS, for example, tries to evaluate the effect of market share on ROI. This is not the same as assessing its impact on the value of the company, although it makes some attempt to do this, as will be described shortly. Ultimately, it is increases in the market value of shares which interests shareholders; hence financial specialists used to researching determinants of market returns might extend their work to incorporate the contents of data bases such as PIMS.

Little work has so far been done to link strategic possibilities with share valuations. Graham (1982) supports such efforts and explores, through PIMS, the relationship between the excess of actual returns on equity over required yields and the excess of market value over book value. He plots companies in the same industry on a cross-section basis to obtain a valuation curve like that shown in figure 6.3.

Graham's results are not very surprising at a conceptual level. All he has done is to show, in a crude way, that, in order to increase the market value of the firm, one needs to identify opportunities where actual

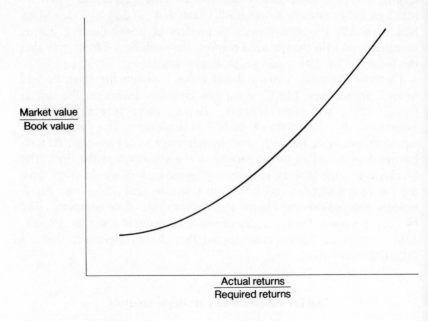

Figure 6.3   Assessing the impact on the market value of the company

returns exceed those required for the risk involved! While financial managers address this question more directly, using the appropriate cost of capital to show how different strategies will increase the market value of the company, Graham does seem to demonstrate that the market does value returns in excess of a required yield allowing for risk.

Readers are also referred back to figure 5.1 and the Bogue and Buffa V-curve. Instead of showing operating margin on the vertical axis, the financial analyst might use the market value of the company (scaled for size) and, possibly, market share on the horizontal axis. This would then test Porter's generic strategies against shareholder value. None of these ideas are very complex, but the search for such relationships between share valuations and strategic data might yield fruitful results for managerial purposes.

A further step in the direction of linking market valuations with strategic concepts has been taken by Buzzell and Chussil (1985), as briefly discussed in chapter 4. Using the PIMS data base, they measured the performance of almost 200 business units over an eight-year period. They measured long-term performance by adding the DCF over a projected five-year period to the discounted future market value

(DFMV) of the unit at the end of that period. The DFMV was derived using the results of the Strategic Planning Institute studies explaining corporate market-value/book-value ratios. These ratios were found to be mainly associated with recent returns on equity, growth rates and debt/equity ratios. Using these relationships, Buzzell and Chussil obtained data on the business-unit ROIs, growth rates and debt/equity ratios to provide notional business-unit market-value/book-value ratios. These ratios were then applied to business-unit book values to obtain notional market values. Hence DCF + DFMV gave a measure of actual performance. In the PIMS book, Buzzell and Gale (1987) say that this measure of performance was highly correlated with five-year averages for accounting ROIs.

Actual performance needed, however, to be evaluated against potential performance given the units' position in the market at the beginning of the five-year period. To obtain a measure of potential performance, Buzzell and Chussil selected 'look-alike' businesses from the PIMS data base, split them between 'winners' and 'losers', and then assumed that the potential performance of each business in the study was mapped by a gradual increase from its initial ROI up to that achieved by the 'winners' by the end of the period.

The results of these calculations indicated that the mean level of performance was only 38 per cent – i.e. actual performance divided by potential performance was only 0.38. It was also found that businesses with strong initial positions outperformed those with weak initial positions. Businesses in the decline phase of their life-cycle achieved only 30 per cent of potential performance.

The implication of all this is not only that weak businesses do worse in absolute terms, but that they do not even realize their own potential. This may, say Buzzell and Chussil, be because businesses are using portfolio analysis too simplistically and not perceiving the remaining potential of 'cash cows' and 'dogs'. For our purposes, it does not really matter exactly what the results of the study were. It was a heroic effort to try to evaluate business units using some notion of market valuation. Much more research is needed in this area, and it is mostly likely to be successful if finance theorists and corporate strategists collaborate.

Summary

The main purpose of this chapter has been to indicate that there is considerable scope for both academic research and practice-oriented analysis of the possible interrelationships between financial management and strategic portfolio analysis. Some of the ideas offered are highly speculative; this reflects the newness of the area of study. There does, however, seem to be some merit in attempting to bring into strategic analysis the finance analyst's tools of valuation, in order to produce a more rigorous consideration of market attractiveness, competitive strengths and the effects of movements of SBUs around the matrix. The objective would be to demonstrate more clearly how to increase the value of the company.

This search for increased value would probably need to be subject to constraints reflecting 'soft rationing' and the need for balanced growth, which are already implicit within strategic portfolio analysis. A series of SBU grids, with one for each year over the next five to ten years, might provide the basis for modelling resource uses and sources in order to plan balanced development to avoid financial distress. Instead of showing the impact of a single additional project, the accounting figures might need analysis over different SBUs so that the impact of variations in their rates of strategic development could be explored.

Also, just as the finance analyst's tools may bring more rigour to strategic considerations, the developments in strategic thinking can help to prevent the financial analyst or modeller from applying his tools to unreliable data. It seems there really is merit in more cross-disciplinary collaboration in this area.

References

Berliner, C. and Brimson, J. 1988: *Cost Management for Today's Advanced Manufacturing*. Cambridge, Mass.: Harvard Business School Press.

Brennan, M. and Schwartz, E. 1986: A new approach to evaluating natural resource investments. In J. Stern and D. Chew (eds), *The Revolution in Corporate Finance*, Oxford: Basil Blackwell.

Bromiley, P. 1986: *Corporate Capital Investment: a behavioural approach*. Cambridge: Cambridge University Press.

Bromwich, M. and Bhimani, A. 1989: *Strategic Investment Appraisal*. London School of Economics, Discussion Papers in Accounting and Finance, 1989/1.

Buzzell, R. and Chussil, M. 1985: Managing for tomorrow. *Sloan Management Review*, Summer.

Buzzell, R. and Gale, B. 1987: *The PIMS Principles: linking strategy to performance*. New York: Collier Macmillan.

Finnie, J. 1988: The role of the financial approach in decisions to acquire advanced manufacturing technology. *Accounting and Business Research*, 18, no. 70.

Graham, M. 1982: Capital market models and their implications for strategy formulation. In T. Naylor (ed.), *Corporate Strategy*, Amsterdam: North Holland.

Gup, B. and Norwood III, S. 1982: Divisional cost of capital: a practical approach. *Financial Management*, Spring.

Hayes, R. and Garvin, D. 1982: Managing as if tomorrow mattered. *Harvard Business Review*, May–June.

Hedley, B. 1977: Strategy and the business portfolio. *Long Range Planning*, 10 (February).

Hill, T. 1985: *Managing Strategy*. London: Macmillan.

Hodder, J. 1986: Evaluation of manufacturing investments: a comparison of US and Japanese practices. *Financial Management*, Spring.

Hodder, J. and Riggs, H. 1985. Pitfalls in evaluating risky projects. *Harvard Business Review*, January–February.

Kaplan, R. and Atkinson, A. 1989: *Advanced Management Accounting*, 2nd edn. Englewood Cliffs, NJ: Prentice-Hall.

Logue, D. 1981: Some thoughts on corporate investment strategy and pure strategic investments. In F. Derkinderen and R. Crum (eds), *Readings in Strategy for Corporate Investment*, London: Pitman.

Lorenz, C. 1988: Divest, diversify or die, Lombard column, *Financial Times*, 2 September.

Marshall, P. 1985: The Experience Curve and Limit Pricing as a means of Integrating Portfolio Matrices into Capital Budgeting. PhD dissertation, University of Bath.

Marshall, P and Tomkins, C. 1988: Incorporating DCF contours onto a BCG portfolio matrix using limit pricing. *Managerial and Decision Economics*, 9.

Peavy III, J. 1984: Modern financial theory, corporate strategy and public policy: another perspective. *Academy of Management Review*, 9, no. 1 (January).

Porter, M. 1985: *Competitive Advantage*. New York: Collier Macmillan.

Prowse, M. 1986: The key to competitiveness. *Financial Times*, 28 October.

Roll, R. and Ross, S. 1984: The Arbitrage Pricing Theory approach to strategic portfolio planning. *Financial Analysts Journal*, May–June.

Simmonds, K. 1987: The accounting assessment of competitive position. In J. Arnold, R. Scapens and D. Cooper (eds), *Management Accounting: expanding the horizons*, vol. 3, London: Chartered Institute of Management Accounting.

Tomkins, C. 1973: *Financial Planning in Divisionalized Companies*. Englewood Cliffs, NJ: Prentice-Hall.

Tsurumi, Y. and H. 1985: Value-added maximizing behavior of Japanese firms and roles of corporate investment and finance. *Columbia Journal of World Business*, Spring.

Wagle, B. and Jenkins, P. 1971: *The Development of a General Computer System to Aid the Corporate Planning Process*. Peterlee, Co. Durham: IBM.

Weaver, S. C., Clemmens, P., Gunn, J. and Dannenburg, B. 1989: Divisional hurdle rates and the cost of capital. *Financial Management*, 18, no. 1 (Spring).

Wensley, R. 1981: Strategic marketing: betas, boxes or basics. *Journal of Marketing*, 45 (Summer).

Discussion questions

6.1   DCF is merely one way of recognizing the cost of funds. Even the Japanese would be foolish to take investment decisions ignoring that money has a cost. Discuss.

6.2   Discuss the problems involved in evaluating proposals to invest in new manufacturing developments such as just-in-time (JIT), flexible manufacturing systems (FMS) or computer-integrated manufacturing (CIM).

6.3   Evaluate Engwall's Multiple Attribute Decision Model (MADM).

6.4   Strategic portfolio matrices are weak at showing how different strategies increase the value of the company, whereas finance theory is strong at making such valuations. To what extent might it be possible, through modelling, to integrate value contours onto portfolio grids? What are the difficulties to be overcome if this is to be developed beyond the simple illustration presented in this chapter?

6.5   A thorough strategic analysis can provide just the information needed to assess an SBU's beta on the basis of the future, rather than historic preformance of that SBU. Discuss and consider what practical difficulties might arise in constructing such forward-looking betas.

7

Organizational Behaviour and Strategic Investment Decisions

The first six chapters of this book have all focused upon the financial and economic analysis underlying major investment decisions. It has been tacitly assumed that someone, somewhere in an organization collates economic facts and integrates them through a rigorous form of evaluation, so that decisions become almost self-evident provided only that the decision-makers realize that no one can make perfect predictions and that some allowance for uncertainties is needed. Investment decisions, at least those of significance and substance, are not made in that way within large organizations. Many persons get involved in the process and have different parts to play. It is therefore most important that students of accounting and economics should see their tools and techniques within the organizational context in which they will have to be used. In general, accounting and economic literature has only begun to do this relatively recently. Accordingly, this chapter will attempt to provide a consideration of key matters which describe the organizational context of investment decision-making and the process of managing the changes associated with major investments or strategic moves.

Multi-disciplinary perspectives of organizational life

As soon as one says that one is going to study organizational life – indeed, any aspect of human life – one runs up against the problem of what lens to use to view the scene. Pennings (1985) is one of the few who has attempted to investigate strategic decision-making taking this simple fact into account. He did this by inviting experts in various fields to contribute economic, political, sociological and anthropological and psychological perspectives on the strategy-formulation process. In summing up his 500-page book Pennings says,

> Rational model advocates are inclined to emphasize economic-perform-
> ance criteria when they pursue research on organizational strategies. They

ignore non-economic criteria, or relegate them to a perfunctory treatment
of 'corporate social responsibility'. . . . The . . . economic-orientated
literature has formed an imagery of the firm . . . that is an organizational
caricature. The profound neglect of psychological, social and political
considerations renders such treatments shallow and incomplete.

(p. 485)

With such an indictment and such a challenge in terms of the variety of
disciplinary insights needed, the reader may well wonder at this stage
whether one brief chapter can even begin to make any impact on this
question. In terms of starkly original insights, the answer is certainly
'no', but I hope that the critical review of non-accounting, non-
economic literature offered here will help those involved in finance and
accounting to gain an overview of theories related to investment and
strategic decisions in organizational life without extensive study of all
the disciplines mentioned.

Of course, many readers will already have studied some aspects of
these other disciplines as well as accounting and finance. This chapter
may stimulate them to contribute to the effort of welding together
insights from different disciplines, rather than, as the majority of
students seem to do, keeping their finance lenses firmly in place when
reading finance texts and then changing to sociological lenses when
reading sociology. Perhaps that is the fault of the examination system.
As indicated later in this chapter, a strong vehicle for changing
behaviour is a change in the reward system.

Organizational structures and roles

Various writers in the late 1950s and 1960s began to move understanding of the investment process in companies away from the strict
neoclassical economic perspective. March and Simon (1958) emphasized that both organizational pressures and lack of information charac-
terize decision-making under uncertainty in organizations. Dean (1951)
stressed the difference between incremental investments and major
additions to the corporate stock of assets. Chandler (1965) demonstrated the link between product diversity and the degree of integration
in the organization structure. All of these provided the basis for
questioning what actually goes on in resource-allocation processes, but a
major step forward came with the work of Bower (1970) and Ackerman
(1970).

These studies independently suggested that, irrespective of whether a
company is more or less integrated in structure, different levels of the
organization have distinct roles in investment decision-making. (Invest-

ments here, as throughout this book, are taken to be significant investments and not just minor replacements of facilities.) Bower and Ackerman's findings may be summarized in the form of figure 7.1, which shows that most investment proposals of any scale or significance are identified at the level of the product line or department. If the divisional managment is convinced, it then takes on the duty of providing impetus and promoting the project through the corporation. Final approval is, however, reserved for decision-making at group headquarters. To repeat: the discussion is about investments which the group sees to be significant. All major companies have rules which permit investments below a certain scale to be undertaken at divisional level without head-office approval. The discussion is also about general patterns of behaviour. Obviously some major initiatives (e.g. mergers) can come from board level.

Ackerman found that, where companies were more integrated in structure, the project was defined to some extent at divisional level and promoted to some degree at head-office level, but the general pattern

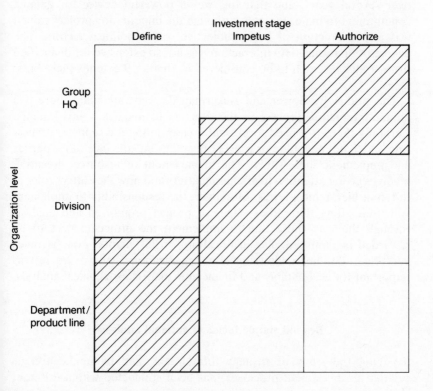

Figure 7.1 Who does what in the investment process

was the progression through the organization indicated in figure 7.1. Projects were evaluated in detail at divisional level. Head office reviewed those proposals on the basis of financial criteria, but also looked for 'strategic fit'. An interesting subsidiary finding was the head-office attitudes to risk assessment described by one interviewee:

> If we're familiar with a project . . . we can rely more heavily on our interpretation of the division's analysis to evaluate it. However, if we're dealing with an unfamiliar area . . . we'll examine the assumptions and market studies more closely *while the analysis is being done*.
>
> (Ackerman, 1970, p. 346)

This suggests that, instead of a once-and-for-all decision at the end of the analysis, there may be a process of evaluation that develops with the project, and that decisions and analyses are not undertaken without consideration of prior experience.

Ackerman also found that in integrated firms there was a great deal of divisional–HQ interaction over significant investments, often extending over several years, and that this was a powerful device for gaining commitment to major projects, although the impetus any project gained was also a function of fairly subjective, often political factors. The degree of divisional–HQ interaction was not so extensive for diversified firms. Later research to be considered in chapter 9 extends these basic ideas.

The studies by Bower and Ackerman demonstrated that there is a human-interaction process in the decision to make key investments. Certainly there is a need to present a case, lobby for support, orchestrate a debate, negotiate or prevent negotiation, convince other parties and implement successfully. The management of resource allocation involves giving attention to all these matters and how they affect roles at different hierarchical levels. Moreover, the responsibility to implement will itself affect the earlier stages of project promotion and analysis through the way those due to implement the project expect to be rewarded or punished. The justification for this chapter now becomes very clear. Studies addressing how organizations behave are just as important for accountants and financial managers as technical analysis.

Beyond simple forms of rational analysis

To date, the study of strategy formulation, and by implication its relation to investment processes, has been conducted within different paradigms. In recent years this has become more widely recognized, with various authors identifying the fundamentally different sets of values upon which different studies have been based. A prerequisite for integrating different approaches to a problem must be the recognition that different appoaches exist, and classification of them according to their basic elements in order to focus upon contradictory factors. Chaffee (1985), for example, identifies three models of the strategy construct: linear analysis (essentially a linear deductive process aimed at achieving specific managerial objectives), adaptive analysis (responding to environmental objectives, and providing the appropriate organizational match) and interpretative analysis (conceptualizing what change means to different individuals; legitimating developments; developing symbols to encourage action and taking action to create symbols of desired behaviour; improving relationships). Chaffee allocates a range of key authors writing on strategy into these three categories, but she argues that the categories need not be seen as separate. The interpretative can be viewed as the broadest perception, into which the adaptive and linear models can be fitted. Her paper is, however, of value more as a codification of different processes of research. It was not intended to show how they might be integrated in practice.

Others, such as Mintzberg (1973), Gluck et al. (1982), and Venkatraman and Camillus (1984), also provide classifications, and these alternative perspectives are now creeping into student textbooks; see, for example, Quinn, Mintzberg and James (1988). There is also some preliminary wrestling with the problem of integrating different disciplinary perspectives in Pennings (1985).

At present, however, we are still essentially at the stage of identifying different approaches to the consideration of strategy. For the purposes of this book, however, and bearing in mind the limitations of space, no attempt will be made to integrate these different classifications. In order to provide a practical précis a different system of classification will be used, but the reader wishing to explore the material presented here in more depth can rapidly extend his or her reading list by reference to the codifying articles already mentioned.

In this chapter a contrast of perspective to the rational models of chapter 3 is needed. 'Rational' – a word that can take on various meanings and get one into all sorts of trouble – is here being used to describe those models that ignore organizational behaviour and suggest that the decision-maker has near-perfect knowledge, power and insight, needing merely to conduct the necessary analysis and implement it.

We shall now explore three alternatives to the rational model: **logical incrementalism**, the **interpretative paradigm** and **action rationality**. This three-way classification is my own and is adopted mainly for convenience of exposition. As will be clear by the end of the chapter, the three categories have overlapping strands and represent related philosophies.

Logical incrementalism

Various authors have contributed to this view of strategic decision-making, but the leader of them all is Quinn (1978, 1980). Quinn's line of thought can be traced back to earlier works such as those of Lindblom (1959) and Wrapp (1967), but he took these general ideas and turned them into a framework for observing organization behaviour and then into practical recommendations for the chief executive who is responsible for strategic change.

Lindblom was mainly interested in the problems of national governments and explaining why it was not appropriate to adopt overall planning models at that level. Wrapp, in contrast, writes from the perspective of the chief executive trying to manage both the organization and his own task. He stresses the need for the chief executive to be informed, but argues that he should focus his attention on just three or four major objectives. He also emphasizes that the chief executive should take into account the power structure of the organization, be careful to choose the right time to promote initiatives, and, in particular, avoid committing himself publicly to a specific objective or action until he knows that it is definitely what he wants and that he can get the support. Management by objectives, says Wrapp, may work at lower levels of the organization where tasks and accountabilities are well defined, but they don't work at the top. Policies emerge in the organization over time. The chief executive may or may not have worked them out in detail beforehand.

Quinn built on this basic theme in a detailed case study (1980) of nine large companies, most with headquarters in the United States, but including also a British company and a Swedish company. As a result of this work, Quinn argues that, while formal (i.e. rational, in the sense defined above) planning systems serve useful purposes, they focus unduly upon measurable quantities and underemphasize 'the vital qualitative organizational and power-behavioral factors that so often determine strategic success' (p. 15). He stresses that formal planning can only be one of the many building blocks which determine corporate strategy.

Quinn sees large companies as similar to large rivers slowly moving in given directions, but containing within them various ebbs, flows and eddies which, while they do not necessarily contribute in any direct analytical way to the general direction, nevertheless in aggregate help to

determine it. Moreover, the flow has direction, but no obvious beginning or end. In a company this is interpreted as the absence of a clear
separation between strategy and implementation. There is, according to
Quinn, no single moment (or relatively short period) in which all the
different aspects of the company are considered together and then each
part given precise goals for the forseeable future according to some
tight, analytical, holistic master plan. Given the size of large corporations, this is impossible, owing not only to the cognitive limits of human
beings, which can tolerate only a severely bounded form of rationality
(March and Simon, 1958, ch. 7), but also to 'process limits'. Process
limits reflect the time needed to create awareness of threats and
opportunities, build commitment and consensus, select and train people
for change, marshal resources, and so on. However, the internal and
external environments of the organization do not stand still while such
processes are worked through. Events, often severe shocks, continue to
occur, and may cause minor or major changes of direction, provided
that no final and irrevocable decision has yet been made. There is,
therefore, an interaction between events, organizational actions and
decisions. Strategic decisions emerge from those on-going processes and
are not formulated by corporate masterplans or mastermatrices.

If Quinn is right, how is such a process to be managed? First, he
stresses that one should *not* view strategic decisions as emerging
randomly. Also, they are *not* just the result of powerplay within the
organization. Power relationships affect outcomes, but so does rational
analysis. What is critical to Quinn is the form of rationality and the
process through which it is formulated.

Quinn's expert manager will be one who recognizes that he has to
guide the organization rather than lead it too definitively. He will
recognize that there are large separable strategic subsystems. These are
not just strategic business units (SBUs), but subsystems relating to
technological development, financial resources, market postures,
product-line development, mergers and acquisitions, employee relations, government relations, and so on. All of these have strategic
aspects to consider, and strategic developments in these areas will not
occur all at the same pace or even, necessarily, in the same direction. As
strategic proposals emerge, each subsystem will evaluate them against
developments in other subsystems, in so far as it perceives them to affect
it too.

In such a process the smart executive does not reveal a strategic
solution (even if he knows one) as soon as he perceives it. He implants
ideas, gives clues, prompts proposals, and avoids committing himself
publicly until the last moment. This gives the organization time to
absorb the idea, to build consensus and to reduce resistance. Also the

smart executive is aware, especially in the early stages of examining a strategic move, that there may be perspectives of which he is unaware. By asking for *proposals* from subordinates, he is able to test his position while being free to reject those proposals without political consequences. This need not suggest a Machiavellian strategy; it may just be sensible caution in the face of uncertainty about both the external and the internal corporate assessment. On the other hand, the approach would also be quite consistent with a concealed move to defeat a rival faction.

Occasionally, severe shocks will rock the system and urgent action will be needed. Quinn has two answers to that. First, if the action must be taken very urgently, it cannot be taken as part of a full corporate strategic analysis; there would not be the time. Nevertheless, actions taken under such stress are often irreversible and set new bounds for strategy in future. Secondly, we should not overestimate the frequency with which really urgent *strategic* decisions are required. Even those countries that formed the oil cartel in the mid-1970s were very careful, says Quinn, about enforcing posted price increases until they were sure that the cartel would hold.

So Quinn gives us a picture of top executives developing mental, or at least private, images of corporate development and, in effect, testing out their ideas through experiments in separable parts of the company. They set broad direction while allowing their views to be influenced by the experience so gained. Such a process is not just 'muddling along', although it might appear to be so. It has the broad direction (as the flowing river does), but it avoids being over-specific. Moreover, the direction is set by powerful clues or 'logics' gradually established in the organization which enable subsystems to bound their search for strategies. The process is selective in addressing issues, but sees each issue within a wider context without, as a rule, seeking a totally holistic view. When each main idea has been sufficiently tested and sufficient knowledge has been gained, the chief executive goes public and announces the decision secure in the knowledge that there will be support for it, because the decision merely 'crystallizes' the views already put to him, whether he subtly induced them or not.

It is important not to read Quinn as calling for the destruction of formal corporate planning or rational analysis. Quinn's fundamental point is simply that it is foolish to try to produce a total group-wide analysis at a given time and then to go ahead rapidly implementing that, ignoring the changing external and internal environments. Rational economic and financial analysis will be vital in presenting proposals, examining relationships between strategic subsystems, and so on. Also, there are clear benefits from bringing proposed actions together in a formal strategic analysis and long-term financial plan. They set down clearly a record of decisions made. They provide a basis for evaluating shorter-term budgets and prevent long-term aims from being forced aside by short-term operational needs. They bring together a range of information not otherwise collected. They encourage managers to think ahead. They reduce uncertainty and hence anxiety about the future. They stimulate ideas for possible improvements. They assist in implementation by assigning responsibilities. None of these benefits is trivial in managing a corporation. But, whatever they do, says Quinn, they do not *determine* strategies. They stand as the essential interface between strategy formulation and tactical decisions.

Before leaving the topic of logical incrementalism, mention needs to be made of a few other relevant studies. Pascale (1984) provides an illuminating analysis of Honda's success in penetrating Western motorcycle markets. After focusing on the Boston Consulting Group (BCG) analysis of the situation, which emphasized the importance of building scale and lower costs through experience-curve effects, Pascale visited Japan to get the story of how the Honda executives planned their entry into American markets. The story is a fascinating description of relatively uninformed risk-taking and opportunism coupled with technological advantage which was only seen as marketable in the United States after the products initially offered in the US market had failed. The story exhibits just the type of learning and experimentation that one would expect from incrementalism, except that, in the Honda case, the experiments were being conducted for real, not just in the executives' minds prior to decision, and the process did not seem all that logical. But it succeeded – largely through a process of persistence and perception of opportunity *as it unfolded*. Pascale says this indicates the distrust in which the Japanese hold single strategic plans, which in their view limit the peripheral vision which is so essential for observing environmental changes. At the very least, this case supports Quinn's stance on incrementalism.

Quinn has been interpreted by some as suggesting that his form of incrementalism leads to a *steady* emergence of change. While this seems to be reading more into Quinn's analysis than is justified, work by Mintzberg (1978), Miller and Friesen (1982), and Pettigrew (1985a, 1985b), supports the notion of incrementalism, but in a form of uneven development with long-term gradual change punctuated by bursts of 'revolutionary' change which may be due to the economic environment, management change or other factors usually, but not necessarily, associated with commercial crisis. At first sight this seems to contradict incrementalism, but incrementalism remains a valid concept if the process of change in these 'revolutionary' bursts does not embrace the group-wide rational analysis.

The intepretative paradigm

The phrase 'interpretative paradigm' is used here as a shorthand description of newer theories of organization that first began to emerge in the early 1970s. These are typified by studies such as those of Cohen, March and Olsen (1972); Hall (1973); Cohen and March (1974); March and Olsen (1976); Weick (1976); Meyer and Rowan (1977); Starbuck (1982); Gioia (1986); and Lord and Foti (1986). The position in the mid-1980s is very economically reviewed and analysed in Weick (1985).

All these theories depend upon the recognition that organizations consist of people and that without the people the organization does not exist. Consequently, we can only understand behaviour in organizations, and, hence, how to manage them, by understanding human cognitive processes and how they influence human behaviour.

Cohen, March and Olsen (1972) provided a stark contrast to the planning-oriented literature on organization design and decision-making with their 'garbage-can model', which in essence claims that people and systems in organizations were in possession of solutions to problems and predispositions to take certain actions when problems or specific situations arise. Organizational direction is therefore primarily determined by problems and reaction rather than pro-active planning.

Later organizational theorists (for example, Starbuck, 1982) argue that the 'garbage-can' view of the world is too extreme in its implications that organizations have no controlled order at all. There will be anarchical aspects of organizations, but order is not completely absent. There will be severe limitations on centralized co-ordination, but there will be 'loose coupling' – that is, some co-ordination, but not in too tight a form.

Large organizations will consist of loosely coupled subsystems, and yet, *within* the subsystems, one would expect to find tighter co-ordination. Even so, the early work of Cohen, March and Olsen was perceptive and catalytic to later developments in ways beyond the general description of the 'garbage-can' model. Irrespective of how much order is or is not present in organizations, Cohen, March and Olsen recognized that people have experience and formulate standard responses to situations. Some of the more recent work on organization behaviour (e.g. Brunnson, 1982, 1985; Gioia, 1986; and Lord and Foti, 1986) reflects this notion of learned response based on prior knowledge, even if it is then referred to as a basis of order rather than disorder.

Doubts about the importance of formal rational planning in organizations grew during the 1970s and 1980s. For example, Starbuck (1982) states that rarely is there a neat sequence of events through from recognition of a problem to definition of the problem, generating possible actions, selection of the appropriate option and implementation. Approximations to such a process might occur if the environment changes slowly with high predictability and where tight control can be exercised centrally. In most large organizations, however, where tight coupling is impossible and no one stakeholder interest predominates, this will not be the situation faced. Moreover, the greater turbulence in the economic and political environment through the 1970s and 1980s means that predictability has decreased.

In such a situation, action is likely to be the product of internal negotiation, with variable dependence upon rational analysis, and one might expect the rational analysis undertaken to have a different orientation according to the stakeholder for whom it is performed (Hall, 1973). Indeed, some stakeholders may take action to prevent a rational analysis of their stance or at least any debate over it. Decisions then emerge in ways more complex than that posited by Quinn (1978, 1980) and yet there has to be a justification of major decisions made both inside and outside the organization.

It is thus not surprising that internal decision-making is loosely coupled with external reporting (Meyer and Rowan, 1977). Not only are the external stakeholders different parties, needing a different rational analysis to justify the decision, but it seems important to convince that group of stakeholders that managers have taken their interests fully into account in the internal negotiation process. The managers' continued legitimation may depend upon convincing the stakeholders that they have done so.

Starbuck (1982) extends this mode of thought into internal management. Organizational members need to have a form of rationality that suits them to justify their continued co-operation and action. In the view of such writers, therefore, rational analyses often serve as *post hoc* devices to justify action rather than accurately reflecting how the decision was actually arrived at. Moreover, it needs to be recognized that a rational, 'value-free' analysis cannot exist in a pluralistic society – or that it would please no one if attempted (Clapham, 1984), unless an action could be shown to benefit all stakeholders. Even then, some may gain more than others, and this could lead to other options being sought which do not produce gain for everyone.

The sort of argument just presented emphasizes that large organizations are not monolithic and that attempts to tighten up the system to make them so do not necessarily yield improvements. Weick (1985) says that, because people persist in simplifying the world, they do not see the differentiations between organizations and within organizations over time. This leads them to see *the* organization as a well-defined unit and not as the heaving, changing mass with fluctuating boundaries that it really is.

People also try to create an ordered and rational existence for themselves. This leads to assumptions about what appeared to happen, did happen and was, usually, intended to happen. There is a natural predisposition to see events as the result of pro-active planning, but, as stressed by March and Olsen (1976), intentions are often overwhelmed by exogenous factors and events or resisted through existing loyalties and perceived duties. Traditional corporate-planning theorists are said to ignore these facts, concluding that rational models lead to effective performance and that highly segmented organizations are really tightly coupled systems (Weick, 1976, 1985). Using hindsight they ignore 'the experiments, the false starts and corrections that enabled people to learn and prepare' (1985, p. 114). Rational analytic systems do not build in opportunities to learn. They assume too much smoothness in the process of unfolding activity based upon the plan. An overall monolithic plan established at one time is therefore impossible.

Weick (1985) also argues that yet other factors show the impossibility of organizational unity. Top managers in large organizations do not manage organizational activity; they manage decision structures. They need those decision structures because it is impossible for them to know enough to control activities directly. They are, therefore, never in full control – they cannot be. All they can do is set trend targets and reward or penalize according to the degree to which they are met. They cannot control the detailed processes. If interdependencies exist between corporate segments, top managers can only see that there are no *major* actions by one segment which adversely affect the others. They cannot totally control the process of interaction. To summarize, 'A loosely coupled system is not a flawed system. It is a social and cognitive solution to constant environmental change, to the impossibility of knowing another mind, and to the limited information-processing capabilities' (Weick, 1985, p. 121). In such segmented organizations with limited overall control it seems inevitable that there will be variable strengths in the links between the segments. This will create a certain amount of ambiguity for everyone attempting to exert control. On the other hand, while ambiguity can never be eradicated, managers can take steps to reduce it (Cohen and March, 1974; Peters and Waterman, 1982).

Managers can act *as if* the elements of a decision process or an organization are tightly coupled. They can do this by establishing clear guiding principles against which all actions need to be evaluated. Examples of such core values might be that customers are always right, that we need 100 per cent product reliability, that we are a computer company and will stick with it, and so on. It is then taken without question by organization participants that observance of these core values leads to success for themselves and 'the organization'.

Even if the core values are not tightly linked to organizational success, they still guide action and promote a more unified view of 'reality'. Consequently, the arguments presented in this section should *not* be used to dismiss centralized corporate planning. The plan itself *does* serve as a binding mechanism to reduce ambiguity, but not too much should be expected of it. It is a coming-together of intentions to create visibility for key strategies and organizational movement. It is a co-ordinating device and a legitimator of subsequent action, but, according to this area of literature, the development of the rational corporate plan is not a dominant decision-making process.

Peters and Waterman (1982) also argue that corporate plans are insufficient for establishing such core values. The underlying values by which organizations are to be run have to be strongly set through a variety of management processes – in particular, through reinforcement by top management and the reward system. The corporate planning process is only one, and perhaps not the best, way of establishing those values throughout the organization.

A little deeper thinking raises the question of why organization participants should accept such core values. As stated, top management can reinforce acceptance through their actions and by biasing the reward system to favour behaviour in accordance with the core values, but will not organization participants seek a form of rational justification for compliance in terms of their own long-run success and survival? The answer is clearly 'yes'. Top management will have to provide a convincing case, but there is, nevertheless, considerable evidence that human cognitive processes provide a natural basis for expecting behaviour according to core values once they have been established, and this fact can be a fundamental mangement aid.

Gioia (1986) stresses that people are not pure information-processors rationally dealing with all available information in an information-rich environment. They also do not process it anew each time it is presented. If problems arise in everyday life, they may begin by *some* rational search and analysis, but they are looking for aspects of the situation that reflect prior experience (that are stereotypical) and, once they recognize those aspects, they switch to a more holistic and intuitive assessment based on their understanding of those stereotyped elements. Also, the stereotyped aspects we recognize in a problem situation depend upon how we look, which in turn is based upon our personal belief and value systems. Finally, our belief systems are not stored in our minds as a complete rational analysis. They may (or may not) have been created that way, but, once they have been determined, we store our beliefs more efficiently in the form of symbols (shorthand words and phrases which reflect a complete attitude to and assessment of a person or situation – e.g. 'She is a poor performer') and **scripts** (models of how we act once certain situations are recognized). There is a *necessity* for us to behave like this in order to cope with the informational complexity with which we are perpetually faced – we 'know' something works so we do it, bracketing off the rest of the world until it becomes clear that there is a need to change our basic beliefs. In the fashion of the philosophers John Locke and David Hume one may say that one cannot *live* as a *total* sceptic or one would achieve nothing.

It is also important to recognize that our basic beliefs (our espoused version of the 'truth') are not necessarily established by rational analysis. Core values, or belief systems, can be created *either* by rational deductive analysis *or* by direct association between action and result through experience. Whichever basis or mix of bases leads to the establishment of those beliefs, they become embedded in the individual and organizational consciousness as 'pre-existing' knowledge systems which are used to interpret events as they occur. In fact some (e.g. Lord and Foti, 1986) like to push this analysis further and find value in analysing these **schemas** (i.e. the knowledge systems) into various categories to reflect our perception of other individuals, of ourselves, of situations and of how specific people will act in given situations. In summary, our understanding of basic cognitive processes suggests that top managers can have a powerful effect on organization behaviour and direction by reducing the variety in subordinates' schemas (core values). This can be done either through rational analysis or through changing experience.

Two further points regarding the ways managers cope with ambiguity will be of relevance to our consideration of strategic management. First, Weick (1985) reminds us how high ambiguity can be reduced by the establishment of networks. This can be interpreted in two ways. Weick interprets it as really a broader application of the basic notion that diversification spreads risks. He quotes the example of diversifying sources of supply. But the basic concept can also be applied to the establishment of networks *within* large organizations. While the break-down of a corporate group into separate SBUs will improve diversification of the total group risk, if there is some interdependence between the SBUs it may be better to have many smaller interdependencies rather than a few large ones. For example, multi-sourcing *within* the corporate group offers less need for co-ordination than single sourcing with the group. It is clear that one cannot give a general rule. Much depends upon the nature of the interdependencies, how critical they are to the success of SBUs and, in turn, how important those SBUs are to total group success. However, it is interesting to note that *some* wider forms of inter-group dependence can, paradoxically, act as a diversification mechanism to reduce organizational ambiguity, and may actually lessen the need for overall planning to ensure that specific interdependencies are always tightly managed. This idea will be picked up again in chapter 8 when we review the corporate-strategy literature from the viewpoint of organization theory.

The second point is that, when ambiguity increases sharply, that is the time when people who can resolve that ambiguity by setting new organizational values to cope with it gain power. There is nothing like a good crisis to lead to a questioning of organizational values, directions and practices (Starbuck, 1982; Blowers, 1983). Crises can therefore be used to legitimize more strategic movement. They do this by acting on the experience mode of establishing truth, and, given the uncertainty associated with any economic analysis relating to a company's future, experience of a crisis is probably far better at getting us to reassess our schemas and scripts than is rational analysis in times of stability and success. Of course, once our schemas are shaken, we may well resort, at least in part, to rational analysis to reformulate them.

Action rationality: the gem in the garbage can?

A direct derivative of the type of thinking traced above is the concept of action rationality, analysed most comprehensively by Brunnson (1982, 1985). Recognizing that people do act according to established beliefs and pre-existing knowledge systems, he focuses upon distinguishing between the establishment of those beliefs (which he calls 'ideologies') and action in accordance with those beliefs.

Brunnson emphasizes that it is the end result of taking action which matters and not just the analysis of what action to take. Successful implementation of decisions, he says, depends on three factors: good motivation, high commitment to the action selected, and common expectations of what is required. On the basis of studies of various enterprises, he then adopts a stance which radically de-emphasizes the degree of *both* rationality and negotiation needed in successful organizations. Under considerable uncertainty, extensive analysis of many options will only highlight the fact that much uncertainty exists and, he argues, create more uncertainty in the minds of organization participants, which will reduce commitment to action. Decisions, then, should be made on a much more impressionistic basis (intuition mixed with analysis of a few alternatives), *provided* that the actions taken do not offend the organization's ideologies.

In Brunnson's view, effective ideologies should have three attributes. They should be **conclusive** – as an example of a conclusive ideology he cites a 'multi-dimensional model of the market' with 'elements which were strongly inter-connected in terms of cause and effect' (1985, p. 92). They should be **consistent** – that is, generally held throughout the organization. Finally, they should be **complex** – meaning that they should be definite, with a full analytical description of why the particular ideology is appropriate, even specifying conditions under which it would cease to be appropriate. A conclusive, consistent and complex ideology provides the basis for *both* a reduction of ambiguity in the organization while the ideology remains appropriate *and* the destruction of that ideology when necessary. While the ideology is appropriate, it enables choices to be made on the basis of far less analysis and with much greater urgency, which certainly seems to be a move in the right direction, even if the choice made is not always the best one in the circumstances. Ideologies of this sort both prevent procrastination through excessive thought and analysis and reduce uncertainty about the right steps to take, thus increasing commitment and motivation. They imply also that the organization is prepared to make more mistakes, but to carry the consequences in view of the greater benefits to the organization as a whole from being action-oriented.

Brunnson clearly follows the line of those who question the need for a totally comprehensive, rational planning system, but his management methodology does contain a considerable element of rational analysis, despite the title of his book. A strong ideology is, in his view, a 'multi-dimensional model' with strong cause-and-effect links. To Brunnson, therefore, the establishment of ideologies (or value systems or *fundamental* strategies) does depend on rigorous, rational analysis. In fact, he may himself be relying too much on rational analysis in setting ideologies. As argued elsewhere (Tomkins, 1987), both Mrs Thatcher in moving to a more competitive economy in the United Kingdom and President Kennedy in declaring that the United States would put a man on the moon established very strong ideologies based more on fundamental beliefs as to what was required than on extensive rational analysis, and they both achieved considerable change.

Brunnson therefore does an excellent job of distinguishing between the formulation and implementation of ideologies, helping us to begin to see how corporate rational analysis and the organizational perspectives may fit together, but his thesis does not sufficiently recognize the degree to which both rationality and negotiation may still underlie the establishment of his ideologies. He seems to sweep aside rational analysis only to let it come back in at the ideological level, and underplays the processes of getting the ideology established in the face of organizational resistance. If we are to adopt an action-rationality stance, and there is considerable merit in so doing, there is still the need to decide at what level ideologies are to be set, what degree of rational analysis needs to be involved, how to sell the ideologies and how much rationality is still needed even within an impressionistic mode of operation. As Weick (1985) says, action rationality contains a dilemma for top managers. Do they conduct more extensive analysis and perhaps provide better solutions but risk dissipating energy to act, or do they focus on forceful implementation of a satisfactory solution? Even Weick doesn't make it clear that this dilemma is not found only at the action level. It is an even bigger dilemma at the ideology-setting level, which relates more to strategic movement. Despite all this criticism, however, Brunnson does point the way towards a system of management which incorporates the implications of cognitive schemes and ideologies. He is also much more positive than many earlier organization theorists, who emphasized the complexities of individual behaviour in organizations but did little to help top managers except to say their task was very difficult and that they might do better if they understood that.

Discovering and changing widely held schemas

In discussing the interpretative paradigm and action rationality, we have seen the importance that a range of authors attach to identifying the commonly held cognitive schemas in an organization. Realizing the importance of schemas and scripts is the first step, but that in itself gets us nowhere unless we push on to consider how a manager can discover *what* schemas actually exist and, if they are inappropriate, how to change them. Only then does schema recognition become a practical managment device.

Very little to date seems to have been written about schema identification. Perhaps that is appropriate. If schemas are widely held, it should usually be obvious to the manager what they are – especially, of course, if he or she aimed to establish them in the first place. On the other hand, in large organizations it may not be so obvious what schemas people at different locations hold. There may be critical differences in schemas between different divisions or hierarchical levels which create conflict or resistance to change. Top managers may well not understand this resistance because they do not recognize the schemas. This is not a rare phenomenon. A colleague and I are currently involved in considering major changes in a very large organization. It is evident that change has not been achieved as rapidly as desired, and to a large extent it is for this reason. Indeed, we were hired to help identify the schemas held at different levels of the organization. There is a need, therefore, for a systematic approach to identifying existing schemas before attempting to establish new ones.

Schema identification may only require some sample interviewing of different internal stakeholder groups. When they are questioned on the attitudes, motivations and beliefs they bring to their tasks, strongly held schemas will often become obvious quite quickly to the trained observer who knows what he (or she) is looking for. It will be important, however, to consider how the organization participants see the interviewer. If the interviewer is closely identified with some head-office group that is known to be contemplating a change that organization participants consider undesirable, he will need considerable skill to tell just how strongly particular schemas are held. It is possible that schemas will be presented in a way which overemphasizes participants' intentions to resist. Alternatively, an apparent readiness to change may conceal an intention to resist in concerted action with others.

Depending upon the issue and situation involved, it may be useful to develop a more systematic procedure for schema identification. In a book (Tomkins, 1987) urging public-sector organizations to consider new ways of evaluating organization effectiveness (not just efficiency), I suggest that the approach of Guba and Lincoln (1981) offers a very practical way of proceeding. Guba and Lincoln base their approach upon the notion that, where stakeholder groups differ in their assessment of the effectiveness of their organizations, this is because of underlying differences in their value systems, which influence their assessment of the importance of different mixes of organizational outputs. A simple methodology has been developed which identifies key stakeholder groups and their concerns about the organization. By comparing concerns of different stakeholder groups, those differences in concerns are divided between those due to misinformation or poor communication and those which are real issues based on differences in value systems. There is no claim that this resolves the differences, but it helps top managers understand where they might focus their efforts in order to improve effectiveness – i.e. it identifies inconsistent schemas. Clearly such an approach is applicable in any organization.

The stakeholder-analysis approach to reviewing strategy developed by Mitroff and Emshoff (1979) has many similarities to the Guba and Lincoln approach. The prime difference is that Mitroff and Emshoff pursue the underlying values each stakeholder group holds with respect to specific strategies. They also say that they have discovered that this tends to produce two dramatically opposed views. For Quinn-style top managers trying to assess current schemas and what steps to take, the less directive Guba and Lincoln approach may raise fewer expectations and prevent a premature confrontation. The Mitroff and Emshoff approach may be more suitable for reviewing strategies already proposed where there is clearly major resistance to those strategies. Nevertheless, both approaches offer ways of thinking about the values guiding organization participants' behaviour.

Finney and Mitroff (1986) develop the earlier Mitroff work further with an approach they call Organizational Self-Reflection (OSR). In their view, corporate strategies fail because they consider problems in the external environment but not those internal to the organization. Compared with Mitroff's earlier paper, there is much more emphasis here on linking stakeholder analysis with research into cognitive schemas, and a greater recognition that there may be problems both in identifying the schemas, often held unconsciously, and in bringing them together to inform the corporate debate about strategy. The paper devotes more attention to establishing basic ideologies than to the problems of how they relate to specific strategies. The approach was developed with the co-operation of a specially formed group of managers, rather than through a company-wide sampling procedure. The result, again, was a recognition of cognitive dissonance between internal stakeholder groups.

Of course, the recognition of cognitive dissonance still does not solve the problem. Top managers still have to decide what to do about it. Given that espoused schemas are inconsistent with the ones top managers would like to establish, how do they go about changing them?

There is a great deal of literature on the process of organizational change, but a reasonable degree of agreement on the basic stages involved. Kanter (1983) is probably as well regarded as any writer on the subject. Like Peters and Waterman (1982), she emphasizes the need for top executives to establish a few clear signals in order to create a felt need for change, and to use 'prime movers' in the organization both to 'talk up' the new strategy and to ensure that the signals or symbols developed to establish the new direction are present in all important interactions – i.e. reflected in reports, agenda for meetings, key events, and so on. She also emphasizes the need to consider the 'action vehicles' which can be used to carry the change. This could be modification to reward systems, management development or training schemes.

This can be so easily set down; indeed, written at such a general level as they are here, these statements become almost obvious. The importance of considering *how, in specific situations*, to change organizational schemas should not, however, be underestimated. While organization theorists have provided a considerable service by focusing our attention upon the notions of ideologies and schemas, once this has been done it is relatively easy to identify what the schemas are. The really difficult task is changing them. Glib statements about the use of prime movers and changing the reward system conceal the considerable difficulties often involved in doing just that.

Figure 7.2 is an attempt to capture the complexity involved. When some thought of major change is initiated, all those affected will have their own interpretations of what is going on, based on their existing knowledge and experience. These perceptions will then be evaluated through a consideration of 'what's in it for me?' This may be expected to lead to a purposeful action, purposeful inaction or indifference. Dependent on the diversity of response, the decision on the proposed change may be resolved or persuasion in some form may be required. In any case, the whole process will be modified by the ability of each group to wield power and influence.

It is clear also that there can be an iteration back from any stage in the process to any previous one as views get modified during the change

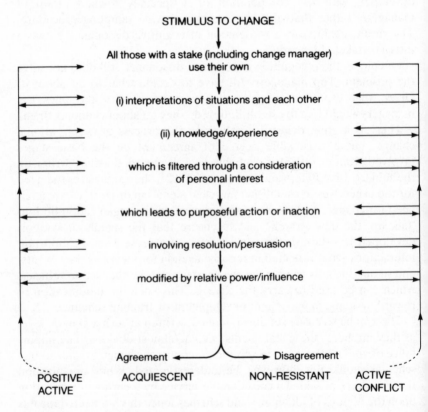

Figure 7.2   Change as a social process

process. Even if the initial reaction to proposed change is generally positive, rethinking can occur during the change as consequences become clarified. It may take some time before matters settle down again and action proceeds quasi-automatically according to revised schemas.

If the change is not well managed *throughout* this process, different groups' interests may be so radically affected that the process has to degenerate into chaos before stability can be regained. I am reminded here of the book on chaos already mentioned in the Preface (Gleick, 1987): it describes how turbulence can be created from a stable physical state. Without trying to push the scientific analogy too far, it is interesting to consider whether there are parallel patterns of development, giving early warnings of 'chaos', in organizations. If so, either the parties most affected need attention, possibly through a change to the proposed reward patterns, or the pace of change may need to be slowed to give those most affected time to adapt. Alternatively, and conversely, it may be recognized that the end goal will not be achieved without a period of turbulence, and the pace of change may actually be accelerated, to get it over as quickly as possible.

In this way change is seen as a developing social process the repercussions of which cannot be completely forecast. On the other hand, the better the change-manager understands each main party's schema, each party's perception of what is risky for it and each party's ability to exercise power to disrupt, the better will he or she be able to develop an appropriate change strategy and recognize where the strategy may be at risk as events unfold. Where some parties gain and lose, as will usually be the case in schema-breaking situations, change can be a complex process.

As noted earlier in this chapter, and by many authors, including Kanter (1983), an attempt to change basic ideologies/schemas of multiple parties is more likely to be successful in times of crisis when it becomes obvious that traditional modes of operation are no longer achieving success. If there is no crisis, top managers will find it much more difficult to achieve fundamental change, since the need for it will be questioned. There are then just two ways in which top managers can proceed. One of these is to attempt to convince the organization that a crisis will occur if current policies are continued. The trouble with that is that others may not be astute as they are in identifying impending crises, and will take some convincing if a crisis is not obvious. It is apparent from the writings of people such as Quinn and cognitive psychologists that schemas are robust and that experience is probably a better instructor for most than deductive logic. (If the reader doubts this and has had an accident driving a car, reflect again!) The further into the future the perceived crisis, the more the chief executive will need to rely on introducing some flexibility into the corporate strategy to facilitate a change in direction in future if it becomes necessary. But at least he or she, by doing that, can create 'thought experiments' in the organization, so that it is ready to move and adopt new schemas if and when the crisis develops. The chief executive may know what change is needed, but has to wait for the right time to introduce it.

If 'crisis management' in this sense (different from the sense in which the phrase is normally used) is impossible, there is only one alternative open to management in creating the felt need for change. Organization participants with majority power must be persuaded that they would be *significantly* better off if a change occurred. This is where the reward/penalty system comes in. Unless the promoter of change has the power to reward the new form of behaviour and/or penalize persistence with the old form of behaviour, schemas are unlikely to change whatever managerial symbols and signals circulate around the organization. This is why it is often stressed that strategic change must be supported by top managers. Usually only they have the power to change the reward systems. It is also interesting to note that often they are severely constrained. In the public sector in the United Kingdom, for example, even top managers have not got complete freedom to reward according to performance.

Of course, rewards and penalties may take non-pecuniary form, but rewards have to be present. Management development and training may be needed to support change, but they have a supporting role. They will not bring about change unless the rewards for change or the resolution of a crisis situation can be delivered. Despite all the theory about schemas, in the absence of a crisis the really critical factor in creating the felt need for change is probably the acquisition of power over the organization's reward/penalty system. This, it seems, is *the* prerequisite for changing schemas. But, given the previous discussion about the complexity of the change process, it may not be obvious in advance what rewards need to be given to whom, or what form, monetary or otherwise, those rewards should take. The change-manager will no doubt contemplate the required strategy before releasing his (or her) proposals, just as Quinn would suggest, but he will still need to be adept at riding the waves of change. He will be wise to have some rewards in hand as oil to pour on any turbulent water he encounters.

Summary

One may summarize the behavioural literature as follows. It emphasizes that totally comprehensive rational analysis and consequent implementation extending right across a major corporate group is completely impossible to achieve in one brief space of time. Such an analysis is so extensive that life moves on before the implementation is complete. Also, people simplify their worlds: they learn through deductive logic but possibly more through experience, and, once learned, the lesson is stored in simplified form as schemas and scripts so that action is not paralysed by thought. The bulk of corporate activity should be within well-set schemas and focus upon the creation of action rationality, but within the corporation there should be a mechanism to warn of impending crises or to recognize opportunities for significant improvement which lead to the questioning and modification of existing schemas. When schemas need to be changed, considerable attention needs to be paid to internal barriers to change, or the best-laid strategies will fail. These internal barriers must be understood as the natural consequence of attempting to combine together multi-interest groups possessing different power and influence. Within a set schema some approximate balance of interests has been achieved. Once the schema is broken some interests will be affected more than others – hence the erection of barriers to change. As some parties will only perceive how they are affected as the change unfolds, successful change needs on-going management until a point is reached where stability is reattained.

With all this in mind, the point of the argument has been reached where an attempt can be made to move towards an integration of the behavioural and strategic perspectives of corporate resource allocation. This will be the goal of chapter 8. Following that, we shall be in a position, in chapter 9, to consider further implications of these other fields of study for accounting and finance.

References

Ackerman, R. W. 1970: Influence of integration and diversity on the investment process. *Administrative Science Quarterly*, September.

Blowers, A. 1983: Master of fate or victim of circumstance – the exercise of corporate power in environmental policy-making. *Policy and Politics*, 11, no. 4.

Bower, J. 1970: *Managing the Resource Allocation Process: a study of corporate planning and investment*. Cambridge, Mass.: Harvard Business School.

Brunnson, N. 1982: The irrationality of action and action rationality: decisions, ideologies and organizational action. *Journal of Management Studies*, 19.

Brunnson, N. 1985: *The Irrational Organization*. New York: John Wiley.

Chaffee, E. E. 1985: Three models of strategy. *Academy of Management Review*, 10, no. 1.

Chandler, A. 1965: *Strategy and Structure*. Cambridge, Mass.: MIT Press.

Clapham, D. 1984: Rational planning and politics: the example of local authority corporate planning. *Policy and Politics*, 12, no. 1.

Cohen, M. D., March, J. G. and Olsen, J. P. 1972: A garbage can model of organizational choice. *Administrative Science Quarterly*, 17.

Cohen, M. D., and March, J. G. 1974: *Leadership and Ambiguity*. New York: McGraw-Hill.

Dean, J. 1951: *Capital Budgeting*. New York: Columbia University Press.

Finney, M. and Mitroff, I. 1986: Strategic plan failures: the organization as its own worst enemy. In H. Sims, D. Gioia et al., *The Thinking Organization*, San Francisco: Jossey-Bass.

Gioia, D. 1986: Symbols, scripts and science-making. In H. Sims, D. Gioia et al., *The Thinking Organization*, San Francisco: Jossey-Bass.

Gleick, J. 1987: *Chaos: making a new science*. London: Cardinal.

Gluck, F., Kaufman, S. and Walleck, W. 1982: The four phases of strategic management. *Journal of Business Strategy*, II, no.3.

Guba, E. and Lincoln, Y. 1981: *Effective Evaluation*. San Francisco: Jossey-Bass.

Hall, P. M. 1973: A symbolic interactionist analysis of politics. *Sociological Inquiry*, 42.

Kanter, R. 1983: *The Change Masters: corporate entrepreneurs at work*. London: Allen and Unwin.

Lindblom, C. 1959: The science of muddling through. *Public Administration Review*, Spring.

Lord, R. and Foti, R. 1986: Schema theories, information processing and organizational behaviour. In H. Sims, D. Gioia et al., *The Thinking Organization*, San Francisco: Jossey-Bass.

March, J. G. and Olsen, J. P. 1976: Organisational choice under ambiguity. In J. G. Marsh and J. P. Olsen (eds), *Ambiguity and Choice in Organizations*, Bergen: Bergen Universitetsforlaget.

March, J. and Simon, H. 1958: *Organizations*. New York: John Wiley.

Meyer, J. W. and Rowan, B. 1977: Institutionalized organizations: formal structure as myth and ceremony. *American Journal of Sociology*, 83.

Miller, D. and Friesen, P. 1982: Structural change and performance: quantum versus piecemeal – incremental approaches. *Academy of Management Journal*, 25, no. 4.

Mintzberg, H. 1973: Strategy making in three modes. *California Management Review*, XVI, no. 2 (Winter).

Mintzberg, H. 1978: Patterns in strategy formation. *Management Science*, 24, no. 9.

Mitroff, I. and Emshoff, J. 1979: On strategic assumption-making: a dialectical approach to policy and planning. *Management Review*, 4, no. 1.

Pascale, R. T. 1984: Perspectives on strategy: the real story behind Honda's success. *Californian Management Review*, XXVI, no. 3.

Pennings, J. M. et al. 1985: *Organizational Strategy and Change*. San Francisco: Jossey-Bass.

Peters, T. and Waterman, R. 1982: *In Search of Excellence*. New York: Harper and Row.

Pettigrew, A. 1985a: *The Awakening Giant: continuity and change in Imperial Chemical Industries*. Oxford: Basil Blackwell.

Pettigrew, A. 1985b: Examining change in the long-term context of culture and politics. In J. M. Pennings et al., *Organizational Strategy and Change*, San Francisco: Jossey-Bass.

Quinn, J. 1978: Strategic change: 'logical incrementalism'. *Sloan Management Review*, Fall.

Quinn, J. 1980: *Strategies for change – logical incrementalism*. Homewood, Ill.: R. D. Irwin.

Quinn, J., Mintzberg, H. and James, R. 1988: *The Strategy Process*. Englewood Cliffs, NJ: Prentice-Hall.

Starbuck, W. H. 1982: Congealing oil: inventing ideologies to justify acting ideologies out. *Journal of Management Studies*, 19.

Tomkins, C. 1987: *Achieving Economy, Efficiency and Effectiveness in the Public Sector*. London: Kogan Page.

Venkatraman, N. and Camillus, J. 1984: Exploring the concept of 'fit' in strategic management. *Academy of Management Review*, 9, no. 3.

Weick, K. 1976: Educational organizations as loosely coupled systems. *Administrative Science Quarterly*, 21.

Weick, K. 1985: Sources of order in underorganized systems: themes in recent organizational theory. In Y. S. Lincoln (ed.) *Organizational Theory and Inquiry: the paradigm revolution*, Beverly Hills: Sage.

Wrapp, H. 1967: Good managers don't make policy decisions. *Harvard Business Review*, September–October.

Discussion questions and exercises

7.1   Describe the roles that different parts of the organization structure are likely to play in making investment decisions.

7.2   Read Finney and Mitroff (1986). Form a group of five or six students and conduct an Organization Self-Reflection analysis using your university department or students' union as the organization. (Readers who are not at an academic instution can use their employing organization.)

7.3   Describe and discuss the various ways of coping with inter-organizational interdependencies over investment decisions.

7.4   Critically evaluate Brunnson's book *The Irrational Organization* (Brunnson, 1985).

7.5   Discuss the following statement.

Organizational theorists have spent much effort attacking analytical corporate strategy models by demonstrating that people act according to schemas and scripts, not rational analyses, but action at that level is operational activity and not strategic movement and so the attack is misdirected.

7.6   Discuss the following statement and consider how to go about changing organizational groups' schemas.

> Internal barriers to change can sink the best of corporate strategies, and if the 'best' strategy is inconsistent with schemas held by key groups it may require much subtlety to change them before the strategy can be implemented.

7.7   The essential truth about organizations is that their attributes and actions reflect a multi-party, purposeful struggle based on a mixture of impressions and rational analysis. Discuss this statement.

7.8   Strategic movement needs a good crisis to create the conditions for change. Discuss.

7.9   What factors determine whether it is better to force the pace of change to limit the 'period of pain' or to implement change more slowly and incrementally? (A consideration of the problems being experienced in effecting far-reaching economic changes in the Soviet Union and Eastern Europe may help here.)

8

Integrating Corporate Strategy and Organizational Approaches to Resource Allocation

In chapters 5 and 6 developments in the literature of corporate strategy were related to financial and economic analyses which might be introduced into both accounting and finance. Up to the end of chapter 6 the approach followed was largely analytical. In chapter 7 the frame of reference was broadened further to provide a behavioural view on strategic decision-making. The final task of this book will be to consider what this wider dimension also implies for accounting and finance. It would, however, be premature to link the thoughts of chapter 7 with accounting and finance without reference back to the corporate-strategy literature discussed in chapter 4. Otherwise the implications for accounting and finance developed from chapters 4 and 7 might appear to be inconsistent. The first task of this chapter is therefore to attempt to link the views of chapters 4 and 7 to provide some integration of the economically oriented strategy literature with the more behaviourally oriented variety. If that can be achieved, we shall have a more unified basis from which to review accounting and finance. It is stressed, nevertheless, that the following attempt to integrate the material of chapters 4 and 7 is exploratory. The links between these two fields have still to be fully worked out, and I do not pretend to provide a complete integration. Rather, I present some ideas which I hope may lead to their integration. On the other hand, I hope to persuade readers that the dichotomous distinction between rational deductive logic and more behavioural approaches is not helpful. Indeed, real-world corporate resource-allocation processes depend on an integration of these perspectives.

Towards an integration of corporate strategy and organizational literature

In one of the few attempts that have so far been made to come to grips with the relationships between strategic planning systems and behavioural processes, Marsh et al. (1987) argue that their observations could not support a polarization of view in which, on the one hand, formal systems were seen as pure ritual, and, on the other, formal systems and capital-budgeting rules were seen as the all-important factor in decision-making. The paper provides a fascinating study of how systems, roles, organization sub-structures and hierarchy, and the organization context all influence strategic decision-making. Moreover, it considers that watching real people make strategy emphasizes that the key managerial task is to make things happen. Marsh et al. say, 'In understanding strategic investment decisions, we need to recognise the importance of promises of action by those who actually do things, and the extent to which the process encourages and reinforces commitment.' Similarly, Kanter (1989) has more recently emphasized that the process of achieving change is all-important and that working out the answers is not enough. Furthermore, she believes that managers will need to work more as partners taking into account the interests of others.

There is, therefore, already recognition that there is a need to integrate analytical with behavioural aspects of corporate resource allocation. An attempt will now be made to develop one possible framework for doing this, with reference to concepts discussed in chapters 4 and 7.

If the concluding section of chapter 7, on Brunnson (1985), is taken as the point of departure, we need first to be clear about what is meant by 'strategy', 'ideologies', 'schemas', and so on. Are they all the same thing? The terms were used interchangeably in chapter 7. Brunnson makes it clear that he considers an ideology to be a very clear and rationally established strategy. It is therefore probably acceptable to use these terms inter-changeably provided that one recognizes that there are different levels of ideology. For example, one might adopt a capitalist market-driven ideology which prevents organization participants from considering options leading to the conversion of the enterprise into a wider co-operative or commune-like organization. With that ideology established, one may then have an ideology that the corporation is in certain markets and not others. This may refer to products, regions (e.g. the company is not prepared to operate in South Africa) or technologies. There may also be ideologies about how the organization does business (no pollution, customer first, and so on) and how it is managed (decentralized, centralized, payment by results, consensus-driven, and so on). All these different levels of thinking about ideology give rise to schemas, which may or may not be linked. Ideally, lower-level schemas should be consistent with higher-level schemas, but they may be only loosely derived from them and there may be influence upward rather than downward or interaction between levels. The basic requirement is not a tight logical link between schemas held at different levels, but the avoidance only of marked inconsistencies between them.

When we are discussing major investment decisions in very large companies and the inevitable link with corporate strategy, we can usually, in the West, take the highest-level ideology (e.g. the capitalist ethic) as given. Moreover, ideologies at that level have little to do with comprehensive rational analysis – they are systems of belief. This may to some extent be the case with some lower-level schemas, where the participants' beliefs may lead them to see a given decision as 'obviously appropriate' (politically wise, socially responsible, and so on). Hence, Brunnson's world of tightly modelled and rationally determined high-level ideologies is too simplistic. On the other hand, it was argued in chapter 7 that most organizational activity is action-oriented and should generally not question the basic assumptions. In between these two levels (i.e. the higher ideological level and the action-rational level) there will, however, be a need for considerable rational analysis. In his model of the organization Brunnson places emphasis on the use of economic rationality to evaluate major alternative strategies to deal wtih the external market. Isn't this what the corporate-strategist literature tries to address? If we see Porter's analysis described in chapter 4 as the setting of *ideologies* about how the market works, there seems to be no major conflict with Brunnson. Both would probably agree that even quite major investments can then be taken on an impressionistic basis given that a strong market model has been established in the executive schemas. Others, such as Quinn and Starbuck, stress that major decisions are not necessarily made with explicit reference to comprehensive rational models, but Brunnson shows us, whether it was his clear intention or not, that considerable economic rational analysis *is* still needed *to set ideologies*. This squares with Newman (1986), who asks whether it is possible for major frame-breaking episodes to be completely avoided through a Quinn-style incrementalism. While, as Starbuck (1982) argues, it may often need a crisis to justify significant change, planning the turn-around usually requires a significant degree of analysis in order to establish the new schema.

In chapter 3 I described how a subsidiary of a major UK group nearly collapsed. This was merely due to its inappropriate schema of success for its operations (its own perception of what it was and what it could do), with inappropriate product-costing systems disguising the early signals of this inadequacy. Once collapse came and everyone became aware of the outdatedness of the schema, it required much analysis and consideration of options before a turn-around strategy could be formulated. More significantly, the rationale for the new strategy had to be well worked through to gain organizational commitment before it could be decided where to seek new business. In such a situation, rational planning starts to fight back, not *just* as a symbolic communication mechanism, but as means of formulating the future progress of the corporation. In fact Quinn himself has stated, 'During times of reorientation, decision rationality will play a major role, but when convergence is necessary, action rationality should dominate' (Gladstein and Quinn, 1986, p. 216). Quinn still believes that decision-rationality belongs within an incremental development process, but he also sees an iteration between symbolic and rational approaches as necessary in cases of major strategic reorientation.

The critical outcome of the discussion of incrementalism and action rationality is the recognition that strategy-making is a more fluid process than one might imagine from the models of chapter 4. Top executives will need, however, to keep a track of how strategy is emerging. They will need to bear in mind established ideologies (or group-wide schemas) for some strategic business units (SBUs) while considering rational analysis as a means of modifying the schemas of others. This in fact lends support to Porter's form of analysis, because it stresses that such an analysis does *not* need to be carried out at one and the same time for *all* the markets in which the group operates. For major corporate groups this would be a huge task. Porter analyses can be performed when the need for a major change in a particular market schema is needed. Otherwise, the outline results of the Porter analysis for any SBU will be crucial as a fixed component in an established corporate schema. The idea of loose coupling between SBUs also supports this form of integration between rational analysis with organizational realism.

If one looks at a McKinsey–GE portfolio grid in the light of the ideas of the previous paragraph, it becomes clear that it should be seen not as a comprehensive, once-and-for-all rational analysis, but rather as a still from a continuing movie, capturing the essence of the corporate group's existing position and providing a focus for communication and for debate about possible changes in that position. The portfolio grid, viewed in that way, enables the corporate executives to identify and focus on where different types of attention are needed. It provides a clear record of established SBU schemas to be kept broadly in mind while schemas under strategic threat are being rigorously, but incrementally, reviewed with the required degree of economic rationality. The portfolio grid does not have to be viewed as a static, analytical tool offering determinate solutions. Its strength is as a provider of 'the corporate picture' as the incremental process unfolds. Also, it does not have to be just a reinforcer of schemas. It can also serve, through the use of *hypothesized* behaviour in each area of the matrix, as a catalyst for reviewing impending strategic movement and as a basis for examining the total corporate balance of activity according to which of several possible strategies is employed. It is through *thought and argument* about the positioning of SBUs on the matrix and their movement round it that participants can obtain real benefit from the portfolio grid, developing shared meanings with regard to both their own position and their contribution to the corporate goals. With this interpretation of the grid, one *can* question whether 'dogs' are not just 'sleepers' to be awakened and moved back to a prominent position. Similarly, one *can* raise questions about both the direction and speed of movement around the matrix.

Hapeslaugh (1982), who reported that the use of portfolio grids was widespread, went on to say that most corporations did *not* make definitive decisions based upon the precise location of SBUs on those grids. So how did they use them? Almost certainly they used them to review, debate and, where necessary, revise SBU schemas through an interactive process. It need not be the only way of focusing attention on key strategic issues, but it is probably a very powerful one. It may also serve as a powerful motivation to 'dogs', indicating what the corporate perception is likely to be if they do not regenerate themselves. The value of portfolio grids should certainly not be overrated – considerable back-up analysis is required and they should not be used in a rigid deterministic manner – but neither should their value as a map of organizational schemas be overlooked, as it is by almost all the corporate-strategy literature.

While contemplating what I had written in this section, I came across this statement by an executive who recently introduced the Boston Consulting Group (BCG) matrix into his company, despite being aware of the criticism of it:

> It was useful . . . when we first used it last year. . . . Now, just a few months later, it's fascinating to see how they [the others] are moving on the grid: several 'dogs' have already shifted across towards more positive positions.
>
> (Philip Candy, Clifford Dairy Products, quoted in the *Financial Times*, 30 March 1988)

Clearly, the value of the matrix is its ability to enforce some sort of analysis of relative SBU positions and to create consensus about the company's 'moving picture'. There is also obviously no automatic destruction of 'dogs' just because of their location on the matrix. Perhaps the very definition of SBUs as 'dogs', viewed through the current lens or schema, leads to the use of different lenses and, hence, the recognition of different potentialities and attractive features, making it possible to devise new, frame-breaking strategies.

Viewed like this, there is no fundamental conflict between the use of portfolio grids and incrementalism, loose coupling, and so on. So what is left of the behavioural 'attack' on corporate-strategy models? Probably just one basic argument, but one which is of critical importance: namely, that portfolio grids are still too simplistic – not in the ways discussed in chapter 4, but through lack of recognition of the *internal* barriers to organizational change. To a limited extent the criticism is wrong, because the McKinsey–GE 'Competitive strengths' axis could be defined to include internal barriers, but there is clearly a need to consider these internal factors much more rigorously than is suggested in the McKinsey literature. If that is done, however (i.e. by extending the competitive-strengths analysis to include the ability to change *internal* barriers within required time-spans), this criticism loses its force.

Herman-Taylor (1986) develops a collegial model of change, in which a participative management style is combined with judgemental decision-making by groups of able people achieving reasoned consensus. In so doing, he distinguishes between a strategic frame of reference, which focuses on the need for change, and an organizational frame of reference, concerned more with identifying internal blockages to change. One can take advantage of this simple dichotomy in frames of reference whether or not one believes in a collegial style of management. There is no necessary conflict between the economic rational analysis and the need to consider internal barriers to change – *both* must be considered. A Porter-style analysis can be conducted first for any SBU contemplating major strategic movement. Alternate strategies can be developed, and in the process they can be 'incrementally' tested against likely internal impediments to change. In fact, it may even be necessary to commence with an analysis of schemas held in the SBU before trying to conduct a Porter analysis which itself will need to rely upon SBU help and information. Established schemas may need to be changed even before analytical strategic thinking can take place, regardless of implementation.

It has become clear, therefore, that any economic analysis within the framework of a portfolio grid needs to be supplemented by an organizational analysis. This may be based on, for example, the Finney and Mitroff Organizational Self-Reflection (OSR) model or the more general Guba and Lincoln approach (both are described in chapter 7). There also needs to be an integrating mechanism to ensure that the economic analysis and the organizational analysis keep in step with each other through the incremental process of strategy development described at the end of chapter 7. There will be no predetermined, obviously correct ordering and timing of the movement from the economic to the organizational frame of reference and back again. Much depends upon the perceived degree of crisis, the strength of established schemas, the origin of proposals for strategic change, the degree of rational analysis required to convince parties to the decision, and so on. It is the successful movement back and forward between these two frames of reference that will illustrate the skill of *managing* as distinct from *analysing*. Also, the pace at which this process proceeds will be as important as the timing of its initiation. That seems to me to focus fairly well on what management, often taken to be so difficult to define, really is. Moreover, it is interesting to note that the incorporation of the organizational frame of reference at the instigation of *critics* of 'rationality' actually introduces *more* rationality into the system. We now have an image of skilled corporate managers quite coolly and *rationally* collecting information, sorting out ideas and thinking through *how to get others to accept change*. Corporate managers, however, may not be the only party rationally considering how to convince others and demanding to be convinced before agreeing to change!

It is not easy to represent such an interactive process between portfolio analysis and the organizational frame of reference diagrammatically, but it seems consistent with the argument for simplifying pictures of reality that an attempt should be made to provide one. Figure 8.1 is such an attempt. The whole organization is seen as operating simultaneously at two levels: (1) the frame-breaking or strategic level, and (2) the action-continuity level. The latter will include regular operations, but also investment selection and implementation which is clearly consistent with established schemas or strategies. At the frame-breaking level there is iterative movement between external (predominantly economic) analysis and internal organizational analysis. Periodically, new schemas or strategic views crystallize and become embedded as the basis for an ongoing stream of influence over action rationality.

Figure 8.1 should not be taken necessarily to imply that frame-breaking analysis only occurs at corporate headquarters, and that action continuity is confined to the lower levels. On the other hand, frame-breaking and continuing action must be clearly separated if the diagram is to be consistent with the idea of action according to established schemas. This may be achieved in several ways. First, there may indeed be a separation by organizational hierarchical level. Second, most corporate SBUs may be operating in an action-rational mode, while a few needing turn-around are being asked to address the frame-breaking level. Third, it may actually be possible for the same organizational sub-unit to be operating simultaneously at both the frame-breaking and

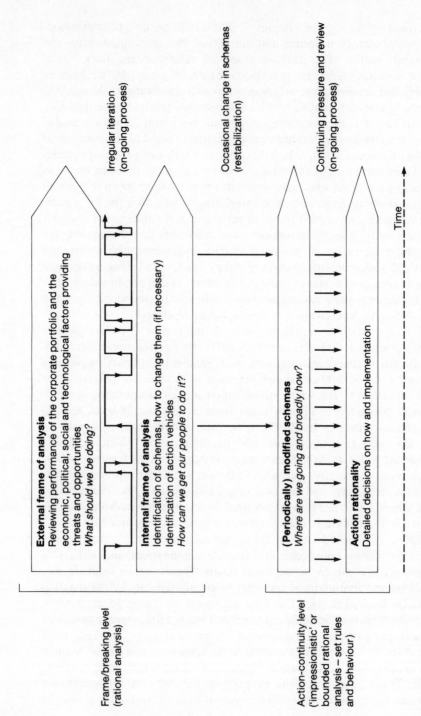

External frame of analysis
Reviewing performance of the corporate portfolio and the economic, political, social and technological factors providing threats and opportunities
What should we be doing?

Internal frame of analysis
Identification of schemas, how to change them (if necessary)
Identification of action vehicles
How can we get our people to do it?

(Periodically) modified schemas
Where are we going and broadly how?

Action rationality
Detailed decisions on how and implementation

Irregular iteration
(on-going process)

Occasional change in schemas
(restabilization)

Continuing pressure and review
(on-going process)

Time

Frame/breaking level
(rational analysis)

Action-continuity level
('impressionistic' or
bounded rational
analysis – set rules
and behaviour)

Figure 8.1 The 'incremental' management process incorporating economic and organizational perspectives

the action-oriented levels. Many of us contemplate future personal strategies while continuing to operate as before, delaying the introduction of a new operational schema until it becomes clear that our strategic thinking demands it. Either individual discipline or an equivalent form of group intelligence can surely be developed to allow the same person or organization unit to indulge in both frame-breaking and action rationality while keeping them separate. The central importance of Brunnson's argument is to stress the need to prevent on-going frame-breaking analysis from creating such uncertainty that action at the operating level is prejudiced. So long as that *is* achieved, it doesn't seem to matter much how it is organized. It *may* be best achieved by ensuring that frame-breaking (schema- and strategy-setting) takes place at one level and action at another, but in most organizations it is probably more complex than that.

It is also vital to recognize in interpreting figure 8.1 that, as chapter 7 emphasized, corporate research allocation involves multiple parties and, to a large extent, a negotiated reality. One might expect a cohesive organization to have a significant level of identity over schemas about what it should be doing, how it should do it and how it is performing, but the motivation for accepting these schemas will vary between interest groups. The word 'frame-breaking' has been used in figure 8.1 to describe marked strategic movement from the whole organization's viewpoint. Each interest group (and individual) will also have its own version of figure 8.1, and what is strategic to it may not be strategic to other interest groups. What is strategic for top managers may not be so for a group of shareholders with widely diversified portfolios. What is strategic for plant workers in South Wales may not be so for top management. Also, those at 'higher levels' may not always be in the most preferred position. Changes at the top of the organization may leave those lower down unaffected. Even takeovers may leave some virtually unaware of any change. Consequently, if top managers recognize the corporate resource-allocation process as depicted by figure 8.1, they also need to recognize that company members' motivations for adopting schemas and the associated action rationality lie within *their own* versions of figure 8.1 with *their own* interpretations of what is frame-breaking *for them* in terms of their own perceptions of what they are, what is critical to their own existence and what they are prepared to do. Hence, if top managers attempt to change schemas in order to bring about *organizational* frame-breaking, they must also be sophisticated enough to understand what *other* groups see as frame-breaking and what capacity these others have to disrupt *both* planning and implementation. Furthermore, top managers must also be aware that what seems like action rationality to them may be seen as strategic elsewhere. Hence, a mechanism is needed at even the action-rationality level to indicate where some critical group is, in effect, asked to indulge in its own perception of frame-breaking.

Hampden Turner and Baden Fuller (1989) put it well:

> Effective management consists in deploying the fullest range of values and differences and incorporating these into what the firm does. In this process informal actions and discoveries need to be combined into formal procedures. *People need to be different and have these differences integrated.*
>
> (p. 4; emphasis added)

The integration comes through being aware of the impact of corporate resource allocation on people's schemas – a matter that at present is not adequately reflected in either the finance, accounting or corporate strategy literature. If all this is the nature of reality in corporate resource allocation, we need to bear it in mind in chapter 9 when considering the contributions of finance and accounting.

A digression to review the problem of interdependencies in portfolio grids given their organizational interpretation

Before proceeding to consider the effect of figure 8.1 on accounting and finance, we need to return to the point reached at the end of chapter 4: namely, that the existence of economic and technological interdependencies seems to strike at the very basis of portfolio grids with their separate SBUs and raise severe questions about their usefulness. This position will now be reviewed in the light of the organizational-theory literature described in chapter 7.

Naylor (1986) is very strong in his criticism of management through a system of SBUs. He says this emphasizes HQ–divisional conflict, and leads to jealously guarded fiefdoms and zero-sum gains, where someone's gain must always be a co-participant's loss. The whole process reflects, in his view, a distorted view of eighteenth-century capitalism and foolish attempts to create the competitive model-market structure within a corporate group. No doubt this state of affairs can exist, indeed does exist, in many companies. Marsh et al. (1987) also show how divisions tend to look inward to their own 'patch' rather than look for benefits to the whole group. In such situations, says Naylor, critical decisions are made within single departments without the benefit of consultation with other managers. Also, in the worst cases, it leads executives to become alienated and opt out of the organization.

The error Naylor makes is his assumption that this must be the inevitable consequence of corporate divisional structures or the use of

SBUs and portfolio grids. The sort of situation he describes results from managerial style, methods of performance evaluation and the reward/penalty system. The portfolio-grid approach is nothing more than a form of analysis; it does not have to be used with confrontational management tactics or an eighteenth-century view of capitalism. There are *always* some areas of possible tension between the parties to a relationship. The method of analysis may resolve such tensions as well as highlight them. It depends how it is handled; it is not inevitable that the outcome will always be damaging for the relationship.

A more significant criticism of portfolio grids relates to their ability to analyse SBUs separately, given the existence of economic, technological or other interdependencies. These issues are much better considered in Prahalad and Doz (1987). The thrust of their book is addressed to the increasing interconnectedness of business operations within international groups. They recognize clearly, however, that there are trade-offs between divisional/SBU interdependence and freedom. Interdependence may bring advantages in the form of cost reduction (common technologies, production, and so on), leverage over common customers and suppliers, increased leverage over governments, and so on. On the other hand, excessive interdependence can produce losses in local task focus and performance visibility, flexibility and diversification, innovation and speed of response, and result in excessive co-ordination costs. Nevertheless, Prahalad and Doz make out a convincing case for the increasing interdependence of business units in many larger corporations and of the need to manage that process. Astley (1984) takes the argument even further and stresses the growing interdependence of different corporate groups in society and the need to manage those 'collectivities'. So it is important to consider the conclusions arrived at so far from the viewpoint of this growing interdependence.

Recall the arguments of Weick (1985). Large organizations are very complex systems. Take into account the economic interactions between market structures and competitive action. Then also take into account the sheer complexity of the problem of managing all possible interactions. It must be concluded that total optimization is impossible; indeed, it can never exist because the parameters change continually. Pitts and Daniels (1984) show, for example, the difficulties of running dual reporting systems in companies organized on a matrix basis, and forecast the demise of the approach in favour of a range of other processes of managing interactions, including management rotation, achieving physical proximity of related parts of the business, worldwide boards for individual businesses, and liaison assignments. As a further example, a major UK bank recently undertook a portfolio analysis. It had fifty-four SBUs on its grid. The scope for interaction is obviously considerable. It is impossible to deal with the required degree of interaction in one formal analysis.

Weick (1985) also emphasizes that links will vary in strength, implying that parts of a system may be coupled, but rather loosely. This suggests, as Prahalad and Doz agree, that tight co-ordination is more likely to be focused on a few linkages which are of critical importance. If we recall also the argument that *increasing* the internal linkages (e.g. diversification of a supply) may also make it *less* necessary to manage the interactions between SBUs, it becomes clear that the existence of interdependence may not necessarily imply tight, central co-ordinating mechanisms or analyses. Much obviously depends on the types of links.

It is likely, then, that there will be a few critical links which do need to be managed at strategic level from head office. This can be achieved in various ways.

First, a strategic *analysis* using the location of SBUs on a portfolio grid does not mean that there must be administrative or organizational responsibility units called SBUs. A large company can, for example, maintain a portfolio analysis over several different 'cross-cuts' of the corporation. It can interpret SBUs as product groups, countries, customer groups or anything else it chooses. Analytical results from one grid can be compared with those from others to see whether there are marked conflicts for particular administrative units (divisions, etc.). If so, they can be specifically discussed with the administrative unit concerned. This process is, moreover, likely to inform top management of the stresses and confused loyalties existing at divisional level, which often lead to the animosity that Naylor describes. In other words, the strategic analysis itself, based on different interpretations of SBUs, does not have to be tightly coupled with the organization structure. There may well be a need for Naylor's 'strategy teams', but that does not do away with the usefulness of SBU matrices.

Second, if it is recognized that portfolio grids can be the basis of an on-going process (rather than a once-and-for-all-grand design), it is straightforward to propose changes in one SBU and then inquire of the others what effect this will have on them. At the next iteration (debate about strategic position), the other SBUs experiencing a major effect can present their analysis. This is quite in keeping with Quinn's incremental movement towards a solution, identifying interaction effects step by step.

Third, identification and consideration of interactions does not necessarily require extensive analysis each time. Some of the interactions, once discovered, will themselves enter part of the SBU schema and script. Salancik and Porak (1986) evoke the familiar cliché of not seeing the wood for the trees. They emphasize the need to focus on key interdependencies, but say that these soon become embedded. Once we have gained experience, we form holistic, and simplified, 'cause-and-effect' maps which encompass a broad feeling for *major* interconnections in decision processes. Salancik and Porak base their views on two studies of university academic departments, but the fundamental concepts apply to any organization. If part of the division's/SBU's schema is the need to check on *major* links with other relevant divisions, and the penalty/reward system creates difficulties for that division if it does not do this, then the interests of other sections of the organization become its own interests.

Finally, even though there may be some (theoretical) loss through a lack of tight co-ordination between SBUs, it is necessary to encourage creativity and a diversity of views feeding into the strategic debate. It is in the group interest to separate some parts of the business for experimentation without risking the whole corporate network through many internal links. It is also important to have some 'conflict of view' to stimulate consideration of a wider range of options. The price of this creativity may be increased ambiguity, but without it there is the danger that divisions, knowing that central mechanisms for co-ordination exist, will leave questions of co-ordination entirely to headquarters. Therein lies the danger of 'group-think' (Janis, 1985). If SBUs or divisions are themselves forced to consider linkages, they may actually question them when they are too constricting and have dysfunctional consequences, suggesting modifications which may benefit everyone. Moreover, there is some evidence (see Goold and Campbell, 1987) that more managers may be moving to reduce linkages within corporate groups in order to gain improved concepts of accountability.

Clearly, the problem of inter-SBU linkages is a complex matter. No corporate group should employ a portfolio-grid analysis ignoring the possibility of creating synergy through SBU linkages. Also, some corporate groups operate with technologies which need much tighter co-ordination than others do. But, given the complexities of organizational life, this is no reason to leap to the naïve assumption that large corporate groups must be managed by means of some comprehensive, tightly coupled, group-wide model. There is a variety of ways of managing linkages. An analysis of an SBU must be *largely* separable, not completely separate. One can gain useful insights from considering an SBU alone, while bracketing off the rest of the complex, messy world. That does not mean, however, that one does not then look at other parts of the SBU network to consider effects there. The process will just tend to be iterative, with a moving focus of attention, and perhaps not even all that systematic. Instant optimization is not possible, but corporate portfolio grids coupled with organizational frame analysis can considerably assist managers to make sense of their worlds, create the appropriate schemas and identify where investment resources are best placed. By using grids within an incremental *process* they take us a step towards integrating corporate analysis with Quinn's reality, which recognizes the difficulties both of internal change and of coping with or even enacting the external environment. A series of portfolio grids can, perhaps, be developed to provide a practical over-arching view of the whole corporate process, a facility that is not afforded by the specific market analyses of Porter or the behavioural commentaries of Weick.

References

Astley, W., 1984: Towards an appreciation of collective strategy. *Academy of Management Review*, 9, no. 1.

Brunnson, N. 1985: *The Irrational Organization*. London: John Wiley.

Gladstein, D. and Quinn, J. 1986: Making decisions and producing action: the two faces of strategy. In H. Sims, D. Gioia et al., *The Thinking Organization*. San Francisco: Jossey-Bass.

Goold, M. and Campbell, A. 1987: *Strategies and Styles*. Oxford: Basil Blackwell.

Hampden Turner, C. and Baden Fuller, C. 1989: *Strategic Choice and the Management of Dilemma: lessons from the domestic appliance industry*. London Business School, Working Paper no. 51.

Hapeslaugh, P. 1982: Portfolio planning: uses and limits. *Harvard Business Review*, January–February.

Herman-Taylor, R. 1986: Finding new ways of overcoming resistance to change. In H. Sims, D. Gioia et al., *The Thinking Organization*. San Francisco: Jossey-Bass.

Janis, I. 1985: Sources of error in strategic decision-making. In J. M. Pennings et al., *Organizational Strategy and Change*. San Francisco: Jossey-Bass.

Kanter, R. M. 1989: *When Giants Learn to Dance*. New York: Simon and Schuster.

Marsh, D., Barwise, P., Thomas, K. and Wensley, R. 1987: Managing strategic investment decisions. Paper presented to the BAM Conference, Warwick.

Naylor, T. 1986: *The Corporate Strategy Matrix*. New York: Basic Books.

Newman, W. 1986: Formulating an integrated view of strategic management. In H. Sims, D. Gioia et al., *The Thinking Organization*. San Francisco: Jossey-Bass.

Pitts, R. and Daniels, J. 1984: Aftermath of the matrix mania. *Columbia Journal of World Business*, Summer.

Porter, M. 1985: *Competitive Advantage*. New York: Collier Macmillan.

Prahalad, C. and Doz, Y. 1987: *The Multi-national Mission: balancing hold demands and global vision*. New York: Collier Macmillan.

Salancik, G. and Porak, J. 1986: Distilled ideologies: values derived from causal reasoning in complex environments. In H. Sims, D. Gioia et al., *The Thinking Organization.* San Francisco: Jossey-Bass.

Starbuck, W. H. 1982: Congealing oil: inventing ideologies to justify acting ideologies out. *Journal of Management Studies,* 19.

Weick, K. 1986: Sources of order in underorganized systems: themes in recent organizational theory. In Y. S. Lincoln (ed.), *Organizational Theory and Inquiry: the paradigm revolution.* Beverley Hills: Sage.

Discussion questions

8.1   During times of strategic change, decision rationality may play a major role, but between such changes action rationality will dominate. Discuss this statement and consider whether these different ways of operating may be fitted into a model of how an organization works.

8.2   While it may be critically important to wait for the right time to initiate thoughts about change, it is also very important to manage the pace at which the iterative process of considering external and internal rationalities takes place. Discuss this statement.

8.3   Review the arguments for and against the use of portfolio grids in strategic management.

8.4   The major weakness of portfolio grids is their inability to allow for interdependencies between SBUs and their deterministic implications for investment and divestment. Discuss this statement.

9

Financial Control in Pluralistic Organizations

Earlier we saw that the corporate-strategy literature provides some insights for developing analyses undertaken by both accountants and corporate-finance specialists. Some speculation on this was provided in chapters 5 and 6. The relevant question now is what has been added by figure 8.1 and the discussion leading up to it in chapters 7 and 8 that may offer *additional* insights for accounting and finance, i.e. beyond those provided in chapters 5 and 6.

The essential additions which figure 8.1 and the discussion in chapters 7 and 8 bring into focus are mainly threefold. First, it is now recognized that organizations consist of multiple groups with variable negotiating powers. These groups come together as coalitions to satisfy their own particular objectives. Hence, one cannot assume a passive response to major change. People with whom top management has to deal both within and beyond the organizational boundary cannot be treated as commodities to be bought and sold, or, at least, they cannot unless top management exercises considerable power over them. (I want to avoid suggesting a moral or political stance here. I am trying to discuss how organizations work, not how, from an ethical viewpoint, they should or should not work.) Second, it is clear that strategy-making is not necessarily just some central corporate-headquarters activity. Third, it is also now recognized that total and comprehensive rationality with full information is impossible. People and hence organizations make sense of their words through schemas and, between changes of schemas, operate 'impressionistically'. The three features must now be considered in relation to financial analysis and control in so far as it affects the major corporate resource-allocation process.

I do not wish to raise readers' expectations too far at this juncture. What follows is speculative and partial. No claim is made to map out a full role for accounting and finance in pluralistic organizations. To do that rigorously requires considerable research, many researchers and many years. What is offered are some of my own thoughts about accounting and finance in the light of figure 8.1. If that helps, to some extent, to set the direction for some future research, I shall be very satisfied.

Thoughts on risk analysis in pluralistic organizations

Our earlier discussion of the concept of risk in investment appraisal, and of the rate of return required to compensate for risk, was conducted from the viewpoint of the current theory of finance. The subject received some further elaboration in chapter 6, after reviewing some of the literature on corporate strategy, but the underlying assumption of the current theory of finance was retained – namely, that the sole objective is to maximize shareholder wealth. Where, however, organizations are coalitions of groups possibly able to affect both the consideration and implementation of projects, it seems appropriate that the risk/return positions of *all* such groups should be analysed. A complete theory of financial management (as distinct from a theory of capital markets) would need to have a framework which showed how to analyse the impact of investment projects on managers, the workforce, governments and other non-shareholder groups.

There is, as yet, no developed theory which addresses financial management from a non-shareholder perspective. It may seem quite legitimate for large companies, with their shares very widely held, to ignore shareholders' attitudes towards risk. It may seem acceptable for directors of such large companies to act on the basis that shareholders are consenting adults and that, if they do not look after their own risk diversification, that is just too bad. That is the world of CAPM man! Corporate men, however, in the shape of the directors, managers and workers themselves, are unlikely to be enthusiastic if their risk attitudes are ignored. If the company suffers a severe setback, they will suffer with it; or, at least, some of them may.

Care should be taken not to assume that different parties' attitudes will be determined solely by financial returns and risk. Nevertheless, these will be important determinants of behaviour. What is needed, therefore, from company financial analysts is a way of analysing the risk/return positions of all major stakeholder groups. It seems obvious that project betas will not capture all the risk of an investment from the viewpoint of non-shareholders. It may also seem, therefore, that financial managers will need to consider the impact of a project upon the variability of the total corporate returns, even though the current theory of finance says that this is not required. A warning, however, is needed: the argument needs to be more complex than this.

First, recall that it was emphasized in chapter 8 that common, widely held corporate schemas may exist, but that each interest group holding such a schema may have a different motivation for doing so. Its motivation will be directly tied to its own perception of risk and return derived from being part of the organization. It is critical, however, to identify each group's *own conception of the organization* to which it belongs. This is because its own view on risk will be tied to that. To clarify: top directors may be happy to have their own risk/return position associated with the performance of the whole corporate group. The case may be similar for the government of the parent company's country. On the other hand, a foreign government is unlikely to be content with a situation where the attractiveness of investments is examined solely from a parent-company viewpoint. Similarly, divisional executives may see their own risk/return situations as tied more to the future of the division (some support is provided by Marsh et al., 1987), while elements of the workforce may identify theirs with the future of product groups or even local plants. The first stage of multi-party risk analysis is, therefore, to identify the '**relevant entity**' (i.e. whole group, division, plant, etc) which determines the risk faced by each party. Of course, an interest group may perceive that it is at risk from several 'relevant entities'.

While one may identify the 'relevant entities' it does *not* then automatically follow that the appropriate notion of risk measurement for each interest group is the variability of the total returns of that entity or indeed the probability of its collapse. The CAPM is applicable to shareholders because they can hold diversified portfolios and modify the mix of securities held to compensate, in part, for risks they do not like which are undertaken by a company in which they are investing. All non-systematic risk can be diversified away. Does a similar logic apply to other types of stakeholder?

To the extent that a wealth-maximizing stakeholder (i.e. a non-shareholder) holds assets not associated with the company, he (or she) might be able to compensate for increased 'relevant entity' risk by modification of his asset portfolio. This might especially be the case for non-shareholder groups external to a company, such as suppliers, customers and governments. It might also apply to some corporate chairmen and executives. In general, however, it seems reasonable to suppose that the scope for home-made risk modification will be limited for most stakeholder groups internal to the corporate group. Even for them, however, one should not automatically think that variability of the total returns of the 'relevant entity' must be the correct concept of risk. They may be diversified in another sense – in their own flexibility of movement. They may be able to adjust their 'portfolio' by changing jobs.

Can one really say that top executives are completely undiversified in terms of interest in the risky activities of the company they manage? Are they not in a better position than shareholders? If the company collapses, the shareholders lose some of the value of their investment. If a manager can walk away to another appointment at no cost, should he not be risk-neutral with regard to the company's investment programme? In assessing *his* risk should one not use a risk-free discount rate?

Of course, there will always be a cost either in money or other terms, but the freedom with which some chief executives seem to change companies suggests that the risk attached to their 'personal portfolio of earning capacity' is not exclusively locked up in the total risk of the company that they are currently managing, even where they do not have substantial other assets. They are diversified through flexibility in terms of their own personal capacities.

The same might apply to the workforce. If jobs of similar (or acceptable) type are readily available without a transfer cost, why should the workforce not be risk-neutral also? Once again, there are usually costs involved in corporate or plant collapse and, in the United Kingdom in recent years, these have sometimes been very harsh indeed. This is not a cavalier attempt to ride roughshod over such personal difficulties, but an attempt to point out that the way in which risk is assessed in project appraisal ought to depend, in part, on the market for the services of those who may be affected by the project.

Consequently, accountants have a potential role in examining the risk/return perspectives of each stakeholder group likely to be affected by major investment proposals. If this examination is not carried out, an apparently worthwhile project from a shareholder viewpoint may fail at implementation or not even be proposed at all. With specified models of risk/return for different stakeholder groups, it may be possible to create a better understanding of others' view of the world, to institute negotiations to modify risks unacceptable to one or other of the parties, and generally to undertake more investment. Of course, such activities already take place informally in practice, but there is no current, rigorously derived financial theory by which to assess them. Hence, justification for behaviour may be left more to the display of power. The exercise of power requires a mobilization of support of some kind. Exposing the risk/return of different parties to more careful analysis may show where that support is and is not justified. Of course, some parties may not want the effect of change upon others' risk/return positions to be perceived. Even so, it may be wise for top managers, for example, to be aware of the effects on other parties, even if they decide not to communicate this information. Eventually the effects will be perceived, and forewarned is forearmed.

It follows from the above argument that general alternatives to maximization of shareholder wealth, such as increases in value added, or Grinyer's Maximization of Monetary Surplus (MMS), or Currie's emphasis on total risk (Grinyer, 1986; Currie, 1989) do make us aware of non-shareholder perspectives, but do not take us very far towards building commitment from relevant stakeholders. These approaches are weak because they do nothing to help us identify the schemas held of their risk/return positions by the various groups which comprise the organization. They may help to emphasize that all stakeholders are in the activity together and that, in general, policies which increase value added enable all types of internal stakeholders to share in the extra surplus gained. That may, however, be of little comfort to the management or employees of a particular plant which is closed down as part of a strategic development without careful specification of their financial risk/return situation, or to any particular group which sees everyone else benefiting from the risk to which it alone is exposed. The corporation may well see a crisis emerging if no strategic movement occurs, but certain stakeholder groups may see a much greater crisis to their own position in the new strategy itself.

Some of the implications of this are obvious. Analysis of local alternatives for employment, costs of employment transfer, adequate compensation for redundancy, promises of adequate compensation or security if the strategy does not work, availability of alternative workers at existing pay rates, perceptions of performance-related pay schemes, executive incentives, and so on, may all be criticial in understanding key stakeholder positions. There is, however, a little more to it than that. There is the need for the financial analyst to identify what those key stakeholders see as 'their' organization and the need to identify the risks which the strategy has for *that part* of the total group. In pluralistic organizations relevant risk analyses are not adequately encompassed within beta risk or even total corporate risk. A variety of risk analyses may be needed from a variety of key stakeholder perspectives. It is only with analysis of risks at different levels that appropriate steps can be taken to gain commitment either by modifying the risks or by providing adequate compensation for taking them.

The question then arises as to how the non-shareholder requirements may be fed into strategic analysis. Once again this will probably be achieved in practice through an iterative, incremental process similar to that shown in figure 8.1. This will be a balancing operation whereby developments are reviewed successively from the viewpoint of key stakeholders rather than just shareholder wealth maximization, with, perhaps, the parties whose risk/return positions are most severely affected receiving a greater part of the value aded. This is presumably what is achieved through the Japanese consensus-building process.

If adequate and reliable risk/return analyses could be developed for different stakeholder groups, less time might need to be spent in constructing consensus. It is recognized that time spent in discussion usually helps, in itself, to build understanding and commitment, but discussion and even negotiation may be conducted more efficiently with the aid of analytical assessments of stakeholders' risk/return requirements. Clancy and Collins (1989) provide a good analysis of the behavioural factors which upset capital budgeting, but all they offer by way of improvement is the comment that behavioural factors should be taken into account, without being allowed to obscure relevant decision data of a more rational nature. They overlook that these 'behavioural factors' are a form of rational behaviour to someone. An approach like that proposed in this section might do more than just make the accountant aware of 'behavioural factors'. He or she might actually start to analyse their financial aspects.

Although executives and the workforce may be the prime internal stakeholders, it must also be remembered that there are other stakeholders with power to disrupt. These may be customers, suppliers, government departments, and so on. Recall that Porter's industrial analysis was essentially about the identification of relative economic power of one's own corporate businesses. Therefore, this also may be the basis for identifying the key external stakeholders whose risk/return perceptions need to be considered. Given that much of Porter's analysis depends on financial figures and economic data, the financial manager also has a key role to play in identifying the external stakeholders with power to disrupt. While they may be external to the organization (as usually conceived), it will be necessary also to see what they need to persuade them to accept strategic developments without opposition.

There is one final point to consider with regard to dealing with non-shareholders' welfare. It is by no means obvious that a wealth-maximizing criterion such as net present value (NPV) is the appropriate criterion for investment selection. The workforce and managers may well be more concerned with continuity of employment and income, inasmuch as they do not have the ability to move employment without cost. Similarly, a government helping to finance a project may be more interested in stability of employment. That does not mean that risk and innovation should be avoided; after all, taking some risk to increase, say, market share may help to ensure longer-run security. Yet it is not obvious that the NPV mechanism provides the correct weighting through time of the benefits to be derived from projects where security of employment is important. It might be argued that if the company maximizes NPV (or net monetary value in Grinyer's model), it should be able to raise finance on the promise of future returns and to keep the workforce together pending the bonanza. It may be able to do so, but are we sure the world functions so perfectly?

The conclusion arrived at is, therefore, simple to summarize, even if it also suggests some confusion in so far as it is not possible to prescribe one simple correct way to appraise major investment projects. A variety of analyses are needed. The analysis will be predominantly in the form of NPV or adjusted present value (APV) calculations backed by appropriate strategic considerations where shareholder welfare is concerned, and at least we know quite a lot about the right and wrong ways to approach that problem.

In addition some attention should be given to the identification of 'relevant entities' and risks attached to their futures. Some groups, however, might even be risk-neutral or face very low risks when their personal market positions are taken into account. Just as the CAPM provided better insights into the required returns of shareholders by seeing their position as located in a market, so similar insights might be gained on other stakeholder perspectives by examining their positions in markets. (It would be interesting to see how far differences in top managers' compensation reflect the risks they face.)

Where stakeholder groups cannot change allegiance with ease, there will be the need to employ criteria other than discounted cash flow (DCF). The principal alternative is probably continuity of activity in some sense, and this may be translated into development of market share or growth, irrespective of NPV *per se*. There is some evidence, for example, that, in Japan it is the dominant job-for-life phenomenon that stimulates the search for organic corporate growth as a means of achieving employment security and scope for promotion (Odagiri, 1988). It also now becomes clear that, if DCF is to be rejected as discussed (and refuted) in chapter 6, it must be on the basis of the objectives of non-shareholder stakeholders, not through some inherent inability of DCF to incorporate long-run effects. What Hayes and Garvin (1982) and Hill (1985) are really arguing for in criticizing DCF is a non-shareholder view of the world. It's as well to get that clear. Shareholders may not worry too much whether *one* company in which they are investing has a 'long-term tomorrow'.

How corporate managers must be concerned with entity risk when maximizing shareholder wealth – despite the CAPM!

It has been stressed that, when the objective is to maximise shareholder wealth, the most complete theory available to us is the CAPM. There is one danger with the theory, however, and that is that it may encourage finance directors totally to ignore corporate risk (or 'relevant entity' risk) and to focus exclusively on the CAPM's systematic risk. This could lead to errors even when only trying to maximize shareholder wealth. Such a statement runs directly counter to the current position in the theory of finance and so needs careful explanation.

The perception that the current theory of finance needs to be handled with care at this point is derived directly from the notion of 'negotiated reality' and the recognition that interest groups other than shareholders are not always passive. Consequently, they can react to affect shareholders' positions. The case is developed by reference to a company getting into financial distress, but it will be seen that this is just a special case of the need to recognize multiple groups' interests.

The CAPM is concerned with the specification of the return shareholders require in the case of risks attached to their portfolios. The implication is that, as this risk is specified only in terms of systematic risk, corporate finance directors can disregard any calls for diversification: they merely should try to see that the company earns the required yield commensurate with its beta. But the value of the corporate equity is a function of both the expected cash flow and the discount rate. Also, if a company gets into serious financial distress, i.e. has a strong possibility of being forced into liquidation, this will affect its ability to generate future cash flows. Once the word is out that the XYZ company is in trouble, customers may start to consider companies where continuity of supply and maintenance is more assured. Suppliers may insist on quicker payment of bills; some may even refuse to supply. Providers of finance may require more restrictive covenants attached to debt instruments and, in order to survive through the short term, the company may be forced to preserve cash by cutting back on R&D or selling off parts of its business at less than its 'true worth'. Consequently, financial distress may itself reduce the ability of the company to generate attractive cash flows.

Recognition that financial distress can directly affect the cash-flow position means that there is a rationale for managers to engage in various sorts of financial hedging techniques in order to convert a given operating stream of expected earnings, with given expected variability, into one with less variance, at least on the downside, in order to reduce the likelihood of financial distress (see Shapiro and Titman, 1986). The CAPM does not therefore completely remove the need for managers to consider more than just the systematic risk attached to the corporate cash flows. Financial managers should evaluate individual projects using the appropriate discount rate based upon the project beta. In addition, however, they should also check whether that project's projected cash flows interact with the cash flows from existing operations and other projects already accepted in such a way as to make financial distress significantly more likely. If they do, there are two steps that the manager can take.

He (or she) can either decide (1) to accept the risk or (2) to take action through financing operations to change the sequence of corporate cash flows so that the threat of financial distress can be removed. If he takes the first option, he must base the estimate of the expected cash flows and the project beta on the net incremental cash flows after allowing for the likelihood of financial distress, but that cannot be done without considering the interaction between the individual project under consideration and the rest of the company's proposed operations. The CAPM and the associated theory of finance are not wrong, but they assume that all the interest-group interactions have been worked out before the projected cash flows and betas are calculated. The practising financial manager does not have the luxury of such an assumption. A consideration of total firm risk is therefore essential in arriving at the project incremental expected cash flow and its beta.

If the manager adopts the second alternative, i.e. that of using financing tools to help the company through a relatively short period in which liquidity will be strained, there will be no need to revise the initial estimates of the project cash flows or the original estimate of the project beta (apart from allowing for any *extra* financing costs). He does not know, however, what financing is needed without looking at the aggregate corporate position.

It is interesting to note, however, that this argument with regard to suppliers and customers is just a special case of the multiple-interest-groups situation highlighted in chapters 7 and 8. If the 'relevant entity' risk as defined in the previous section of this chapter is recognized, any relevant stakeholder group may not be passive as assumed in the theory of finance. It may well exercise power and take steps which will affect both the level of projected cash flows and their covariance with the market portfolio. Hence, *even if trying only to maximize shareholder behaviour, the financial director has to consider 'relevant entity' risk before estimating the projected cash flows and, indeed, the project beta.* This arises from the perception that shareholder-wealth maximizers still have to operate in negotiated environments and may not be able to treat other interest groups as mere commodities in their project-appraisal calculation. Of course, the extent to which this is a problem in practice will depend upon the strategic significance of the project to various interest groups and may often be ignored where investments are marginal to those groups' interests, but the point may have more than theoretical relevance where major strategic change is being undertaken.

In sum, the above argument establishes that companies cannot consider major projects in isolation. Their evaluation of them must proceed in two stages. First, projects must be assessed separately on the basis of what might be called their 'direct' incremental cash flows and their associated beta, determined by the likely covariance of those 'direct' cash flows and the market portfolio. Second, the impact of the marginal project on 'relevant entity' risk must be assessed, as a result of which it may be concluded (a) that no modification of the projected cash flows is necessary, in which case the original project NPV calculations can stand, or (b) that financing operations are needed in order to modify the 'relevant entity' risk in order to allow those original calculations to stand, or (c) that the original estimates of the 'direct' incremental cash flows and the associated project beta need to be modified in the light of a change in 'relevant entity' risk, which will affect the payments made to other stakeholders. Even if the result is (a) or (b), the second stage of project assessment is still needed.

Also, it is interesting to note that, if the result is (c), incorporating recognition of changed 'relevant entity' risk could lead, in theory, to an increase in the NPV for the project. This might occur if the project's cash-flow distribution under a situation of, say, financial distress were less correlated with the market-portfolio returns. Then the decreased beta effect might outweigh the decreased cash-flow effect. This would seem to depend upon how deep the financial distress is likely to be. In the extreme case of financial distress leading to complete bankruptcy, the expected project cash flows might be converted to near zero, such that no decreases in beta would give an increased NPV.

It is interesting to note, furthermore, that large companies often do adopt a two-stage evaluation of major projects on the lines of that specified above, even if they do not apply the CAPM approach to the determination of discount rates. Some sort of financial model will usually be run in the second stage in order to assess the impact of a large additional project upon the total corporate position. The CAPM theory does not invalidate such action if the main purpose of looking at the aggregate position is to assess the likelihood of financial distress or other changes in 'relevant entity' risk which may affect the project cash flows.

The location of frame-breaking responsibility in the organization and its relevance to financial control: ROI revisited, yet again!

In chapter 5 it was largely accepted that return on investment (ROI) is dysfunctional if used as a performance measure to motivate investment, but that, when applied sensibly, it is useful for short-term diagnosis. It was argued that early signs of success in investment are to be sought by reference to its effects upon critical success factors and key result areas. Now that argument will be qualified. It will not be discarded, but it will be argued that exactly how this is implemented will depend upon the nature of the company and where frame-breaking is located within it. In particular, it will be suggested that, if the company's divisions are loosely coupled, all seeking to innovate to ensure their own future existence, ROI does, after all, have a very useful role to play in motivating investment. To establish the argument it is necessary first to explain recent work on corporate structure and associated management styles; this will give insight into how ROI is used.

It is clear from figure 8.1 that a sharp distinction needs to be made between the frame-breaking process and the action-rationality level, but it has been stressed that it would be a mistake to assume that this simply reflects the distinction between head-office and divisional roles. While the general thrust of the Bower and Ackerman findings (see chapter 7) still holds, those results were published in 1970, and in the meantime there has been much development in strategic management and many corporate groups have become multi-business operations. The growing size and complexity of large corporate groups have probably made practices more diverse, Goold and Campbell (1987) suggest.

Goold and Campbell studied sixteen large UK corporations and classified them into three categories of management control:

1 **strategic-planning companies** (SPCs)
2 **financial-control companies** (FCCs)
3 **strategic-control companies** (SCCs)

In SPCs the head office gets significantly involved in setting strategies for the group's businesses. Their philosophy is that there are just two or three major strategic decisions to be made in each decade for each business, as a result of which that business will succeed or fail. It is deemed unwise to leave business managers to make those critical path-determining decisions. Head office is concerned most of the time with whether each subsidiary business is moving in the right direction in accordance with its set strategy.

In contrast, in the FCCs head offices give their subsidiary businesses financial targets, and usually quite short-term ones. Business managers are left to determine their own strategy to ensure *continued* good financial performance. The head office also seems less committed to the continuation of any business. Compared to corporations in the other two categories, an FCC tends to be more widely diversified and its board much more readily inclined to sell or buy businesses.

Head offices in SCCs are involved in the formulation of business strategy less than head offices in SPCs but more than their counterparts in FCCs. They assist businesses in devising their strategies, but expect to take the main responsibility for this themselves. Control over businesses is exercised by a balance of short- and long-term performance indicators.

As stated by Goold and Campbell, companies such as Cadbury Schweppes, BP and United Biscuits are SPCs. Hanson Trust and GEC are FCCs, and ICI, Imperial Group and Plessey are SCCs. While this chapter was being written, Alan Pink (ICI's current general manager in charge of planning) stated at a conference on the subject 'Routes to Global Leadership' that ICI now classifies all its businesses into four categories: growth businesses, cash cows, problem businesses and new businesses (see *Financial Times*, 3 February 1988). As a result there has been a shift from an organization structure based on geographical territories to one where global business managers work closely with heads of territorial divisions to ensure that businesses are developed on a truly international basis. This indicates two things of relevance to this book. First, it confirms the view that there is merit in the portfolio-grid classification system and that its use does not necessarily conflict with the need to manage interdependencies within the group. Second, it illustrates how an SCC operates, with international businesses being prime movers in developing their own strategy within a broad portfolio perspective maintained by head office.

Goold and Campbell also discovered that the profitability performance of all three categories was good, although this was achieved in different ways. For example, organic business growth was good in SPCs, whereas FCCs tended to improve profitability through acquisition. In SCCs it was also found that short-term measures of performance tended to take precedence over long-term ones. In general, no one management style emerged as clearly the best way of developing strategy, and the role of head office tended to vary with the structure of the group. For example, one would expect a group with five or six main businesses to be strategically managed by head office, but in the case of a group such as Hanson Trust the company has too many businesses for top management to understand all their needs. Consequently, groups with many subsidiary businesses may be managed more like FCCs. This, however, ought not to mean that the distinction between the strategic-analysis (external and internal) and action-rationality levels of figure 8.1 is meaningless. The strategic analysis still needs to be done somewhere. In FCCs and SCCs, it is just done lower down the corporate hierarchy. We do *not* have to map the process description of figure 8.1 onto the HQ–division organizational divide. The same process can be accommodated within different structures. The portfolio-grid analysis will be useful wherever a unit *within* a corporate group wishes to balance the development of different business activities. This unit may be the whole group, but in larger corporations it is increasingly being seen as the subsidiary or some subdivision of the group, with that unit itself expected to have *continued* good financial performance. In other words, a division which can produce a *consistently* good ROI (not necessarily a growing one) will retain control over its own affairs and be more able to satisfy its own executive needs. ROI is used to exert pressure in divisions to keep their *strategic analysis* up-to-date so as to retain their independence and thereby manage their own 'relevant entity' risk. If divisions are sufficiently large, there will be continuity of employment and most managers in the division will have a long-run interest in its success. If they employ sensible strategic analyses for the division's constituent SBUs (and do not place investment in those SBUs by reference only to ROI), continuing pressure for *total* divisional ROI at a minimum level need not be dysfunctional at all: quite the reverse, it allows divisions to be loosely coupled without loss of accountability and financial control by head office. Given a minimum sustained ROI achievement, the division may assume its continued independence.

The argument in the previous paragraph needs to be borne in mind when evaluating recent claims in the financial press that General Electric itself now has less regard for portfolio matrices and their related concepts. For example, in the *Financial Times* of 16 May 1988 C. Lorenz wrote,

> The new GE is very far indeed from the company which in the 1960's and 1970's was a uniquely fertile breeding ground for 'model' strategy and organisation concepts which were copied across the world by enterprises of all shapes and sizes; in many cases, they are still in the process of being installed. . . . Yet Welch's creation [i.e. the changes introduced by the new chief executive, Jack Welch] has either abandoned them [SBUs and sectors] entirely or downgraded them to secondary status [portfolio techniques].

Essentially what GE seems to have done is to recognize the problems associated with linkages between SBUs, combining its forty-three SBUs into just eighteen larger and more separable businesses. These larger businesses are then expected by group headquarters to recognize the need for rapid change while simultaneously recognizing the *continuous* need to provide good financial results. Given the size of GE and each of its businesses, this seems sensible. Though the term 'SBU' has been dropped, strategic analysis cannot possibly have been. It has been pushed down the hierarchy in order to adapt and respond more rapidly to more dynamic markets. Each business manager undoubtedly still manages a portfolio of products, product groups or product markets – indeed, with the increased rate of change in the environment, it would be difficult to see how sustained financial performance could be achieved without carefully planning for a balanced portfolio of business segments in different stages of their life-cycles. It was argued earlier that, in designing strategy, it is important not to have SBUs lost within organizational units. The GE development shows that it *is* acceptable, indeed perhaps inevitable, for this to occur in very large companies to some extent. Those at the top cannot possibly plan and control all SBUs, but those lower down must still be able to distinguish clearly between separate businesses and organization units within their own realms of responsibility. As Lorenz says in a follow-up article, 'What GE has done is not to dump the discipline or the rigour of strategic planning, but to stream-line and de-bureaucratise the process, shifting the main planning responsibility away from the centre and out to line management' (*Financial Times*, 18 May 1988). *But it can only do this by reintroducing accounting controls at the topmost level.* Those corporate strategists who have criticized the use of ROI in assessing *SBUs* are correct, but they have overlooked its *higher level* control features in very large corporate groups. Also, the strategic portfolio analysis has been decoupled from the organizational structure, but the concepts discussed in chapter 4 are still quite relevant – even SBUs. GE's abandonment of the term was obviously symbolic of the change. However, the notion of a separable business segment, which is all that an SBU is, can hardly be dropped completely in an organization so big as GE, which seems increasingly to be run like a large conglomerate.

Goold and Campbell's finding that organic growth was less in FCCs than in SPCs or SCCs might appear to suggest that the strategic analysis was not being conducted so effectively at business level in FCC groups. Care is needed, however, not to confuse the *process* of strategic analysis with its *objectives*. If FCC businesses are expected to maintain *continued* good financial performance and little variation, they will still need to conduct strategic analysis to achieve that end, and this may well lead them to forgo some degree of organic growth.

Much also depends upon the nature of the competitive environment in which businesses operate. If that environment provides no significant threat to the longer-run maintenance of current results and these are deemed satisfactory, performance measurement may be adequately monitored in terms of short-term financial indicators without much need to consider growth strategies (see Donaldson, 1985, p. 65). That does not mean, however, that the businesses need not watch the environment for new threats and opportunities.

Moreover, Goold and Campbell were emphasizing differences in styles of managerial *control*. Obviously, head offices in FCCs *will* need to undertake significant strategic analysis to back up their central acquisition policy. Also, the GE example shows how in very large organizations, consisting of divisions consisting of sub-businesses, an emphasis on short-term financial results *at higher levels* over divisions as a whole is not inconsistent with organic growth.

The argument in this section emphasizes that there is a need to keep a balance between the pressures for continuing good financial performance and those for longer-term achievement. The accounting system will be instrumental in setting organizational schemas to achieve this balance, but the extent to which ROI is dysfunctional will in turn depend upon the organizational schemas within which it is used.

It is opportune to emphasize that a short-term financial emphasis is not all bad. A focus on 'short-termism' with no regard for continued success is clearly inadvisable, but so is forever planning the future while overlooking how to stay in business in order to guarantee a future. McWilliams, chief economist at IBM (UK), recently said, 'The short-term results provide the financial strengths to support the longer-term strategy' (address, Kingston Business School, 25 May 1988). He also argued that the main factor bringing about the recent turn-around in British business performance was 'financial pressure'. That financial pressure can only be affected through the financial accounts and, where a considerable degree of delegation is required, by the use of ROI (or a similar construct).

Swieringa and Weick (1987), drawing upon Brunnson (1982), are among the few who recognize the importance of accounting to induce an appropriate action rationality. This property of accounting is often overlooked by its critics, who usually, on a rational-deductive basis, believe that the only result of pressure to achieve short-term results is cutbacks in investment, marketing and training expenditure, with dire long-term consequences. Well-run companies should recognize those dangers. The company needs to be managed to avoid *excessive* short-termism, but *continual* financial pressure will not only induce an action orientation at the operational level, but also fulfil the same function at the strategic level by ensuring that managers cannot leave until tomorrow strategic moves needed now. The strength of ROI is derived, therefore, from an understanding of organizational behaviour and corporate ideologies rather than a deductive logic associated with the hypothesized use of ROI or NPV as maximands. One should not allow pressure substantially to increase short-run ROI to lead to considerable under-investment, but some pressure to maintain ROI is vital to motivate investment.

The accountant as schema-reinforcer for SBUs

Chapters 7 and 8 stressed the need for schema-setting in order to create a basis for action and prevent continual doubts about what one is doing. It would appear that accounting measurement, especially through its control dimension, has a considerable role to play in reinforcing the existing schemas and indicating when they may need revision.

The use of accounting to induce financial pressure was discussed at a general corporate level in the previous section. The implication was that, in some very large companies, *divisions* would not be classed as 'stars', 'cash cows', and so on, but would be given resources where they promised maintenance of an acceptable ROI (for the aggregate level of risk) over the longer run. They would then be left to manage their own SBUs. When one moves to the level of analysing individual *SBUs*, the use of accounting measures to induce financial pressure can be more precise.

Where there is emphasis on short-term profitability as well as longer-term growth, the conventional, rather woolly argument is that there must be a sensible balance between short-term and long-term goals. Strategic analysis of SBUs indicates *where* there should be greater emphasis on short-term net cash inflows for the next few years and where a longer view should be taken. With this in mind, accounting for SBUs has just as important a role to play on the right-hand side of the strategic portfolio grid. It is no use rewarding a 'cash cow' manager on the basis of long-term growth. Such businesses must be pressured through the accounting system and related rewards to generate increased short-term cash flows in the later stages of their life-cycles. To illustrate: in a piece on Reckitt and Colman dated 8 April 1988 the *Financial Times* noted, while one of that company's SBUs was aiming for a breakthrough in a new anti-ulcer drug, this was to be complemented by one thing that Reckitt and Colman's management does rather well: 'squeezing the last bit of margin out of mature businesses and doing it in parts of the world which demonstrate the company's substantial skills at currency management'. That cannot be achieved without tight budget standards and considerable reliance upon the accounting system.

A consultancy colleague of mine has emphasized how essential this is in achieving the full projected profitability of the product line. SBUs (product groups) classified as 'cash cows' may be expected to be in the mature or declining stage of their life-cycles. In this phase, my colleague suggests, what happens in many companies is that the sales people start to look more to the next product to be established, while manufacturing starts to focus more on the next product development; so, if the accounting function does not focus on the proper management of products in their later years, no one will, and the SBU will end up carrying unnecessary working capital and overheads. The accountant, therefore, has a prime role to play with 'cash cows' and 'dogs'. The general direction of control will be to manage these product groups down, but the accountant should be aware of all possible options. These certainly include closing-down, but it may be preferable to extend the product's life by changing the manufacturing method for reduced volume or by contracting out small volumes. The portfolio-grid classification sets an *a priori* schema for the SBU, and in response the accountant should determine exactly what form of financial analysis and management is needed. Is the answer 'euthanasia', or can the product's life be extended? Occasionally there will be the opportunity for rebirth, but, if there is, this will be tantamount to creating a new SBU.

The problem remains, of course, that 'cash cows' and 'dogs' may produce outstanding new investment ideas with 'star' potential. This can, however, be catered for by allowing each such SBU to have a small unit following up potentially very attractive investment opportunities. It is not necessary to make growth central to the whole effort and schema of the 'cash cow' SBU, nor should such investment opportunities be generally expected. Indeed, if they are identified, then, as just stated, the consequence is more likely to be a new SBU than a continuation of the old one. The distinction between an SBU and a division is essential here. The division may well contain both the original and the new SBUs, but the relevant units for management of the strategy should be the individual SBUs – not the divisions.

In theory, wealth will be optimized, in a capital-rationing situation, by considering all positive-NPV projects and selecting a mix of projects to maximize the NPV achievable within the resource constraints, irrespective of which SBUs the projects come from. The argument against using this approach is a pragmatic, not a theoretical, one. It is just that most SBUs finding themselves in the 'cash cow' area of the grid will *by definition* have fewer long-term investment outlets. Again the distinction between an SBU and an organization division is stressed. As companies become more conscious of strategic management, the more careful they will be to prevent SBUs from sliding around to the 'cash cow' position prematurely. At the same time they should become more aware of the pointlessness of raising investment expectations in 'cash cows' which are not achievable.

From a pragmatic management viewpoint, top-level executives may well want to set investment-appraisal rules under which SBU managers will generally hold attitudes towards investment consistent with the grid location of their SBU. Otherwise there could be a perpetual battle for funds on a scale much wider than necessary, confusion over SBUs' central roles, and much waste of time and energy by 'cash cow' managers who could probably contribute better to the corporation by ensuring that some surplus revenues are earned now. The rationale for this lies within the notion of 'action rationality' and not within the thought pattern that is obsessed with ensuring that no profitable opportunity is lost. The opportunity cost of searching for and evaluating other opportunities may be too high.

This *may* mean, for example, a greater emphasis on payback for 'cash cows' and 'dogs', but a longer-run analysis with DCF for non-frame-breaking investments in 'stars'. Also, the capital-expenditure limit on investments that an SBU can undertake without reference to head office may be much lower for SBUs on the right-hand side of the McKinsey–GE matrix than for those on the left. (Or the reference might be to divisional head office in companies that Goold and Campbell would define as FCCs or SCCs.)

Companies do of course classify investment projects and do not treat them all the same in terms of the attention devoted to them and the selection rules applied. No company, for example, is likely to treat the replacement of a small boiler as a matter requiring the same degree of analysis as a major company acquisition. This is not a weakness in the analysis but a strength, because it suggests behaviour similar to that hypothesized in this book. What is not clear from the literature is whether companies do classify projects with careful attention to their strategic schemas. Research here would be helpful.

In addition to more general schema-setting through portfolio-grid categories, chapter 5 proposed a series of possible accounting analyses suggested by a reading of the corporate-strategy literature. Most of these analyses may also have a role as schema-setters. We considered what might be needed if the strategic schema adopted for an SBU were cost leadership. Moreover, we observed a distinction within this category between learning curves for single products with long lives and generic product groups with cost reductions through redesign.

If a business is pursuing a cost-leadership/strategic-pricing policy based on an experience curve, that strategy will fail unless the business is *perpetually* seeking ways to use its experience to lower costs. There must be a frequent challenging of the existing manufacturing practices with regard to capital intensity, flexible manufacturing, automation, set-up times, materials, work-in-progress levels, finished-goods stock levels, and so on. Each cost-saving investment, although in itself apparently relatively insignificant, can aid the implementation of the strategy. The strategy therefore needs to be thoroughly understood and the accounting function can do much to establish the schema of perpetual searching for operating-cost reduction throughout the business.

It is also vital to consider the **internal frame** aspects of strategy based on the experience curve. The workforce may see a continual movement down the experience curve as one of ever-tightening standards, with workers being squeezed in the unreasonable expectation that they should work harder and harder. If an experience-curve strategy is to be successful, it must be fully understood by all levels of the workforce, and regular procedures must be established to search for ways of bringing about cost reductions to the benefit of all, without ever-increasing operating effort from the workforce. The schema of cost reduction through exercising intellect, rather than ever-increasing physical effort, needs to be established. The strategic literature has not adequately considered these interactions between the external and internal frames of reference, and the part that negotiation over accounting targets and standards can play, if properly developed, in bringing these two frames of reference together.

Accounting measurements may therefore play a significant part in reinforcing existing schemas in different parts of the organization, but this is not enough. Brunnson (1985) stresses that it should be clear from the schema itself when it is no longer appropriate (part of his definition of a 'complex' schema). This, after chapter 8, may be viewed in two ways: (1) providing an early warning of when a particular SBU's strategic policy is no longer appropriate, and (2) providing a signal of an impending change in 'relevant entity' risk for a key stakeholder of the SBU – for instance, through a shift in either the external economic or internal organizational critical factors. As Quinn (1980) stresses, executives struggle with uncertainty, trying gradually to clarify the interpretation of fuzzy signals. This interpretation may be helped by a complex schema which indicates critical levels in key variables which will suggest that it is time to go frame-breaking again. In fact the situation may be rather more complex; one is reminded of Ansoff's proposals for phased responses to environmental signals as they change from weak to strong (Ansoff, 1975). Perhaps the complex schema should incorporate such staged responses to a changing situation, such that, when a signal reaches a certain strength, the issue and possible response are brought to the forefront of attention and debate. This may be of comfort to Buzzell and Gale (1987) and Wensley (1981), who suggest that companies use portfolio grids too simplistically. Complex SBU schemas may avoid such simplicity while enabling managers to be action-rational (i.e. treating a 'star' as a 'star') in the absence of signals which indicate otherwise.

In addition to considering how to link financial and more general performance indicators directly to SBU schemas, chapter 5 made it clear that even more general changes in accounting systems may be required to ensure recognition of a crisis. Activity-based costing was discussed as means of revealing more appropriate product strategies. This, in effect, is changing organizational schemas about product groups. There may, however, be conflict over which are the important schemas to be stressed at any time.

Hiromoto (1988) argues that Japanese industry is well aware of activity-based costing, but much of it continues to use a fairly crude system of charging out overheads on a labour-hour basis. The justification given is that, if managers are held responsible for their costs constructed in that way, they will be motivated to cut labour costs as much as possible. So, if the corporate schema is that automation is the secret of success in that industry, a labour on-cost rate, while distorting product costs, may still be preferable because it encourages the appropriate strategic behaviour. Once significant progress has been made in this direction, the overhead-allocation method may be changed to encourage a focus elsewhere.

Hiromoto therefore argues that it is what people do in response to accounting measures that is most important, not a crusade for accurate costs *per se*. Hiromoto is stressing the schema-reinforcing properties of accounting. In discussing this with me, an executive in the engineering industry suggested that perhaps Kaplan and the activity-based costing school were falling into the same sort of trap as manufacturing got into during the 1970s. While Western manufacturing was developing better and better devices to calculate the required levels of inventories accurately, the Japanese quietly did away with the need for them – they did distinguish the wood from the trees. However, it is my opinion that this argument, and Hiromoto's are doing Kaplan an injustice. Kaplan says that he does not necessarily recommend activity-based costing for routine control. His aim is to provide better estimates of product costs, on a *periodic* basis, in order to determine product-mix policies. The positions of Hiromoto and Kaplan should not necessarily be presented as alternatives, as Hiromoto does; they may be quite compatible. If one followed Hiromoto one might get more automation – but of the wrong products! It is unlikely that the Japanese are so naïve. They probably work out their product costs informally, but carefully, *ex ante* (as Kaplan proposes), *then* motivate the on-going search for ways of reducing labour through the schema-setting labour on-cost rate. The two views of accounting really stem from a different emphasis on the critically important success factors in corporate strategy. What Hiromoto overlooks is that both perspectives are important and that an appropriate *complex schema* could emphasize both through a combination of accounting and non-accounting methods. It is interesting to note too that most of Kaplan's cases advocating activity-based costing deal with companies in difficulty. Hence they need frame-breaking analysis to turn around the company by altering product-profitability schemas. If the Japanese firms are not in such difficulties they have no need for such an analysis – they simply need to reinforce the move towards more automation. Hence the West (USA and UK), with many 'turn around situations', may need activity-based costing to move to a more focused product strategy. Hiromoto's comments are less relevant to such situations. He obviously has in mind the situation in Japanese companies, which usually have well-focused product strategies. He may not be recognizing that different situations may require the establishment of different schemas.

The perpetually innovating company: does this invalidate the notion of set schemas?

A matter which bothered me for a considerable time in developing the ideas put forward in chapters 7 and 8 was how one could reconcile the idea of well-set schemas with occasional major change with the notion of success through continual improvement and innovation, which, we are told, is what underlies the success of many Japanese companies and is increasingly being adopted in the West. Brunnson's observation of set schemas and of 'impressionistic' decision-taking at the action-oriented level might explain why Western business fell behind, through not innovating enough. And yet Brunnson's underlying logic, building on a long tradition in organization theory, that perpetually replanning rather than taking action is dysfunctional seems, now that he has explained it, irrefutable. It obviously reflects so much of how we all, as human beings, act.

The resolution of this problem comes, however, through recognizing that innovation is not all of one type. There are 'frame-breaking' innovations and 'action-oriented' innovations. The latter might represent, for example, the perpetual search for lower costs or improved quality *within* the current schemas for market success, such as cost leadership or product differentiation. Innovations at this level are probably just as likely to be adopted 'impressionistically' (or experimentally) as to be arrived at through extensive rational analysis. An enterprise working to an established schema of perpetual innovation will probably be continually innovating at this action-oriented level. This is to be distinguished from the occasional outputs from the frame-breaking level in the form of radically new products or processes or changes to the competitive criteria in specific product groups or markets. A production director in a well known hi-tech firm recently told me that his company's customers simply did not want a major change in technology more than once a decade. They couldn't handle it: it diverted their attention from selling in their own markets. And yet this same hi-tech company revises its product specification every eighteen months or so in the perpetual search for minor improvements which over time accumulate to significant advances. This seems to provide some limited evidence that even the perpetual innovators don't break frames very often, but they do succeed between frame-breaking episodes by continual incremental improvement. If this is so, it seems that there is no paradox to refute figure 8.1 as a (rough) model of corporate reality that accountants and financial managers should get to grips with in order to learn what it implies for them. Moreover, the expectation of perpetual innovation *within* major strategies is not something that the Japanese initiated and that hi-tech computer companies have just taken up. Corporate readers of this book will probably recognize this scenario: 'impressionistic' acceptance of relatively major orders by sales personnel on the basis that the projects fit the general corporate strategy; the subsequent discovery that the project has been priced low to get the business; considerable pressure on the technical, engineering or manufacturing staff to carry out the project at that price. While the Japanese may have introduced a more planned and systematic approach to 'target pricing' in product design in a range of their businesses, the idea of pressured innovation within set strategies is, on reflection, far from new.

The accountant as a change-manager

The main goal of this chapter has been to consider how the accountant or financial manager might extend his (or her) role regarding major resource allocation in an organization which recognizes its pluralistic features. We have looked at this in relation to the analysis of multiple interests, differences in the role of ROI depending on the level of the organization responsible for frame-breaking, and the role that accounting can play as a schema-reinforcer. If the view of corporate resource allocation captured in the latter part of this book approaches reality, this is one further topic which warrants consideration.

Just as the strategic-change process needs to be managed as depicted in figure 7.2, so any change of accounting measurement or control system to ensure that the need to change existing schemas is signalled and recognized, or to facilitate the change to new schemas, will itself need to be managed as a change process. In other words, changing to, say, an activity-based costing system or to a system which more clearly measures an SBU's performance using critical success factors relevant to the 'cash cow' will itself offer gains and losses to different parties. The process of changing the accounting systems may, therefore, be seen as inextricably linked with the change in strategy itself. It follows that accountants may need to recognize the implications of figure 7.2 if they wish to install their own new systems carefully.

In one of Kaplan's cases, Schrader-Bellows, it was recognized that producing a rational new accounting analysis of product costs does not in itself guarantee widespread acceptance of that analysis and its implications. This has been corroborated by the relatively few other studies of attempts to change accounting systems: for example, Palepu (1987), Bruns (1987), Dent (1987) and Schreuder (1987). All these studies also provide *some* insights into why the new systems failed, but their reasons seem to be partial. If failures in system implementation are to be understood, there is a need for more systematic studies using a model (like figure 7.2, which itself may need further elaboration) which provides a more comprehensive coverage of the change process. This suggestion comes directly from the conclusion to chapter 7, where the development of figure 7.2 suggested that broad statements such as the need for top-level involvement do not go very far towards explaining why change succeeds or fails in specific circumstances.

The importance of a model like figure 7.2 has been emphasized to a colleague and me in our work to help a major government department change its mode of operation upon the introduction of extensive new management-information systems and changes in the locus of control within the UK Financial Management Initiative (Colville and Tomkins, 1989; Tomkins and Colville, 1989). It soon also became clear, however, that devising a general model like figure 7.2 is the easy part of the task. Identifying the inputs to such a model is far from problem-free, and, when one does discover the variety of schemas held, there is still the considerable problem from the top manager's viewpoint of what to do about them. In addition, once the 'schema equilibrium' is broken, different interest groups will explore alternative stances for themselves in the light of events *as they unfold*. A static analysis is inadequate. In fact, depending on the system-changer's remit, he (or she) may need to try to prevent the emergence of too great a variety of views, which may take the change situation beyond control.

It is *not* new to recognize generally that accounting reports and controls are not just analyses of objective reality, but also have a role in moulding attitudes and behaviour. For many years, accountants have been warned by 'behavioural accountants' of the possible 'dysfunctional effects' of their measures, which may undo the 'good effects' of 'correct' economic analysis. The discussion in this book suggests, however, that such statements are too general. Upon recognition of the pluralistic organization, the phrase 'dysfunctional effects' has no strict meaning except in relation to a specific group interest, *unless* it is possible to mould the variety of group schemas into one common, widely held corporate schema. But, in order to do that, one needs a knowledge of those individual group schemas and what *they* would see as dysfunctional. Without that knowledge, accountants may not even be effective changers of their own systems.

If corporate resource allocation approximates the process described, aided and abetted by accounting, it becomes clear that accounting analyses are mainly needed (1) to persuade different parties to co-operate and (2) to provide critical indicators of the need to review organizational schemas. This suggests that accounting data need only be good enough to persuade people to join the party or to refrain, as yet, from leaving it. This may well explain why some organizations do not seem over-concerned about inaccuracies in specifying, say, DCF calculations or about conducting extensive strategic analyses. Accounting then seems to serve rather as a smoother of the inter-group process of corporate resource allocation rather than as an assessor of the accurate and *full* economic facts about how each party is affected by a given strategy or investment. Accounting has become a 'sufficiently rational' system. On the other hand, the manager who seeks too ready a refuge in such an interpretation may find that his system is not rational enough when his corporate coalition begins disintegrating, as constituent groups judge their benefits no longer good enough in comparison to those achievable in other companies. Those other companies may offer better rewards by virtue of a better strategy derived from a better understanding of their competitive position and the relevant supporting calculations of product costs, and better specification of schema-reinforcers. There is, therefore, no optimal design for accounting systems, but a continual tension between the internal and external frame of reference and between undertaking analysis and taking action – just as there is for the process of corporate resource allocation itself. Also, it is quite possible that, just when the system seems to be adequately serving both needs, something occurs internally or externally to make it no longer adequate.

References

Ackerman, R. W. 1970: Influence of integration and diversity on the investment process. *Administrative Science Quarterly*, September.

Ansoff, H. I. 1975: Managing strategic surprise by response to weak signals. *California Management Review*, Winter.

Bower, J. 1970: *Managing the Resource Allocation Process: a study of corporate planning and investment*. Cambridge, Mass.: Harvard Business School.

Brunsson, N. 1982: The irrationality of action and action rationality: decisions, ideologies and organizational actions. *Journal of Management Studies*, 19.

Brunnson, N. 1985: *The Irrational Organization*. New York: John Wiley.

Bruns, W. 1987: A field study of an attempt to change an embedded cost accounting system. In W. Bruns and R. Kaplan (eds), *Accounting and Management, Field Study Perspectives*, Cambridge, Mass.: Harvard Business School.

Buzzell, R. and Gale, B. 1987: *The PIMS Principles: linking strategy to performance*. New York: Collier Macmillan.

Clancy, D. and Collins, F. 1989: The behavioural factors of capital budgeting. In G. Siegel and H. Ramananskas-Marconi (eds), *Behavioural Accounting*, Cincinnati: South Western.

Colville, I. and Tomkins, C. 1989: Changing attitudes to innovation in the Civil Service. Memorandum submitted to the Treasury and Civil Service Committee, 5th Report, *Developments in the Next Steps Programme*, House of Commons 348, London: HMSO.

Currie, J. 1989: Capital budgeting in the managment-controlled firm. *The British Accounting Review*, September.

Dent, J. 1987: Tension in the design of formal control systems: a field study in a computer company. In W. Bruns and R. Kaplan (eds), *Accounting and Management, Field Study Perspectives*, Cambridge, Mass.: Harvard Business School.

Donaldson, G. 1985: Financial goals and strategic consequences. *Harvard Business Review*, May–June.

Goold, M. and Campbell, A. 1987: *Strategies and Styles*. Oxford: Basil Blackwell.

Grinyer, J. 1986: An alternative to maximization of shareholders' wealth. *Accounting and Business Research*, Autumn.

Hayes, R. and Garvin, D. 1982: Managing as if tomorrow mattered. *Harvard Business Review*, May–June.

Hill, T. 1985: *Manufacturing Strategy*, London: Macmillan.

Hiromoto, T. 1988: Another hidden edge – Japanese management accounting. *Harvard Business Review*, July–August.

Marsh, D., Barwise, P., Thomas, K. and Wensley, R. 1987: Managing strategic investment decisions. Paper presented to the BAM Conference, Warwick.

Odagiri, H. 1988. *Japanese Management: an 'economic' view*. London Business School, Working Paper Series, no. 60.

Palepu, K. 1987: The anatomy of accounting change. In W. Bruns and R. Kaplan (eds), *Accounting and Management, Field Study Perspectives*, Cambridge, Mass.: Harvard Business School.

Quinn, J. B. 1980: *Strategies for Change – Logical Incrementalism*. Homewood, Ill.: R. D. Irwin.

Schreuder, H. 1987: Organization, information and people: a participant observation of an MIS-carriage. In W. Bruns and R. Kaplan (eds), *Accounting and Management, Field Study Perspectives*, Cambridge, Mass.: Harvard Business School.

Shapiro, A. and Titman, S. 1986: An integrated approach to corporate risk management. In J. Stern and D. Chew (eds), *The Revolution in Corporate Finance*. Oxford: Basil Blackwell.

Swieringa, R. and Weick, K. 1987: Management accounting and action. *Accounting Organizations and Society*, 12, no. 3.

Tomkins, C. and Colville, I. 1989: Managing for greater innovation in the Civil Service: Customs and Excise. *Public Money*, Winter.

Wensley, R. 1981: Strategic marketing: betas, boxes or basics. *Journal of Marketing*, 45 (Summer).

Discussion questions

9.1   The accountant or financial manager can play a significant part in developing an understanding of different stakeholder risk/benefit attitudes by reference to the basic market concepts underlying the derivation of the CAPM. Discuss.

9.2   Despite advice from the current theory of finance, the financial manager cannot afford to disregard entity risk even if he wishes solely to maximize shareholder wealth – and yet the theory of finance is not wrong. Discuss and explain this apparent contradiction.

9.3   Examine the role of accounting as a schema-setter at SBU and sub-SBU levels.

9.4   To what extent might corporate investment appraisals be designed mainly to serve as a means of persuading multi-group compliance rather than maximizing wealth? Does this mean that such analyses are 'economical with the truth'? What is meant by 'sufficiently rational' systems? Discuss these questions.

9.5   Companies already classify investment projects and treat those classes in terms of the analysis needed to justify acceptance or rejection of the project. How do you think they classify them now? Do you think a knowledge of organization schemas would help improve classification?

9.6   Innovation itself can be based on 'impressionistic' behaviour or derived from extensive rational analysis. Discuss.

9.7   The role required of ROI in the management control process is quite different according to the precise location of strategic decision-making in the corporate group. Discuss.

10

Some Concluding Thoughts

It is hoped that the various arguments in this small book stand for themselves without the need for an extensive summarizing chapter. I set out to think about the problems of major resource allocation in large organizations. I started near to home, within financial management and accounting, but then moved abroad through strategy and organizational behaviour before returning home to view finance and accounting again with the experience gained on the journey. The choice of sights abroad reflects my own idiosyncrasies. No doubt the native would point out some other things, but it is unlikely that most of the things selected for examination in this book are far from the central, well-trodden paths.

The journey proved thought-provoking for me as I attempted to see relationships between different views. No doubt the links proposed between the different areas are sometimes weak and perhaps even misconceived. Some suggestions have more direct practical relevance than others. Some are presented in very general terms: some are more precise. But I am satisfied that there is considerable work to be done in exploring a wider role which both accounting and financial managers can play in the resource-allocation process.

On the other hand, I am dissatisfied with the amount of progress that I have been able to make. I have suggested some new analyses accountants and financial managers might make which reflect thinking in other disciplines, but I have certainly not provided a complete synthesis of different disciplinary perspectives. Also, while various further analyses have been proposed, we are still far from understanding how to balance analysis with pragmatism and action. This book may not, therefore, warrant a conclusion. It is more a tentative search for a beginning. It is nevertheless clear from the perspective beyond accounting and financial management that financial managers may play a considerable part in resource allocation in ways not fully appreciated in their own literature. They are not just problem-solvers; but also problem-finders. They do not just monitor passively; they provide signals and set schemas. Their constraining influence can be interpreted positively as an encouragement to action provided that their constraints are based on sound models of what is necessary for success in competition. On the other hand, the models must not become so set that change is inhibited when required. The models must themselves signal when it is time for them to self-destruct. Accountants and financial managers may also ease the management process by recognizing the interactive nature of decisions and clarifying different groups' risk/benefit positions and perceptions. The word *process* needs emphasis. Corporate resource allocation contains analysis, but it is a dynamic, interactive process. Hence financial managers need to see the place of their roles in negotiation and managing change.

All this seems to suggest that one can no longer adequately understand financial management and accounting from within. In practice accountants and financial managers interact with other functional managers, and yet much of the literature inadequately reflects this. I urge students to begin to cross such functional boundaries. The future of corporate controllership lies in a fusion of different functions and disciplines. The financial dimension will remain critically important, but the financial-controllership function cannot achieve its full potential in isolation.

If I were asked to indicate only one key message which I would like students to take from this book, it would be that organizational life is really about the apparently paradoxical combination of careful analysis before action and action taken with little previous thought. It is a combination of routine action, incrementalism and rigorous weighting of options. The secret of success seems to be to find the right balance for the situation faced. Those interested in developing financial management and control have many challenges in trying to fit their techniques and roles into such a paradoxical process.

I end by offering some very broad questions (perhaps more for pondering in the bath or at a late-night student discussion) which may help to bring home this basic message.

1 Select one of the most important decisions that you have ever made. (For mature readers it might be the choice of career, buying a house, marriage, or even divorce. For younger readers it might be the decision to continue in education or the choice of university or university course.) Consider *carefully* the processes you went through in order to make that decision. What degree of strategic analysis was involved? What evidence was there of incrementalism (as described by Quinn) or escalating responses to signals gaining in strength (as outlined by Ansoff)? To what extent was the decision determined by pre-set 'ideologies' you held (as described by

Brunnson) and action taken on an 'impressionistic' basis? How did you come to hold those 'ideologies'? Was it through experience or analysis or a combination of both? What tended to reinforce them? What tended to change them? Did you have to consider the position of other persons? If so, what form of negotiation took place and was this supported by rational analysis? In retrospect, would a better analysis of either your own or other persons' 'risk/return' perspective have improved the action you took?

2 Take another key decision you have made. Was there a different mixture of rigorous analysis, incrementalism and impressionistic analysis? If so, why was that?

3 Why should decision-making in organizations be any different in any fundamental sense from the way you make key personal decisions? What implications does this have for managerial control?

If, like many readers, you turn to the end of the book first to see if the conclusion suggests that the book is worth reading, you may wonder what on earth these discussion questions have to do with financial control in large organizations and be tempted to dig into the book itself in order to find out. If so, the decision to have no real conclusion will have been a good one. So, why not read the book and provide your own conclusions? This is an embryonic area and *your* carefully developed ideas are needed and will probably be as good as most given the current state of the art. The important point, at present, is that a number of thinking people address themselves seriously to the way we might fit together the separate fields of strategy, organization behaviour and financial analysis. It is also one thing to read a travelogue and quite another to make the journey. Read the former, but then try the latter. It is likely to be more rewarding and you may see many things that I have missed.

Index